Christian Festivals
Through the Year

Anita Ganeri

W
FRANKLIN WATTS
LONDON • SYDNEY

© 2003 Franklin Watts

First published in Great Britain by
Franklin Watts
96 Leonard Street
LONDON EC2A 4XD

Franklin Watts Australia
45–51 Huntley Street
Alexandria
NSW 2015

ISBN: 0 7496 4445 1
A CIP catalogue record for this book is available
from the British Library

Printed in Hong Kong, China

Editor: Kate Banham   Designer: Joelle Wheelwright
Art Direction: Jonathan Hair   Illustrations: Peter Bull
Picture Research: Diana Morris
Educational and Faith Consultant: Alan Brown
Roman Catholic Faith Consultant: Martin Ganeri, O.P.

Acknowledgements
The publishers would like to thank the following for permission to reproduce
photographs in this book:
Anthony Blake Photo Library/Photothèque Culinaire: 14b; Britstock-IFA/HAGA: 21t; Michael Dalder/
Reuters/Popperfoto: 19b; Dick Doughty/Britstock-IFA/HAGA: 13t, 25t; Bernd Ducke/Britstock-IFA:
8t, 16b; Franklin Watts Photo Libary: 6t, 16t, 23b, 26 (Steve Shott); 6b, 7t, 9t, 18b, 20t, 27t (Chris
Fairclough); 13b, 17t, 24b; Grant V. Faint/The Image Bank/Getty Images: front cover, 15;
G. Graefenhain/ Britstock-IFA: 12t; Hideo Haga/Britstock-IFA: 8b; Atsuko Isobe/Britstock-IFA/HAGA:
7c; Bruco Lucas/ Britstock-IFA: 12b; Caros Reyes-Manzo/Andes Press Agency: 14t, 17b, 20b, 22;
Akiro Nakata/ Britstock-IFA/HAGA: 23t; A. Diaz Neira/Britstock-IFA: 19t; © Trip/Viesti Collection:
27b; Waldenfels/Britstock-IFA: 24t; Heidi Weidner/Britstock-IFA: 18t; Jennifer Woodcock/Reflections
Photo Library/Corbis: 10; Masakatsu Yamazaki/Britstock-IFA/HAGA: 11b

Whilst every attempt has been made to clear copyright should there be any inadvertent omission
please apply in the first instance to the publisher regarding rectification.

Contents

Words printed in **bold** are explained in the glossary.

Introduction

Christians are people who follow the religion of Christianity. They believe in God and in the teachings of a man, called Jesus Christ. He was a preacher and healer who lived about 2,000 years ago in the Middle East. Christians believe that Jesus was the Son of God who came to Earth to save people from their sins, or wrong-doings.

This painting shows Jesus teaching.

Spreading the word

After Jesus's death, his **disciples** spread his message far and wide. Today, with some 2,000 million followers all over the world, Christianity is the largest religion. There are many different groups of Christians. The three largest are the Roman Catholics, Protestants and Orthodox Christians.

Many Christian buildings are decorated with beautiful stained-glass windows like this.

Christian worship

On Sundays, and other special occasions, many Christians go to church. They take part in services that include prayers, **hymns**, readings from the **Bible** (the Christian holy book), and a talk or sermon. One of the services is the sharing of bread and wine to remember the Last Supper (see page 18). This is called the **Eucharist**, Mass or Holy Communion. Christians also pray in private to thank and praise God.

Christians worshipping in a church.

A statue of Jesus is carried through the streets in this Easter procession in Guatemala.

The Christian year

Festivals are joyful times when people remember the lives of their teachers and leaders, and events from their religion's history. These are occasions for people to celebrate and share their beliefs, with special services, ceremonies, gifts and food. Many Christian festivals mark important times in the life of Jesus. The Christian year begins with preparations for Christmas and Jesus's birth.

Festival dates

Some festivals, such as Christmas, use the everyday calendar and fall on the same date every year. Other festivals are called moveable feasts. Easter is one of these. It is based on the appearance of the springtime full moon and can change by over a month each year. Festivals in the Orthodox Church fall on different dates because it uses an old calendar which runs several days behind.

Advent

On 25 December, Christians celebrate Christmas Day and the birth of Jesus. This is one of the most important festivals in the Christian year. The period leading up to Christmas Day is called Advent, and it is the start of the Christian year. The word 'Advent' means 'arrival' or 'coming'.

In Germany, people can buy all sorts of Christmas goods at cheerful Advent markets.

An Advent service in a church in Australia.

Advent Sunday

Advent begins four Sundays before Christmas, and is a time for reflecting on Jesus's birth. The first Sunday of Advent is called Advent Sunday. On this day, many Christians attend a special service in church. There are readings from the Bible and Advent hymns which look to the coming of a great saviour. It is a time for looking forward with hope and expectation.

Light of the world

In some churches, Christians light candles on an Advent ring, or crown. This is a circle of holly and ivy leaves with four small candles around the outside, one for each Sunday of Advent, and a large white one in the centre. The outer candles can be red or purple, the special colours used in Christian churches at times of preparation such as Advent or Lent (see page 16). One of these outer candles is lit for each Sunday of Advent. On Christmas Day, the centre candle is also lit. Christians use the candles as symbols to stand for Jesus, because he brought light and hope into the world.

← *Lighting a candle on the Advent ring.*

Advent calendars

Some people mark off the days leading up to Christmas on an Advent calendar.

To make an Advent calendar:

1. Draw a Christmas scene on a large sheet of card, showing the story of Jesus's birth.

2. On top of the scene draw 23 small windows and one larger window. Number the small windows 1–23, and the larger one 24. Carefully score round three sides of all the windows so they can be opened.

3. Place the window card on top of a second piece of card, the same size. Open the windows carefully and draw round the boxes. Then press the windows shut again.

4. On the second piece of card, stick a picture in each of the boxes you have drawn. You can either draw your own pictures or cut them from old Christmas cards. Then spread glue around the edge of the card and place the first sheet on top, facing outwards.

5. Starting on 1 December, open one window each day to show a Christmas picture.

The Christmas Story

Christians celebrate Jesus's birthday on 25 December, but no one knows exactly when Jesus was born. The early Christians chose this date about 300 years after Jesus's birth. It was also the date of an ancient Roman winter festival, when people looked forward to spring and the return of the sun. In the Orthodox Church, Christmas falls on 7 January (see page 7).

(see page 7)

A Christmas Carol

'O little town of Bethlehem,
How still we see thee lie!
Above thy deep and dreamless sleep
The silent stars go by.
Yet in thy dark streets shineth
The everlasting light.
The hopes and fears of all the years
Are met in thee tonight.'

The Christmas story

The story of Jesus's birth is told in the books, or **Gospels**, of St Luke and St Matthew in the Bible. Luke tells how the angel **Gabriel** appeared to a **Jewish** woman called Mary and told her that she would have a son who would be the saviour of the world. Mary and her husband, Joseph, had to travel to **Bethlehem** to pay their taxes, and there Jesus was born. Soon afterwards, shepherds tending their flocks on the nearby hills came to the stable to worship him.

At Christmas, children act out the story of Jesus's birth with nativity plays at school and in church.

Christmas in church

Christmas is a joyful time for Christians because it celebrates the coming of Jesus. On the night before Christmas, Christmas Eve, many churches hold a special service called Midnight Mass. On Christmas morning, people go to church to sing carols, listen to readings of the Christmas story from the Bible, and thank God for sending Jesus to them.

A Christingle

Some churches hold a Christingle service at Christmas to celebrate God's gifts to the world. The word 'Christingle' means 'Christ light'.

To make a Christingle:

1. Push a small candle into the top of an orange.

2. Then add four cocktail sticks, full of nuts, raisins and sweets.

3. Tie a red ribbon around the orange.

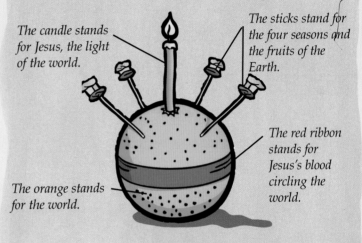

The candle stands for Jesus, the light of the world.

The sticks stand for the four seasons and the fruits of the Earth.

The red ribbon stands for Jesus's blood circling the world.

The orange stands for the world.

St Lucia's Day

In Sweden, Christmas celebrations begin on 13 December. This is St Lucia's Day. Legend says that Saint Lucia helped the early Christians, hiding from **persecution** in Rome. She is also the **patron saint** of light. On this day, girls take turns to be Saint Lucia and dress in long white robes with red sashes. On their heads they wear crowns of evergreen leaves and candles to light up the winter darkness.

Girls in Sweden dress up for St Lucia's Day.

Christmas Customs

Christmas is a happy time when Christians thank God for Jesus's birth and remember the Christmas message of peace on Earth and goodwill towards everyone. Christmas customs include putting up Christmas trees and decorations, exchanging gifts and cards, and enjoying delicious Christmas food. Today, Christmas is celebrated all over the world, by Christians and non-Christians alike.

Christmas Day on the beach!

Giving gifts

Exchanging Christmas presents reminds Christians of the wise men's visit to Jesus and the gifts they brought (see page 14). Christians also give gifts to remember that Jesus was God's gift to the world. Many children leave out socks, stockings, shoes and pillowcases, hoping they will be filled with presents. There are many stories about who delivers the Christmas gifts. In the Netherlands, children receive their presents on 6 December, St Nicholas's Day. Legend says that Saint Nicholas, or Sinterklaas (Santa Claus), was a **bishop** who lived long ago in Myra, Turkey. A story tells how he secretly left three bags of gold as gifts for three girls who were too poor to get married.

St Stephen's Day

The day after Christmas is the feast of Saint Stephen, the first Christian **martyr**. He was put to death for teaching about Jesus. In Britain, it is also called Boxing Day. In the past, boxes of money, clothes and food were opened and shared out among the poor.

Christmas dinner is a time for families to get together to tuck into a special meal.

A delicious Christmas pudding. ....▶

Festive food

Many special types of food are eaten at Christmas. In Britain and many other places, Christmas Day dinner is traditionally roast turkey, followed by Christmas pudding and mince pies. In some countries, the main Christmas meal is eaten on Christmas Eve. In Italy, fish with lentils is a favourite Christmas dish. In Poland, people traditionally tuck into poppy seed cake, beet soup and prune dumplings. An empty setting is often left at the table for the baby Jesus.

Epiphany

T welve days after Christmas, on 6 January, Christians celebrate Epiphany. St Matthew's Gospel tells how a bright star guided the kings or wise men to Bethlehem where they found Jesus. They brought three precious gifts for him, which have special meanings for Christians. There was gold fit for a king, frankincense for use in worship, and myrrh to foretell a death.

The Festival of the Three Kings in Panama. ············▶
The Bible does not say how many wise men there were. We think there were three because they brought three gifts.

Three Kings' Day

In Spain, Epiphany is called Three Kings' Day. This is the day on which children receive their Christmas presents. On Epiphany eve, they leave their shoes by the window or door, for the wise men to fill with gifts as they pass by. They also leave straw and water for the wise men's camels. If children misbehave, the wise men leave them lumps of coal instead.

◀············
Epiphany is also the end of the Twelve Days of Christmas. In many countries, a special Twelfth Night cake is baked. It often contains lucky gifts or money.

Candlemas

The festival of Candlemas falls on 2 February, 40 days after Christmas. For some people, this marks the real end of Christmas. The festival gets its name from the procession of lighted candles that took place in church. In Roman Catholic churches, there are still candlelit processions.

Jesus in the temple

On Candlemas, Christians also remember the presentation of Jesus in the **Temple** in **Jerusalem**. According to Jewish customs, Jewish boys were taken to the Temple by their parents 40 days after their birth to be 'presented', or shown, to God. This was a way of thanking God for the baby's birth. At this time, Mary, Jesus's mother, was also blessed.

Candle light is a symbol for Jesus as a guiding light in the world.

A Candlemas prayer

An old man, called Simeon, spoke these words when he saw Jesus in the Temple. They show that Simeon knew how special Jesus was. They are known as the *Nunc Dimittis*, which is **Latin** for 'Now let us depart', and are often said as part of a church service:

'Lord, now let your servant go in peace.
Your word has been fulfilled.
My own eyes have seen the salvation
Which you have prepared in the sight of every people.
A light to reveal you to the nations
And the glory of your people Israel.'
(The Bible, Luke 2: 29–32)

Lent

For Christians, Easter is the most important festival of the year. This is when they remember how Jesus was put to death on the cross, and how he rose again from the dead. Lent is the name for the period of 40 days before Easter (not counting Sundays). This is a solemn time for Christians when they reflect on and prepare for the great festival of Easter.

*Jesus was put to death by being **crucified**, or nailed to a cross. Many churches have models or statues commemorating this. The models are called crucifixes.*

Carnival time is particularly colourful in Rio de Janeiro, Brazil.

Carnival!

Lent begins in February or March. The day before Lent is called Shrove Tuesday. In many countries, particularly in South America, Shrove Tuesday, or Mardi Gras, is carnival time! Spectacular processions of floats, singers and dancers fill the streets with colour and noise. This is a time for having fun before the solemn days of Lent begin. The word 'Shrove' comes from an old word which means 'to confess your sins'. Some Christians go to church to ask God to forgive them for their wrong-doings.

Fasting

During Lent, Christians try to live good lives and think about Jesus's suffering. Before he began his teaching, Jesus spent 40 days in the wilderness. There he was tempted by the Devil who tried to turn him away from God. Lent used to be a time for **fasting**, or going without food, as Jesus did in the wilderness. Today, many people still give up luxuries such as sweets. They may also give money to charity and spend more time reading the Bible.

Pancake Day

Because Christians traditionally ate plain, simple food during Lent, on Shrove Tuesday they had to use up their rich foods, such as fat, eggs and milk, which would go bad if kept. In Britain, these were made into delicious pancakes, and Shrove Tuesday is often called Pancake Day.

Ash Wednesday

The first day of Lent is called Ash Wednesday. In Roman Catholic churches, a special Mass is said. Last year's palm crosses (see page 18) are burned and the ashes mixed with holy water. Then the priest makes a cross shape with the ash on each person's forehead. Lent is a time for thinking of the things you have done wrong, and ashes are a sign of being sorry.

Mothering Sunday

Mothering Sunday, or Mother's Day, falls on the fourth Sunday of Lent. In church, special prayers are said for mothers to thank them for all their hard work. Children often give their mothers gifts of cards and flowers.

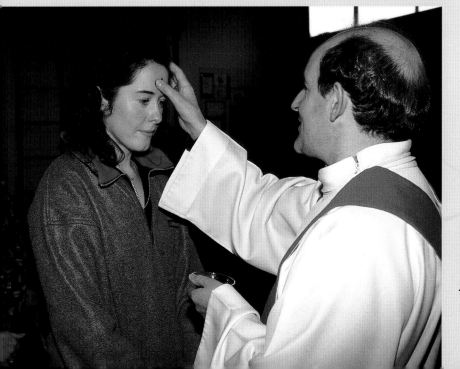

On Ash Wednesday, the priest makes an ash mark on the forehead of each worshipper.

Holy Week

The last week of Lent is called Holy Week. It is the most important time in the Christian year, when Christians remember the final week of Jesus's life. There are many special church services, prayers and processions.

Palm Sunday

Holy Week begins with Palm Sunday, when Jesus rode into Jerusalem on the back of a donkey for the festival of **Passover** (Pesach). Crowds of people greeted him as a great king and saviour. They waved palm branches to welcome him. Today, people who go to church are given small palm-leaf crosses or even palm branches to remind them of that day.

On Palm Sunday in Germany, people are given catkin twigs instead of palm crosses or branches.

The Last Supper

On Thursday of Holy Week, Jesus ate a final meal with his 12 disciples. This is called the Last Supper. At the meal, he took some bread and wine, and shared them out among the disciples. He told them that the bread and wine represented his body and his blood, which he was about to sacrifice for the sins of mankind. Today, most Christians share bread and wine as part of a special church service, to remember Jesus. The service has different names, such as Mass, Holy Communion or the Eucharist and happens regularly throughout the year, not just during Holy Week.

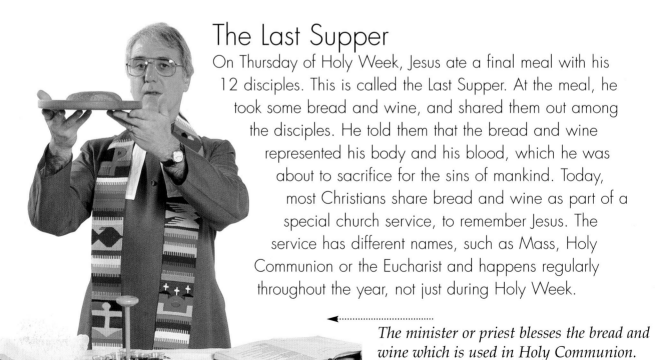

The minister or priest blesses the bread and wine which is used in Holy Communion.

Maundy Thursday

This Thursday is called Maundy Thursday. 'Maundy' is from the Latin word *mandatum* which means 'a command'. On this day, Jesus gave his disciples the commands to share bread and wine, and to love one another. He showed his love for them by washing their feet, as a humble servant would. In some churches, the priest washes the feet of 12 worshippers.

The Semana Santa, or Holy Week, procession in Seville, Spain. Some people dress in hoods and robes as a sign of sorrow. ⋯⋯⋯⋯⟶

Good Friday

On Friday of Holy Week, Christians remember how Jesus was crucified. It is called Good Friday because Christians believe that Jesus gave up his life for the good of everyone. This is a solemn day when most churches are cleared of their flowers and decorations, and left dark and plain with a simple cross on the **altar**. There is often a service of silent prayer between midday and three o'clock, the time that Jesus hung on the cross. On Good Friday, people eat spicy hot cross buns. The cross on the top reminds them of how Jesus died.

⟵⋯⋯⋯

Every ten years in Oberammergau, Germany, the story of Holy Week is acted out on a grand scale.

Easter Day

After the sadness of Good Friday, Easter Sunday is a joyful day. This is the day on which Christians believe Jesus was resurrected, or rose from the dead. Christians believe that this shows that death is not the end, but the start of a new life with God. Many Christians go to church to thank God for Jesus's life. Churches are filled with beautiful flowers and the church bells ring out.

On Easter Day

When Jesus died, his friends took his body down from the cross and placed it in a tomb. They rolled a large stone across the entrance. Three days later, on Sunday morning, they went to visit the tomb. To their astonishment, the tomb was empty. Jesus had risen from the dead.

Easter vigil

The Easter *Vigil* is the most important service of the year for Roman Catholics. After dark on Easter eve, a large fire is lit outside the church. The Paschal, or Easter, candle is lit from the fire. Then everyone lights a candle from the Easter candle. They process into the church as an ancient hymn called the *Exultet*, which means 'rejoice', is sung (see opposite). A similar service is held in Orthodox churches.

Lighting the Paschal, or Easter, candle at an Easter vigil in South Africa.

Easter customs

Easter customs, such as giving Easter eggs, celebrate new life. They remind Christians of how Jesus rose from the dead. But they also celebrate spring, and a time of new life in nature.

The Easter egg rolling competition happens every year on the lawn of the White House, in Washington DC, the home of the US president.

Decorated Easter eggs

In some countries, like Poland, people decorate their own Easter eggs.

To decorate an Easter egg:

1. Use a needle to make a tiny hole in each end of an egg. Gently blow through one hole so that the egg comes out of the other. (You could use a hard-boiled egg instead.)

2. Draw a pattern on the empty shell with a wax crayon.

3. Dip the egg in a bowl of fabric dye or food colouring. It will stain the shell, except where the pattern appears.

The Exultet

'Rejoice, heavenly powers!
Sing, choirs of angels!
Exult, all creation around God's throne!
Jesus Christ, our King, is risen!
Sound the trumpet of salvation!'

Summer Festivals

Ascension Day

Forty days after Easter, Christians remember the end of Jesus's time on Earth after his resurrection and his going into heaven to be with God for ever. This is called Ascension Day and always falls on a Thursday. (To ascend means 'to go up'.)

Pentecost

The festival of Pentecost, 50 days after Easter, marks the birthday of the Christian Church. The Bible tells how, at Pentecost, a strong wind blew through the house where Jesus's disciples were praying in Jerusalem, and flames rested on their heads. They were filled with the Holy Spirit and began to speak in many different languages about God's work. This is when they began to go out and teach people about Jesus. Christians believe that the Holy Spirit is always with them, helping and guiding them.

*Pentecost is a favourite time for people to be **baptised**, and join the Christian Church. Traditionally, they dressed in white to signify the start of a new life.*

Trinity Sunday

The Sunday after Pentecost is called Trinity Sunday. On this day, Christians think about the three ways of seeing God – God the Father who made and cares for the world; God the Son, who came to Earth as Jesus; and God the Holy Spirit, the power of God. Saint Patrick, the patron saint of Ireland, explained that the three parts of God were like the three parts of a shamrock leaf – separate but part of the same whole. (Shamrock is similar to clover.)

Corpus Christi

The Thursday after Trinity Sunday is the Roman Catholic festival of *Corpus Christi*, meaning 'the body of Christ'. The festival was begun in 1264 and celebrates the Last Supper. The bread used for Mass is carried through the streets as part of a procession. Often the path of the procession is scattered with flowers. Some people kneel as the procession passes, to honour the bread which is a symbol of Jesus Christ. In the Middle Ages this was also a time when **mystery plays** would be performed.

During the Corpus Christi procession in Italy, the bread is carried through the town under a canopy.

The Assumption

For Roman Catholics and Orthodox Christians, the Blessed Virgin Mary, Jesus's mother, is a very special person whom they honour and worship. On 15 August they remember how Mary, at the end of her life, was taken up into heaven. Roman Catholics call this the Feast of the Assumption of Our Lady. (Here 'assumed' means 'taken up'.) It is a holiday in many Roman Catholic countries. In the Orthodox Church, it is called the Dormition, or Falling Asleep, of the Blessed Virgin Mary.

A painting of the Blessed Virgin Mary, Jesus's mother.

Harvest Festival

In September or October, many Christians in Britain go to special services to celebrate Harvest Festival. This is a time for thanking God for all the good things that come from the Earth. Churches are decorated with flowers, fruit and vegetables, and loaves of harvest bread. These are later given to charity to share out God's goodness. In other countries, the harvest is celebrated at different times of the year.

A colourful display of fruit and vegetables in church for Harvest Festival.

Harvest bread is often baked in the shape of a wheatsheaf.

Harvest supper

For farmers, autumn was traditionally the time for bringing in the crops. When the last stalks of grain had been cut, a great feast was held to thank God for the harvest. Some churches still hold a harvest supper. Long ago, a loaf was baked from wheat cut at the start of the harvest. The bread was used at a Holy Communion service on 1 August. This became Lammas, or Loaf Mass, Day.

Thanksgiving

On the fourth Thursday in November, people in the USA celebrate the first harvest of the early settlers in America almost 400 years ago. Life was hard, so when the harvest was safely gathered in, the settlers gave heartfelt thanks to God. Many families dress up in their best clothes and go to church. Then they share a delicious Thanksgiving dinner of turkey and pumpkin pie. Thanksgiving is a very important festival and a national holiday.

A family enjoying a delicious Thanksgiving dinner in the USA.

A harvest altar cloth

A church's altar is covered by an altar cloth. The design of the cloth changes to reflect the church's year. At festival times it is usually white or gold, with an appropriate design.

To make a harvest altar cloth:

1. Cut a piece of white or gold cloth, about 200 cm long by 50 cm wide. Turn over the edges, and sew or stick the hems down.

2. Cut out the shapes of a cross, loaves of bread, sheaves of corn, fruit and vegetables from coloured cloth. Sew or stick them on to your altar cloth.

A Harvest Hymn

'We plough the fields,
and scatter
The good seed on the land,
But it is fed and watered
By God's almighty hand.
He sends the snow in winter,
The warmth to swell the grain,
The breezes and the sunshine,
And soft refreshing rain.
All good gifts around us
Are sent from heaven above.
Then thank the Lord,
O thank the Lord,
For all his love.'

All Saints' and All Souls'

On 1 November, some Christians celebrate All Saints' Day when they give thanks for the life and works of all the saints. For all Christians, saints are especially holy people who devoted their lives to God. Roman Catholics and Orthodox Christians pray to the saints for help and guidance. Apart from All Saints' Day, each of the saints has a special day throughout the year, on which he or she is remembered. This is called a feast day. In the Roman Catholic Church, feast days are important festivals.

Saint Peter

Saint Peter was one of Jesus's disciples who became the leader of the Christian Church. Tradition says that Peter travelled to Rome where he became the first bishop. The leader of the Roman Catholic Church, the Pope, is also called the Bishop of Rome. Saint Peter was crucified for his beliefs. His feast day is 29 June, and he shares it with Saint Paul.

Saints are an important focus of worship in the Orthodox Church. Orthodox Christians celebrate All Saints' Day earlier in the year, in June.

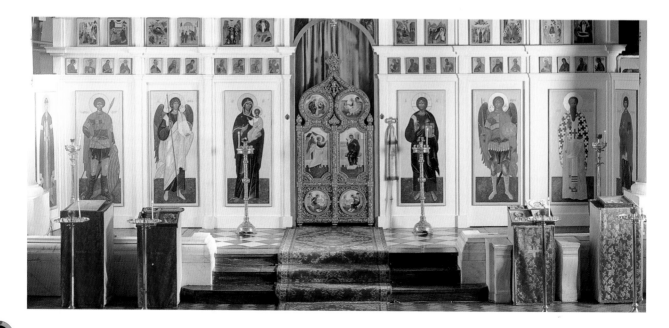

All Souls' Day

The day after All Saints' Day is called All Souls' Day. This is when Christians remember those who have died, and pray that their souls may rest in peace in heaven. Some people visit the graves of loved ones and put flowers on them. Even so, this is not a gloomy day, but a day for happy memories.

In many countries, on All Souls' Day, people place flowers on the graves of their loved ones.

Day of the Dead

In Mexico, All Souls' Day is called the Day of the Dead. People used to believe that this was when the souls of the dead came back to life, just for one night. At home and in cemeteries, people leave out flowers, water and food to welcome the souls of the dead. Among the offerings are models of skulls, skeletons and coffins, made from sugar.

Sugar model-making in Mexico dates back more than 100 years. The hollow models are formed from hard white sugar and decorated with bright colours.

Festival Calendar

Date	Month	Event
	November/December	Advent Sunday
6	December	St Nicholas's Day
13	December	St Lucia's Day
25	December	Christmas Day
26	December	St Stephen's Day
6	January	Epiphany
7	January	Christmas Day (Orthodox)
2	February	Candlemas
	February/March	Shrove Tuesday
	February/March	Lent
	March/April	Mothering Sunday
	March/April	Holy Week
		• Palm Sunday
		• Maundy Thursday
		• Good Friday
		• Holy Saturday
		• Easter Day (Sunday)
	April/May	Ascension Day
	May/June	Pentecost/Whitsun
	May/June	Trinity Sunday
	May/June	Corpus Christi
29	June	Feast of St Peter and St Paul
15	August	Feast of the Assumption Dormition (Orthodox)
	September/October	Harvest Festival
1	November	All Saints' Day
2	November	All Souls' Day
	November	Thanksgiving Day (USA)

Glossary

Altar   A table in a Christian church, used for the Eucharist.

Baptism   A ceremony at which a person becomes a full member of the Christian Church. They are sprinkled with or bathed in water to wash away their sins.

Bethlehem   A town in Israel where Jesus was born.

Bible   The holy book of the Christians. It is made up of the Old Testament and the New Testament. The Old Testament dates back to Jewish times, before the birth of Jesus; the New Testament contains the life and words of Jesus Christ.

Bishop   A leading priest, responsible for all the Church affairs in a particular area.

Carol   A religious song, usually sung at Christmas.

Crucified   Put to death by being nailed to a cross.

Disciples   The 12 men chosen by Jesus to be his close companions and followers.

Eucharist   The service at which bread and wine are shared, in remembrance of Jesus. It is also called Mass or Holy Communion.

Fasting   Going without food.

Gabriel   The angel who appeared to Mary and told her that she would be the mother of Jesus.

Gospels   The first four books of the New Testament. They tell of the life and work of Jesus. The word 'gospel' comes from an old word meaning 'good news', because the Gospels contain the good news about Jesus.

Hymns   Religious songs which praise God.

Jerusalem   A city in Israel where Jesus spent his last days on Earth and where he was crucified.

Jewish   To do with the faith of Judaism. Jesus's family were Jewish and he was born and raised as a Jew.

Latin   An ancient language, spoken in the Roman Empire.

Martyr   Someone who suffers and even dies for his or her religious beliefs.

Mystery plays   Medieval religious plays presenting Bible stories or the miracles of the saints. They are still performed today in many cities, such as York and Coventry in Britain and Oberammergau in Germany. They are also known as 'miracle plays'.

Passover (Pesach)   A Jewish festival, celebrated in March or April. It remembers the escape of the early Jews from slavery in Egypt.

Patron saint   A saint regarded as the protector or supporter of a particular group or country. For example, Saint Christopher is the patron saint of travellers and Saint Patrick is the patron saint of Ireland.

Persecute   To injure or harass someone (usually because of what they believe in).

Temple   The ancient Jewish Temple in Jerusalem. It was the holiest building for the Jews.

Vigil   Keeping awake at a time when you would normally be asleep, as part of worship during a festival.

Further Resources

Books

A World of Festivals: Christmas
Catherine Chambers, Evans Brothers, 1997

A World of Festivals: Easter
Catherine Chambers, Evans Brothers, 1998

Beliefs and Cultures: Christian
Carol Watson, Franklin Watts, 1996

Celebration!
Barnabas and Anabel Kindersley,
Dorling Kindersley, 1997

High Days and Holidays
David Self, Lion Publishing, 1993

Festivals in World Religions
The Shap Working Party on World Religions
in Education, 1998

Websites

www.festivals.com
Information about festivals, holy days
and holidays.

www.christmas.com
Christmas greetings from around the world.

www.antiochian-orthodox.co.uk
Information about festivals in the Orthodox Church.

In Australia you can check out the websites of the
Christian Research Association, **www.cra.org.au**,
and the Christian Churches of God, Australia,
www.ccg.org/_region/ Australia.

Index

decided I would be better off with neither of them around. If there was no possibility of talking about something easy and entertaining, I preferred not to talk at all.

Poirot appeared in the drawing room, still wearing his hat and coat, and closed the door behind him. I expected a barrage of questions from him, but instead he said with an air of distraction, 'It is late. I walk and walk around the streets, looking, and I achieve nothing except to make myself late.'

He was worried, all right, but not about me and whether I had eaten or was going to eat. It was a huge relief. 'Looking?' I asked.

'*Oui.* For a woman, Jennie, whom I very much hope is still alive and not murdered.'

'Murdered?' I had that sense of the ground dropping away again. I knew Poirot was a famous detective. He had told me about some of the cases he'd solved. Still, he was supposed to be having a break from all that, and I could have done without him producing that particular word at that moment, in such a portentous fashion.

'What does she look like, this Jennie?' I asked. 'Describe her. I might have seen her. Especially if she's been murdered. I've seen two murdered women tonight, actually, and one man, so you might be in luck. The man didn't look as if he was likely to be called Jennie, but as for the other two —'

'*Attendez, mon ami,*' Poirot's calm voice cut through my desperate ramblings. He took off his hat and began to unbutton his coat. 'So Madame

elegant building that was at most three hundred yards away. 'You live *there*?' I said. I thought it must be a joke.

'*Oui.* I do not wish to be far from my home,' Poirot explained. 'It is most pleasing to me that I am able to see it: the beautiful view!' He gazed at the mansion block with pride, and for a few moments I wondered if he had forgotten I was there. Then he said, 'Travel is a wonderful thing. It is stimulating, but not restful. Yet if I do not take myself away somewhere, there will be no *vacances* for the mind of Poirot! Disturbance will arrive in one form or another. At home one is too easily found. A friend or a stranger will come with a matter of great importance *comme toujours* — it is always of the greatest importance! — and the little grey cells will once more be busy and unable to conserve their energy. So, Poirot, he is said to have left London for a while, and meanwhile he takes his rest in a place he knows well, protected from the interruption.'

He said all this, and I nodded along, as if it made perfect sense, wondering if people grow ever more peculiar as they age.

Mrs Unsworth never cooks dinner on a Thursday evening — that's her night for visiting her late husband's sister — and this was how Poirot came to discover Pleasant's Coffee House. He told me he could not risk being seen in any of his usual haunts while he was supposed to be out of town, and asked if I could recommend 'a place where a person like you might go, *mon ami* — but where the food is excellent'. I told him about Pleasant's: cramped, a little eccentric, but most people who tried it once went back again and again.

On this particular Thursday evening — the night of Poirot's encounter with Jennie — he arrived home at ten past ten, much later than usual. I was in the drawing room, sitting close to the fire but unable to warm myself up. I heard Blanche Unsworth whispering to Poirot seconds after I heard the front door open and shut; she must have been waiting for him in the hall.

I couldn't hear what she was saying but I could guess: she was anxious, and I was the cause of her anxiety. She had arrived back from her sister-in-law's house at half past nine and decided that something was wrong with me. I looked a fright — as if I hadn't eaten and wouldn't sleep. She'd said all this to me herself. I don't know quite how a person manages to look as if he hasn't eaten, incidentally. Perhaps I was leaner than I had been at breakfast that morning.

She inspected me from a variety of angles and offered me everything she could think of that might set me right, starting with the obvious remedies one offers in such situations — food, drink, a friendly ear. Once I'd rejected all three as graciously as I could, she proceeded to more outlandish suggestions: a pillow stuffed with herbs, something foul-smelling but apparently beneficial from a dark blue bottle that I must put in my bath water.

I thanked her and refused. She cast her eyes frantically around the drawing room, looking for any unlikely object she might foist upon me with the promise that it would solve all my problems.

Now, more likely than not, she was whispering to Poirot that he must press me to accept the foul-smelling blue bottle or the herb pillow.

Poirot is normally back from Pleasant's and reading in the drawing room by nine o'clock on a Thursday evening. I had returned from the Bloxham Hotel at a quarter past nine, determined not to think about what I had encountered there, and very much looking forward to finding Poirot in his favourite chair so that we could talk about amusing trivialities as we so often did.

He wasn't there. His absence made me feel strangely remote from everything, as if the ground had fallen away beneath my feet. Poirot is a regular sort of person who does not like to vary his routines — 'It is the unchanging daily routine, Catchpool, that makes for the restful mind' he had told me more than once — and yet he was a full quarter of an hour late.

When I heard the front door at half past nine, I hoped it was him, but it was Blanche Unsworth. I nearly let out a groan. If you're worried about yourself, the last thing you want is the company of somebody whose chief pastime is fussing over nothing.

I was afraid I might not be able to persuade myself to return to the Bloxham Hotel the following day, and I knew that I had to. That was what I was trying not to think about.

'And now,' I reflected, 'Poirot is here at last, and he will be worried about me as well, because Blanche Unsworth has told him he must be.' I

Blanche, she is correct — you are troubled? Ah, but how did I not see this straight away? You are pale. My thoughts, they were elsewhere. They arrange to be elsewhere when they see that Madame Blanche approaches! But please tell Poirot *immédiatement*: what is the matter?'

★ ★ ★

'Three murders are the matter,' I said. 'And all three of them like nothing I've seen before. Two women and one man. Each one in a different room.'

Of course, I had encountered violent death before many times — I had been with Scotland Yard for nearly two years, and a policeman for five — but most murders had about them an obvious appearance of lost control: somebody had lashed out in a fit of temper, or had one tipple too many and lost his rag. This business at the Bloxham was very different. Whoever had killed three times at the hotel had planned ahead — for months, I guessed. Each of his crime scenes was a work of macabre art with a hidden meaning that I could not decipher. It terrified me to think that this time I was not up against a chaotic ruffian of the sort I was used to, but perhaps a cold, meticulous mind that would not allow itself to be defeated.

I was no doubt being overly gloomy about it, but I couldn't shake my feelings of foreboding. Three matching corpses: the very idea made me shudder. I told myself I must not develop a phobia; I had rather to treat this case as I would any other, no matter how different it seemed on the surface.

'Each of the three murders in a different room in the same house?' Poirot asked.

'No, at the Bloxham Hotel. Up Piccadilly Circus way. I don't suppose you know it?'

'*Non.*'

'I had never been inside it before tonight. It's not the sort of place a chap like me would think to go. It's palatial.'

Poirot was sitting with his back very straight. 'Three murders, in the same hotel and each in a different room?' he said.

'Yes, and all committed earlier in the evening within a short space of time.'

'This evening? And yet you are here. Why are you not at the hotel? The killer, he is apprehended already?'

'No such luck, I'm afraid. No, I . . . ' I stopped and cleared my throat. Reporting the facts of the case was straightforward enough, but I had no wish to explain to Poirot how my mood had been affected by what I had seen, or to tell him that I had been at the Bloxham for no more than five minutes before I succumbed to the powerful urge to leave.

The way all three had been laid out on their backs so formally: arms by their sides, palms of their hands touching the floor, legs together . . .

Laying out the dead. The phrase forced its way into my mind, accompanied by a vision of a dark room from many years ago — a room I had been compelled to enter as a young child, and had been refusing to enter in my imagination ever

24

since. I fully intended to carry on refusing for the rest of my life.

Lifeless hands, palms facing downwards.

'*Hold his hand, Edward.*'

'Don't worry, there are plenty of police crawling about the place,' I said quickly and loudly, to banish the unwelcome vision. 'Tomorrow morning is soon enough for me to go back.' Seeing that he was waiting for a fuller answer, I added, 'I had to clear my head. Frankly, I've never seen anything as peculiar as these three murders in all my life.'

'In what way peculiar?'

'Each of the victims had something in his or her mouth — the same thing.'

'*Non.*' Poirot wagged his finger at me. 'This is not possible, *mon ami*. The same thing cannot be inside three different mouths at the same time.'

'Three separate things, all identical,' I clarified. 'Three cufflinks, solid gold from the look of them. Monogrammed. Same initials on all three: PIJ. Poirot? Are you all right? You look — '

'*Mon Dieu!*' He had risen to his feet and begun to pace around the room. 'You do not see what this means, *mon ami*. No, you do not see it at all, because you have not heard the story of my encounter with Mademoiselle Jennie. Quickly I must tell you what happened so that you understand.'

Poirot's idea of telling a story quickly is rather different from most people's. Every detail matters to him equally, whether it's a fire in which three hundred people perish or a small dimple on a child's chin. He can never be induced to rush to the nub of a matter, so I settled into my chair and let him tell it in his own way. By the time he had finished, I felt as if I had experienced the events first-hand — more comprehensively, indeed, than I experience many scenes from my life in which I personally participate.

'What an extraordinary thing to happen,' I said. 'On the same night as the three murders at the Bloxham, too. Quite a coincidence.'

Poirot sighed. 'I do not think it is a coincidence, my friend. One accepts that the coincidences happen from time to time, but here there is a clear connection.'

'You mean murder on the one hand, and the fear of being murdered on the other?'

'*Non*. That is one connection, yes, but I am talking about something different.' Poirot stopped promenading around the drawing room and turned to face me. 'You say that in your three murder victims' mouths are found three gold cufflinks bearing the monogram 'PIJ'?'

'That's right.'

'Mademoiselle Jennie, she said to me quite clearly: 'Promise me this: if I'm found dead, you'll tell your friend the policeman not to look for my killer. *Oh, please let no one open their mouths!* This crime must never be solved.' What do you think she meant by 'Oh, please let no one open their mouths'?'

Was he joking? Apparently not. 'Well,' I said, 'it's clear, isn't it? She feared she would be murdered, didn't want her killer punished and was hoping no one would say anything to point

26

the finger at him. She believes *she* is the one who deserves to be punished.'

'You choose the meaning that at first seems obvious,' said Poirot. He sounded disappointed in me. 'Ask yourself if there is another possible meaning of those words: 'Oh, please let no one open their mouths'. Reflect upon your three gold cufflinks.'

'They are not mine,' I said emphatically, wishing at that moment that I could push the whole case very far away from me. 'All right, I see what you're driving at, but — '

'What do you see? *Je conduis ma voiture à quoi?*'

'Well . . . 'Please let no one open their mouths' could, at a stretch, mean 'Please let no one open the mouths of the three murder victims at the Bloxham Hotel.'' I felt an utter fool giving voice to this preposterous theory.

'*Exactement!* 'Please let no one open their mouths and find the gold cufflinks with the initials PIJ.' Is it not possible that this is what Jennie meant? That she knew about the three murder victims at the hotel, and that she knew that whoever killed them was also intent on killing her?'

Without waiting for my answer, Poirot proceeded with his imaginings. 'And the letters PIJ, the person who has those initials, he is very important to the story, *n'est-ce pas?* Jennie, she knows this. She knows that if you find these three letters you will be on your way to finding the murderer, and she wants to prevent this. *Alors*, you must catch him, before it is too late

27

for Jennie, or else Hercule Poirot, he shall not forgive himself!'

I was alarmed to hear this. I felt a pressing sense of responsibility for catching this killer as it was, and did not wish also to be responsible for Poirot never forgiving himself. Did he really look at me and see a man capable of apprehending a murderer with a mind of this sort — a mind that would think to place monogrammed cufflinks in the mouths of the dead? I have always been a straightforward person and I work best at straightforward things.

'I think you must go back to the hotel,' said Poirot. He meant immediately.

I shuddered at the memory of those three rooms. 'First thing tomorrow will be soon enough,' I said, studiously avoiding his gleaming eyes. 'I should tell you, I'm not going to make a fool of myself by bringing up this Jennie person. It would only confuse everybody. You have come up with a possible meaning for what she said and I have come up with another. Yours is the more interesting, but mine is twenty times more likely to be correct.'

'It is not,' came the contradiction.

'We shall have to disagree about it,' I said firmly. 'If we were to ask a hundred people, they would all agree with me and not with you, I suspect.'

'I too suspect this.' Poirot sighed. 'Allow me to convince you if I can. A few moments ago, you said to me about the murders at the hotel, 'Each of the victims had something in *his* or *her* mouth', did you not?'

28

I agreed that I had.

'You did not say, 'in *their* mouth', you said, 'his or her' — because you are an educated man and you speak in the singular and not the plural: 'his or her', to go with 'each' — it is grammatically correct. Mademoiselle Jennie, she is a housemaid, but she has the speech of an educated person and the vocabulary also. She used the word 'inevitable' when talking about her death, her murder. And then she said to me, 'So you see, there is no help to be had, *and even if there were, I should not deserve it.*' She is a woman who uses the English language as it should be used. Therefore, *mon ami . . .*' Poirot was up on his feet again. 'Therefore! If you are correct and Jennie meant to say, 'Please let no one open their mouths' in the sense of 'Please let no one give information to the police', why did she not say, 'Please let no one open his or her mouth?' The word 'no one' requires the singular, not the plural!'

I stared up at him with an ache in my neck, too bewildered and weary to respond. Hadn't he told me himself that Jennie was in a frightful panic? In my experience, people who are stricken with terror tend not to fuss about grammar.

I had always thought of Poirot as among the most intelligent of men, but perhaps I had been wrong. If this was the sort of nonsense he was inclined to spout then no wonder he had judged it time to submit his mind to a rest cure.

'Naturally, you will now tell me that Jennie was distressed and was therefore not careful about her speech,' Poirot went on. 'However she spoke with perfect correctness apart from in this one instance — unless I am right and you are wrong, in which case Jennie said nothing that was grammatically incorrect at all!'

He clapped his hands together and seemed so gratified by his announcement that I was moved to say rather sharply, 'That's marvellous, Poirot. A man and two women are murdered, and it's my job to sort it out, but I'm jolly pleased that Jennie, whoever she is, didn't slip up in her use of the English language.'

'And Poirot also, he is *jolly pleased*,' said my hard-to-discourage friend, 'because a little progress has been made, a little discovery. *Non*.' His smile vanished and his expression became more serious. 'Mademoiselle Jennie did not make the error of grammar. The meaning she intended was, 'Please let no one open the mouths of the three murdered people — *their* mouths'.'

'If you insist,' I muttered.

'Tomorrow after breakfast you will return to the Bloxham Hotel,' said Poirot. 'I will join you there later, after I look for Jennie.'

'You?' I said, somewhat perturbed. Words of protest formed in my head, but I knew they would never reach Poirot's ears. Famous detective or not, his ideas about the case had so far been, frankly, ridiculous, but if he was offering his company, I wouldn't turn it down. He was very sure of himself and I was not — that was what it boiled down to. I already felt bolstered by the interest he was taking.

'*Oui*,' he said. 'Three murders have been

committed that share an extremely unusual feature: the monogrammed cufflink in the mouth. Most assuredly I will go to the Bloxham Hotel.'

'Aren't you supposed to be avoiding stimulation and resting your brain?' I asked.

'*Oui. Précisément.*' Poirot glared at me. 'It is not restful for me to sit in this chair all day and think of you omitting to mention to anybody my meeting with Mademoiselle Jennie, a detail of the utmost importance! It is not restful for me to consider that Jennie runs around London giving her murderer every opportunity to kill her and put his fourth cufflink in her mouth.'

Poirot leaned forward in his chair. 'Please tell me that this at least has struck you: that cufflinks come in pairs? You have three in the mouths of the dead at the Bloxham Hotel. Where is the fourth, if not in the pocket of the killer, waiting to go into the mouth of Mademoiselle Jennie after her murder?'

I'm afraid I laughed. 'Poirot, that's just plain silly. Yes, cufflinks normally come in pairs but really, it's quite simple: he wanted to kill three people, so he only used three cufflinks. You can't use the notion of some dreamed-up fourth cufflink to prove anything — certainly not to link the hotel murders to this Jennie woman.'

Poirot's face had taken on a stubborn cast. 'When you are a killer who decides to use cufflinks in this way, *mon ami*, you invite the thought of the pairs. It is the killer who has put before us the notion of the fourth cufflink and the fourth victim, not Hercule Poirot!'

31

'But . . . then how do we know he doesn't have six victims in mind, or eight? Who is to say that the pocket of this killer doesn't contain *five* more cufflinks with the monogram PIJ?'

To my amazement, Poirot nodded and said, 'You make a good point.'

'No, Poirot, it's not a good point,' I said despondently. 'I conjured it up out of nowhere. You might enjoy my flights of fancy but I can promise you my bosses at Scotland Yard won't.'

'Your bosses, they do not like you to consider what is possible? No, of course they do not,' Poirot answered himself. 'And they are the people in charge of catching this murderer. They, and you. *Bon.* This is why Hercule Poirot must go tomorrow to the Bloxham Hotel.'

3

At the Bloxham Hotel

The following morning at the Bloxham, I could not help but feel unsettled, knowing that Poirot might arrive at any moment to tell us simple police folk how foolishly we were approaching the investigation of our three murders. I was the only one who knew he was coming, which set me rather on edge. His presence would be my responsibility, and I was afraid that he might demoralize the troops. If truth be told, I feared that he might demoralize me. In the optimistic light of an unusually bright February day, and after a surprisingly satisfactory night's sleep, I couldn't understand why I hadn't forbidden him from coming anywhere near the Bloxham.

I didn't suppose it mattered, however; he would not have listened to me if I had.

I was in the hotel's opulent lobby when Poirot arrived, talking to a Mr Luca Lazzari, the hotel's manager. Lazzari was a friendly, helpful and startlingly enthusiastic man with black curly hair, a musical way of speaking, and moustaches that were in no way the equal of Poirot's. Lazzari seemed determined that I and my fellow policemen should enjoy our time at the Bloxham every bit as much as the paying guests did — those that did not end up getting murdered, that is.

I introduced him to Poirot, who nodded curtly. He seemed out of sorts and I soon learned why. 'I did not find Jennie,' he said. 'Half the morning I waited at the coffee house! But she did not come.'

'Hardly 'half the morning', Poirot,' I said, for he was prone to exaggeration.

'Mademoiselle Fee also was not there. The other waitresses, they were able to tell me nothing.'

'Bad luck,' I said, unsurprised by the news. I hadn't for a moment imagined that Jennie might revisit the coffee house, and I felt guilty. I should perhaps have tried harder to make Poirot see sense: she had run away from him and from Pleasant's, having declared that confiding in him had been a mistake. Why on earth would she return the following day and allow him to take charge of protecting her?

'So!' Poirot looked at me expectantly. 'What do you have to tell me?'

'I too am here to provide the information you need,' said Lazzari, beaming. 'Luca Lazzari, at your disposal. Have you visited the Bloxham Hotel before, Monsieur Poirot?'

'*Non.*'

'Is it not superb? Like a palace of the belle époque, no? Majestic! I hope you notice and admire the artistic masterpieces that are all around us!'

'*Oui.* It is superior to the lodging house of Mrs Blanche Unsworth, though that house has the better view from the window,' Poirot said briskly. His glum spirits had certainly dug themselves in.

34

'Ah, the views from my charming hotel!' Lazzari clasped his hands together in delight. 'From the rooms facing the hotel gardens there are sights of great beauty, and on the other side there is splendid London — another exquisite scene! Later I will show you.'

'I would prefer to be shown the three rooms in which murders have taken place,' Poirot told him.

That put a momentary crimp in Lazzari's smile. 'Monsieur Poirot, you may rest assured that this terrible crime — three murders on one night, it is scarcely credible to me! — that this will *never* happen again at the world-renowned Bloxham Hotel.'

Poirot and I exchanged a look. The point was not so much preventing it from happening again but dealing with the fact that it had happened on this occasion.

I decided I had better take the reins and not allow Lazzari the chance to say too much more. Poirot's moustaches were already twitching with suppressed rage.

'The victims' names are Mrs Harriet Sippel, Miss Ida Gransbury and Mr Richard Negus,' I told Poirot. 'All three were guests in the hotel and each one was the sole occupant of his or her room.'

'Each one? *His or her* room, you say?' Poirot smiled at his little joke. I attributed the rapid improvement in his spirits to the fact that Lazzari had fallen silent. 'I do not mean to interrupt you, Catchpool. Continue.'

'All three victims arrived here at the hotel on

Wednesday, the day before they were murdered.'

'Did they arrive together?'

'No.'

'Most definitely not,' said Lazzari. 'They arrived separately, one by one. They checked in one by one.'

'And they were murdered one by one,' said Poirot, which happened to be exactly what I was thinking. 'You are certain of this?' he asked Lazzari.

'I could not be more so. I have the word of my clerk, Mr John Goode, the most dependable man of my entire acquaintance. You will meet him. We have only the most impeccable persons working here at the Bloxham Hotel, Monsieur Poirot, and when my clerk tells me a thing is so, I know that it is so. From across the country and across the world, people come to ask if they can work at the Bloxham Hotel. I say yes only to the best.'

It's funny but I didn't realize how well I had come to know Poirot until that moment — until I saw that Lazzari did not know how to manage him at all. If he had written 'Suspect This Man of Murder' on a large sign and hung it around Mr John Goode's neck, he could not have done a better job of inciting Poirot to distrust the fellow. Hercule Poirot will not allow anyone else to dictate to him what his opinion should be; he will, rather, determine to believe the opposite, contrary old cove that he is.

'So,' he said now, 'it is a remarkable coincidence, is it not? Our three murder victims — Mrs Harriet Sippel, Miss Ida Gransbury and Mr Richard Negus — they arrive separately

36

and appear to have nothing to do with one another. And yet all three share not merely the date of their deaths, which was yesterday, but also their date of arrival at the Bloxham Hotel: Wednesday.'

'What's remarkable about it?' I asked. 'Plenty of other guests must also have arrived on Wednesday, in a hotel of this size. I mean, ones that have not been murdered.'

Poirot's eyes looked as if they were about to burst forth from his head. I couldn't see that I had said anything particularly shocking, so I pretended not to notice his consternation, and continued to tell him the facts of the case.

'Each of the victims was found inside his or her locked bedroom,' I said, feeling rather self-conscious about the 'his or her' part. 'The killer locked all three doors and made off with the keys — '

'*Attendez*,' Poirot interrupted. 'You mean that the keys are missing. You cannot know that the murderer took them or has them now.'

I took a deep breath. 'We *suspect* that the killer took the keys away with him. We've done a thorough search, and they are certainly not inside the rooms, nor anywhere else in the hotel.'

'My excellent staff have checked and confirmed that this is true,' said Lazzari.

Poirot said that he would like to perform his own thorough search of the three rooms. Lazzari joyously agreed, as if Poirot had proposed a tea party followed by dancing.

'Check all you like, but you won't find the three room keys,' I said. 'I'm telling you, the murderer took them. I don't know what he did with them, but — '

'Perhaps he put them in his coat pocket, with one, or three, or five monogrammed cufflinks,' Poirot said coolly.

'Ah, now I see why they speak of you as the most splendid detective, Monsieur Poirot!' Lazzari exclaimed, though he can't have understood Poirot's remark. 'You have a superb mind, they say!'

'Cause of death is looking very much like poisoning,' I said, disinclined to linger over descriptions of Poirot's brilliance. 'We think cyanide, which can work with great speed if the quantities are sufficient. The inquest'll tell us for sure, but . . . almost certainly their drinks were poisoned. In the case of Harriet Sippel and Ida Gransbury, that drink was a cup of tea. In the case of Richard Negus it was sherry.'

'How is this known?' Poirot asked. 'The drinks are still there in the rooms?'

'The cups are, yes, and Negus's sherry glass. Only the remaining few drops of the drinks themselves, but it's easy enough to tell tea from coffee. We will find cyanide in those drops, I'll wager.'

'And the time of death?'

'According to the police doctor, all three were murdered between four o'clock in the afternoon and half past eight in the evening. Luckily, we've managed to narrow it down further: to between a quarter past seven and ten minutes past eight.'

'A stroke of luck indeed!' Lazzari agreed. 'Each of the . . . ah . . . deceased guests was last seen alive at fifteen minutes after seven o'clock, by three unquestionably dependable representatives of this hotel — so we know this must be true! I myself found the deceased persons — so terrible, this tragedy! — at between fifteen and twenty minutes after eight o'clock.'

'But they must have been dead by ten past eight,' I told Poirot. 'That was when the note announcing the murders was found on the front desk.'

'Wait, please,' said Poirot. 'We will get to this note in due course. Monsieur Lazzari, it is surely not possible that each of the murder victims was last seen alive by a member of hotel staff at a *quarter past seven precisely?*'

'Yes.' Lazzari nodded so hard, I feared his head might fall off his neck. 'It is very, very true. All three ordered dinner to be brought to their rooms at a quarter past the hour, and all three deliveries were exceptionally prompt. That is the way of the Bloxham Hotel.'

Poirot turned to me. 'This is another coincidence *énorme*,' he said. 'Harriet Sippel, Ida Gransbury and Richard Negus all arrive at the hotel on the same day, the day before they are murdered. Then on the day of the murders *they all order dinner to be brought to their rooms at a quarter past seven exactly?* It does not seem very likely.'

'Poirot, there's no point debating the likelihood of something we know happened.'

'*Non.* But there is a point in making sure that it happened in the way that we have heard. Monsieur Lazzari, I have no doubt that your

39

hotel contains at least one very large room. Please assemble in that room everybody who works here, and I will speak to them all at their — and your — earliest convenience. While you do this, Mr Catchpool and I will begin the inspection of the three victims' rooms.'

'Yes, and we'd better be quick about it, before they come for the bodies,' I said. 'In normal circumstances, they would have been removed by now.' I did not mention that the delay in this instance had been caused by my own dereliction of duty. In my hurry to put distance between myself and the Bloxham Hotel last night, and to think about something — anything — more pleasant than these three murders, I had neglected to make the necessary arrangements.

* * *

I hoped Poirot might warm up a few degrees once Lazzari had left us alone, but there was no change to his stern demeanour, and I realized that he was probably always like this 'at work', as it were — which seemed a bit rich since it was my work and not his, and he was doing nothing to lift my spirits.

I had a master key, and we visited the three rooms one by one. As we waited for the lift's elaborate gold doors to open, Poirot said, 'We can agree on one thing, I hope: Monsieur Lazzari's word cannot be relied upon with regard to those working in the hotel. He speaks of them as if they are above suspicion, which they cannot be if they were here yesterday when the murders

40

were committed. The loyalty of Monsieur Lazzari is commendable, but he is a fool if he believes that all the staff of the Bloxham Hotel are *des anges*.'

Something had been bothering me, so I made a clean breast of it: 'I hope you don't also think I'm a fool. What I said before about plenty of other guests also arriving on Wednesday . . . That was a hare-brained thing to say. Any guests that arrived on Wednesday and *didn't* get murdered on Thursday are irrelevant, aren't they? I mean, it's only a noteworthy coincidence that three or any number of apparently unconnected guests arrive on the same day if they also get murdered on the same evening.'

'*Oui.*' Poirot smiled at me with genuine warmth as we stepped into the lift. 'You have restored my faith in your mental acuity, my friend. And you hit the head of the nail when you say 'apparently unconnected'. The three murder victims will turn out to be connected. I will swear to it now. They were not selected at random from among the hotel's guests. The three were killed for *one* reason — a reason connected with the initials PIJ. It is for the same reason that they all came to the hotel on the same day.'

'It's almost as if they received an invitation to present themselves for slaughter,' I said in a cavalier fashion. 'Invitation reads: 'Please arrive the day before, so that Thursday can be devoted entirely to your getting murdered.''

It was perhaps undignified to joke about it, but joking is what I do when I feel despondent, I'm

41

afraid. Sometimes I succeed in tricking myself into imagining that I feel all right about things. It didn't work on this occasion.

'Devoted entirely . . . ' Poirot muttered. 'Yes, that is an idea, *mon ami*. You were not being serious, I understand. Nevertheless, you make a point that is very interesting.'

I did not think I had. It was an asinine joke and nothing more. Poirot seemed intent on congratulating me for my most absurd notions.

'One, two, three,' said Poirot as we went up in the lift. 'Harriet Sippel, Room 121. Richard Negus, Room 238. Ida Gransbury, Room 317. The hotel has a fourth and a fifth floor also, but our three murder victims are on the consecutive floors 1,2 and 3. It is very neat.' Poirot usually approved of things that were neat, but he looked worried about this one.

We examined the three rooms, which were identical in almost every respect. Each contained a bed, cupboards, a basin with an upturned glass sitting on one corner, several armchairs, a table, a desk, a tiled fireplace, a radiator, a larger table over by the window, a suitcase, clothes and personal effects, and a dead person.

Each room's door closed with a thud, trapping me inside . . .

'Hold his hand, Edward.'

I couldn't bring myself to look too closely at the bodies. All three were lying on their backs, perfectly straight, with their arms flat by their sides and their feet pointing towards the door. Formally laid out.

(Even writing these words, describing the

posture of the bodies, produces in me an intolerable sensation. Is it any wonder I could not look closely at the three victims' faces for more than a few seconds at a time? The blue undertone to the skin; the still, heavy tongues; the shrivelled lips? Though I would have studied their faces in detail rather than look at their lifeless hands, and I would have done anything at all rather than wonder what I could not help wondering: whether Harriet Sippel, Ida Gransbury and Richard Negus would have wanted somebody to hold their hands once they were dead, or whether the idea would have horrified them. Alas, the human mind is a perverse, uncontrollable organ, and the contemplation of this matter pained me greatly.)

Formally laid out . . .

A thought struck me with great force. That was what was so grotesque about these three murder scenes, I realized: that the bodies had been laid out as a doctor might lay out his deceased patient, after tending him in his illness for many months. The bodies of Harriet Sippel, Ida Gransbury and Richard Negus had been arranged with meticulous care — or so it seemed to me. Their killer had ministered to them after their deaths, which made it all the more chilling that he had murdered them in cold blood.

No sooner had I had this thought than I told myself I was quite wrong. It was not ministration that had taken place here; far from it. I was confusing the present and the past, mixing up this business at the Bloxham with my unhappiest childhood memories. I ordered myself to think

43

only about what was here in front of me, and nothing else. I tried to see it all through Poirot's eyes, without the distortion of my own experience.

Each of the murder victims lay between a wing-backed armchair and a small table. On the three tables were two teacups with saucers (Harriet Sippel's and Ida Gransbury's) and one sherry glass (Richard Negus's). In Ida Gransbury's room, 317, there was a tray on the larger table by the window, loaded with empty plates and one more teacup and saucer. This cup was also empty. There was nothing on the plates but crumbs.

'Aha,' said Poirot. 'So in this room we have two teacups, and many plates. Miss Ida Gransbury had company for her evening meal, most certainly. Perhaps she had the murderer's company. But why is the tray still here, when the trays have been removed from the rooms of Harriet Sippel and Richard Negus?'

'They might not have ordered food,' I said. 'Maybe they only wanted drinks — the tea and the sherry — and no trays were left in their rooms in the first place. Ida Gransbury also brought twice as many clothes with her as the other two.' I gestured towards the cupboard, which contained an impressive array of dresses. 'Have a look in there — there isn't room to squeeze in even one petticoat, the number of garments she brought with her. She wanted to be certain of looking her best, that's for sure.'

'You are right,' said Poirot. 'Lazzari said that they all ordered dinner, but we will check exactly what was ordered to each room. Poirot, he would

44

not make the mistake of the assumption if it were not for Jennie weighing on his mind — Jennie, whose whereabouts he does not know! Jennie who is more or less the same age as the three we have here — between forty and forty-five, I think.'

I turned away while Poirot did whatever he did with the mouths and the cufflinks. While he conducted his forays and emitted various exclamations, I stared into fireplaces and out of windows, avoided thinking about hands that would never again be held, and pondered my crossword puzzle and where I might be going wrong. For some weeks I had been trying to compose one that was good enough to be sent to a newspaper to be considered for publication, but I wasn't having much success.

After we had looked at all three rooms, Poirot insisted that we return to the one on the second floor — Richard Negus's, number 238. Would I find it any easier to enter these rooms, I wondered, the more I did it? So far the answer was no. Walking once again into Negus's hotel room felt like forcing my heart to climb the most perilous mountain, in the certain knowledge that it will be left stranded as soon as it reaches the top.

Poirot — unaware of my distress, which I concealed effectively, I hope — stood in the middle of the room and said, 'Bon. This is the one that is most different from the others, n'est-ce pas? Ida Gransbury has the tray and the additional teacup in her room, it is true, but here there is the sherry glass instead of the teacup,

45

and here we have one window open to its full capacity, while in the other two rooms all the windows are closed. Mr Negus's room is intolerably cold.'

'This is how it was when Monsieur Lazzari walked in and found Negus dead,' I said. 'Nothing's been altered in any way.'

Poirot walked over to the open window. 'Here is Monsieur Lazzari's wonderful view that he offered to show me — of the hotel's gardens. Both Harriet Sippel and Ida Gransbury had rooms on the other side of the hotel, with views of the 'splendid London'. Do you see these trees, Catchpool?'

I told him that I did, wondering if he had me down as a colossal idiot. How could I fail to see trees that were directly outside the window?

'Another difference here is the position of the cufflink,' said Poirot. 'Did you notice that? In Harriet Sippel's and Ida Gransbury's mouths, the cufflink is slightly protruding between the lips. Whereas Richard Negus has the cufflink much further back, almost at the entrance to the throat.'

I opened my mouth to object, then changed my mind, but it was too late. Poirot had seen the argument in my eyes. 'What is it?' he asked.

'I think you're being a touch pedantic,' I said. 'All three victims have monogrammed cufflinks in their mouths — the same initials on each one, PIJ. That's something they have in common. It isn't a difference. No matter which of their teeth the cufflink happens to be next to.'

'But it is a very big difference! The lips, the

entrance to the throat — these are not the same place, not at all.' Poirot walked over so that he was standing right in front of me. 'Catchpool, please remember what I am about to tell you. When three murders are almost identical, the smallest divergent details are of the utmost importance.'

Was I supposed to remember these wise words even if I disagreed with them? Poirot needn't have worried. I remember nearly every word he has spoken in my presence, and the ones that infuriated me most are the ones I remember best of all.

'All three cufflinks were in the mouths of the victims,' I repeated with determined obstinacy. 'That's good enough for me.'

'This I see,' said Poirot with an air of dejection. 'Good enough for you, and good enough also for your hundred people that you might ask, and also, I have no doubt, for your bosses at Scotland Yard. But not good enough for Hercule Poirot!'

I had to remind myself that he was talking about definitions of similarity and difference, and not about me personally.

'What about the open window, when all the windows in the other two rooms are closed?' he asked. 'Is that a difference worth noting?'

'It's unlikely to be relevant,' I said. 'Richard Negus might have opened the window himself. There would be no reason for the murderer to close it. You've said it often yourself, Poirot — we Englishmen open windows in the dead of winter because we believe it's good for our character.'

47

'*Mon ami*,' said Poirot patiently. 'Consider: these three people did not drink poison, fall out of their armchairs and quite naturally land flat on their backs with their arms at their sides and their feet pointing towards the door. It is impossible. Why would one not stagger across the room? Why would one not fall out of the chair on the other side? The killer, he *arranged* the bodies so that each one was in the same position, at an equal distance from the chair and from the little table. *Eh bien*, if he cares so much to arrange his three murder scenes to look exactly the same, why does he not wish to close the window that, yes, perhaps Mr Richard Negus has opened — but why does the murderer not *close* it in order to make it conform with the appearance of the windows in the other two rooms?'

I had to think about this. Poirot was right: the bodies had been laid out in this way deliberately. The killer must have wanted them all to look the same.

Laying out the dead . . .

'I suppose it depends where you choose to draw your frame around the scene of the crime,' I said hurriedly, as my mind tried to drag me back to my childhood's darkest room. 'Depends whether you want to extend it as far as the window.'

'Frame?'

'Yes. Not a real frame, a theoretical one. Perhaps our murderer's frame for his creations was no larger than a square like this.' I walked around Richard Negus's body, turning corners

48

when necessary. 'You see? I've just walked a small frame around Negus, and the window is outside the frame.'

Poirot was smiling and trying to hide it beneath his moustaches. 'A theoretical frame around the murder. Yes, I see. Where does the scene of a crime begin and where does it end? This is the question. Can it be smaller than the room that contains it? This is a fascinating matter for the philosophers.'

'Thank you.'

'*Pas du tout.* Catchpool, will you please tell me what you believe happened here at the Bloxham Hotel yesterday evening? Let us leave motive to one side for the moment. Tell me what you think the killer did. First, and next, and next, and so on.'

'I have no idea.'

'Try to have an idea, Catchpool.'

'Well . . . I suppose he came to the hotel, cufflinks in pocket, and went to each of the three rooms in turn. He probably started where we did, with Ida Gransbury in Room 317, and worked his way down so that he would be able to leave the hotel fairly quickly after killing his final victim — Harriet Sippel in Room 121, on the first floor. Only one floor down and he can escape.'

'And what does he do in the three rooms?'

I sighed. 'You know the answer to that. He commits a murder and arranges the body in a straight line. He places a cufflink in the person's mouth. Then he closes and locks the door and leaves.'

'And to each room he is admitted without

49

question? In each room, he finds his victim waiting with a most convenient drink for him to drop his poison into — drinks that were delivered by hotel staff at precisely a quarter past seven? He stands beside his victim, watching as the drink is consumed, and then he stands for a little longer as he waits for each one to die? And he stops to eat supper with one of them, Ida Gransbury, who has ordered a cup of tea for him too? All these visits to rooms, all these murders and putting of cufflinks in mouths and very formal arranging of bodies in straight lines, with feet pointing towards the door, he is able to do between a quarter past seven and ten past eight? This seems most unlikely, my friend. Most unlikely indeed.'

'Yes, it does. Have you got any better ideas, Poirot? That's why you're here — to have better ideas than mine. Do please start any time you wish.' I was regretting my outburst by the time I'd finished the sentence.

'I started long ago,' said Poirot, who thankfully had not taken umbrage. 'You said that the killer left a note on the front desk, informing of his crimes — show it to me.'

I took it out of my pocket and passed it across to him. John Goode, Lazzari's idea of perfection in the form of a hotel clerk, had found it on the front desk ten minutes after eight o'clock. It read, 'MAY THEY NEVER REST IN PEACE. 121. 238. 317.'

'So the murderer, or an accomplice of the murderer, was brazen enough to approach the desk — the main desk in the lobby of the hotel

50

— with a note that would incriminate him if anyone saw him leaving it,' said Poirot. 'He is audacious. Confident. He did not disappear into the shadows, using the back door.'

'After Lazzari read the note, he checked the three rooms and found the bodies,' I said. 'Then he checked all the other rooms in the hotel, he was very proud to tell me. Fortunately no other dead guests were found.'

I knew I oughtn't to say vulgar things, but it made me feel better somehow. If Poirot had been English, I probably would have made a greater effort to keep myself in check.

'And did it occur to Monsieur Lazzari that one of his still-living guests might be a murderer? *Non*. It did not. Any person who chooses to stay at the Bloxham Hotel must have a character of the utmost virtue and integrity!'

I coughed and inclined my head towards the door. Poirot turned. Lazzari had let himself into the room and was standing in the doorway. He could hardly have looked happier. 'So true, so true, Monsieur Poirot,' he said.

'Every single person who was in this hotel on Thursday must speak to Mr Catchpool and account for their movements,' Poirot told him sternly. 'Every guest, everyone who was here to work. All of them.'

'With the greatest pleasure, you may speak to whomsoever you wish, Mr Catchpool.' Lazzari bowed in deference. 'And our dining room will soon be at your disposal, once we have cleared away the breakfast — ah, how do you say? — *paraphernalia*, and gathered everybody together.'

51

'*Merci*. Meanwhile, I will conduct a thorough examination of the three rooms,' said Poirot. This came as a surprise to me. I thought that was what we had just done. 'Catchpool, find out the addresses of Harriet Sippel, Ida Gransbury and Richard Negus. Find out who in the hotel took their reservations, what food and drinks they each requested to be delivered to their rooms, and when. And from whom.'

I started to edge towards the door, fearing that Poirot would never stop dreaming up more tasks to add to the list.

He called after me, 'Find out if anyone by the name of Jennie is staying in the hotel, or working here.'

'There is not a Jennie employed at the Bloxham, Monsieur Poirot,' said Lazzari. 'Instead of asking Mr Catchpool you should ask *me*. Everybody here is well known to me. We are a very large happy family here at the Bloxham Hotel!'

4

The Frame Widens

Sometimes, remembering something a person said months or even years ago still makes you chuckle, and this, for me, is true of what Poirot said to me at some point later on that day: 'It is hard for even the most ingenious detective to know what to do if his desire is to be free of Signor Lazzari. If one's praise of his hotel is insufficient, he stays by one's side and supplements it with his own; if one's praise is fulsome and lengthy, he stays to listen.'

Poirot's efforts were eventually successful, and he finally managed to persuade Lazzari to leave him to his own devices in Room 238. He walked over to the door that the hotel manager had left open, closed it, and sighed with relief. How much easier it was to think clearly when there was no babble of voices.

He made straight for the window. An open window, he thought as he stared out of it. The murderer might have opened it to escape, after killing Richard Negus. He could have climbed down a tree.

Why escape thus? Why not simply leave the room in the expected way, using the corridor? Perhaps the killer heard voices outside Negus's room and did not want to risk being seen. Yes, that was a possibility. And yet when he strolled up to the front desk to leave his note announcing his three murders, he risked being seen. More than seen — he risked being caught in the act of leaving incriminating evidence.

Poirot looked down at the body on the floor. No gleam of metal between the lips. Richard Negus alone of the three victims had the cufflink right at the back of his mouth. It was an anomaly. Too many things about this room were anomalous. For this reason, Poirot decided he would search Room 238 first. He was . . . Yes, there was no virtue in denying it — he was *suspicious* of this room. Of the three, it was his least favourite. There was something disorganized about it, something a little unruly.

Poirot stood beside Negus's body and frowned. Even by his exacting standards, one open window was not enough to render a room chaotic, so what was it that was giving him this impression? He looked around, turning in a slow circle. No, he must be mistaken. Hercule Poirot was not often wrong but it did happen very occasionally, and this must be one such instance, because 238 was an undeniably tidy room. There was no mess or muddle. It was as tidy as Harriet Sippel's room and Ida Gransbury's.

'I shall shut the window and see if that makes a difference,' said Poirot to himself. He did so, and surveyed the territory anew. Something was still not right. He did not like Room 238. He would not have felt comfortable if he had arrived at the Bloxham Hotel and been shown to this . . .

Suddenly the problem leapt out at him,

54

putting an abrupt end to his meditations. The fireplace! One of the tiles was not aligned correctly. It was not straight; it jutted out. A loose tile; Poirot could not sleep in a room with such a thing. He eyed the body of Richard Negus. 'If I were in the condition that you are in, *oui*, but not otherwise,' he said to it.

His only thought as he bent to touch the tile was that he might straighten it and push it back in so that it was flush with the others. To spare future guests the torment of knowing that there was something amiss in the room and being unable to work out what it was — what a service that would be! And to Signor Lazzari also!

When Poirot touched it, the tile fell clean out, and something else fell with it: a key with a number on it: 238. '*Sacre tonnerre*,' Poirot whispered. 'So the thorough search was not so thorough after all.'

Poirot replaced the key where he had found it, then set about inspecting the rest of the room, inch by inch. He discovered nothing else of interest, so he proceeded to Room 317 and then to Room 121, which was where I found him when I returned from my errands with exciting news of my own.

Poirot being Poirot, he insisted on telling me his news first, about his finding of the key. All I can say is, in Belgium it is evidently not considered unseemly to gloat. He was quite puffed up with pride. 'Do you see what this means, *mon ami?* The open window was not opened by Richard Negus, it was opened after his death! Having locked the door of Room 238

55

from the *inside*, the murderer needed to escape. He did so using the tree outside Mr Negus's window, after he had hidden the key behind a tile in the fireplace that had come loose. He perhaps loosened it himself.'

'Why not conceal it in his clothing, take it with him and leave the room in the customary way?' I asked.

'That is a question I have been asking myself — one that, for now, I am unable to answer,' Poirot said. 'I have satisfied myself that there is no hidden key in this room, 121. Nor is there a key anywhere in Room 317. The killer must have taken two keys with him when he left the Bloxham Hotel, so why not the third? Why is the treatment of Richard Negus different?'

'I haven't the faintest idea,' I said. 'Listen, I've been talking to John Goode, the clerk — '

'The most dependable clerk,' Poirot amended with a twinkle in his eye.

'Yes, well . . . dependable or not, he's certainly come up trumps for us on the information front. You were right: the three victims *are* connected. I've seen their addresses. Harriet Sippel and Ida Gransbury both lived in a place called Great Holling, in the Culver Valley.'

'*Bon.* And Richard Negus?'

'No, he lives in Devon — place called Beaworthy. But he's connected too. He booked all three hotel rooms — Ida's, Harriet's and his own — and he paid for them ahead of time.'

'Did he indeed? This I find very interesting . . . ' Poirot murmured, stroking his moustaches.

56

'Bit puzzling, if you ask me,' I said. 'The main puzzle being: why, if they were coming from the same village on the same day, did Harriet Sippel and Ida Gransbury not travel together? Why did they not arrive together? I went over it several times with John Goode and he is adamant: Harriet arrived two hours before Ida on Wednesday — two full hours.'

'And Richard Negus?'

I resolved henceforth to include all details relating to Negus at the earliest opportunity, if only so that I wouldn't have to hear Poirot say, 'And Richard Negus?' over and over again.

'He turned up an hour *before* Harriet Sippel. He was the first of the three to arrive, but it wasn't John Goode who dealt with him. It was a junior clerk, a Mr Thomas Brignell. I also found out that all three of our murder victims travelled to London by train, not car. I'm not sure if you wanted to know that, but — '

'I must know everything,' said Poirot.

His obvious desire to be in charge and make the investigation his own both irritated and reassured me. 'The Bloxham has some cars that it sends out to fetch guests from the station,' I told him. 'It's not cheap, but they're happy to sort it out for you. Three weeks ago, Richard Negus made arrangements with John Goode for the hotel's cars to meet him, Harriet Sippel and Ida Gransbury. Separately; a car each. All of it — the rooms, the cars — it was all paid for in advance, by Negus.'

'I wonder if he was a wealthy man,' Poirot mused aloud. 'So often, murder turns out to be about money. What are your thoughts, Catchpool, now that we know a little more?'

'Well . . . ' I decided to throw myself into it, since he'd asked. Imagining what was possible was a good thing in Poirot's book, so I would allow myself to concoct a theory, using the facts as a starting point. 'Richard Negus must have known about all three arrivals, since he reserved and paid for the rooms, but perhaps Harriet Sippel didn't know that Ida Gransbury was also coming to the Bloxham. And perhaps Ida didn't know that Harriet was.'

'*Oui, c'est possible.*'

Encouraged, I went on: 'Maybe it was essential to the murderer's plan that neither Ida nor Harriet should know about the presence of the other one. But if that's so, and if Richard Negus, meanwhile, knew that he and both women would be guests at the Bloxham . . . ' My well of ideas ran dry at that point.

Poirot took over: 'Our trains of thought proceed along similar tracks, my friend. Was Richard Negus an unwitting accomplice in his own murder? Perhaps the killer persuaded him to entice the victims to the Bloxham Hotel supposedly for another reason, when all along he planned to murder all three of them. The question is this: *was it vital for some reason that Ida and Harriet should each be ignorant of the presence of the other in the hotel?* And if so, was it important to Richard Negus, to the murderer, or to both?'

'Perhaps Richard Negus had one plan, and the murderer had another?'

58

'Quite so,' said Poirot. 'The next thing is to find out all that we can about Harriet Sippel, Richard Negus and Ida Gransbury. Who were they when they were alive? What were their hopes, their grievances, their secrets? The village, Great Holling — this is where we will look for our answers. Perhaps we will also find Jennie there, and PIJ — *le mystérieux!*'

'There's no guest here called Jennie, now or last night. I checked.'

'No, I did not think that there would be. Fee Spring, the waitress, told me that Jennie lives in a house across town from Pleasant's Coffee House. That means in London — not Devon and not the Culver Valley. Jennie has no need of a room at the Bloxham Hotel when she lives only 'across town'.'

'Speaking of which, Henry Negus, Richard's brother, is on his way here from Devon. Richard Negus lived with Henry and his family. And I've got some of my best men lined up to interview all the hotel guests.'

'You have been very efficient, Catchpool.' Poirot patted my arm.

I felt obliged to advise Poirot of my one failure. 'This business with the dinners in the rooms is proving difficult to pin down,' I said. 'I can't find anyone who was personally involved in taking the orders or making the deliveries. There seems to be some confusion.'

'Do not worry,' said Poirot. 'I will do the necessary pinning when we gather in the dining room. In the meantime, let us take a walk around the hotel gardens. Sometimes a gentle

59

perambulation causes a new idea to rise to the surface of one's thoughts.'

* * *

As soon as we got outside, Poirot started to complain about the weather, which did seem to have taken a turn for the worse. 'Shall we go back inside?' I suggested.

'No, no. Not yet. The change of environment is good for the little grey cells, and perhaps the trees will afford some shelter from the wind. I do not mind the cold, but there is the good kind and the bad kind, and this, today, is the bad kind.'

We stopped as we came to the entrance to the Bloxham's gardens. Luca Lazzari had not exaggerated their beauty, I thought, as I stared at rows of pleached limes and, at the furthest end, the most artful topiary I had ever seen in London. This was nature not merely tamed but forced into stunning submission. Even in a biting wind, it was exceptionally pleasing to the eye.

'Well?' I asked Poirot. 'Are we going in or not?' It would be satisfying, I thought, to stroll up and down the green pathways between the trees, which were Roman-road straight.

'I do not know.' Poirot frowned. 'This weather . . . ' He shivered.

' . . . will extend, unavoidably, to the gardens,' I completed his sentence somewhat impatiently. 'There are only two places we can be, Poirot: inside the hotel or outside it. Which do you prefer?'

'I have a better idea!' he announced

triumphantly. 'We will catch a bus!'

'A bus? To where?'

'To nowhere, or somewhere! It does not matter. We will soon get off the bus and return on a different one. It will give us the change of scenery without the cold! Come. We will look out of the windows at the city. Who knows what we might observe?' He set off determinedly.

I followed, shaking my head. 'You're thinking of Jennie, aren't you?' I said. 'It's extremely unlikely that we will see her — '

'It is more likely than if we stand here looking at twigs and grass!' said Poirot fiercely.

Ten minutes later we found ourselves trundling along on a bus with windows so fogged up that it was impossible to see anything through them. Wiping them with a handkerchief didn't help.

I tried to talk some sense into Poirot. 'About Jennie . . . ' I began.

'Oui?'

'She might well be in danger, but, really, she's nothing to do with this business at the Bloxham. There's no evidence of a connection between the two. None at all.'

'I disagree, my friend,' said Poirot sorrowfully. 'I am more than ever convinced of a connection.'

'You are? Dash it all, Poirot — why?'

'Because of the two most unusual features that the . . . situations have in common.'

'And what are those?'

'They will come to you, Catchpool. Really, they cannot fail to strike you if you open your mind and think about what you know.'

In the seats behind us, an elderly mother and

61

her middle-aged daughter were discussing what made the difference between pastry that was merely good and pastry that was excellent.

'Do you hear that, Catchpool?' whispered Poirot. '*La différence!* Let us focus not on similarities but on differences — this is what will point us towards our murderer.'

'What sort of differences?' I asked.

'Between two of the murders at the hotel and the third. Why are the circumstantial details so different in the case of Richard Negus? Why did the killer lock the door from the *inside* of the room instead of from the outside? Why did he hide the key behind a loose tile in the fireplace instead of taking it with him? Why did he leave by the window, with the help of a tree, instead of by walking along the corridor in the normal way? At first I wondered if perhaps he heard voices in the corridor and did not want to risk being seen leaving Mr Negus's room.'

'That seems reasonable,' I said.

'*Non.* I do not, after all, think that was the reason.'

'Oh. Why not?'

'Because of the positioning of the cufflink in Richard Negus's mouth, which was also different in this one case: fully inside the mouth, near the throat, instead of between the lips.'

I groaned. 'Not this again. I really don't think — '

'Ah! Wait, Catchpool. Let us see . . . '

The bus had stopped. Poirot craned his neck to inspect the new passengers who boarded, and sighed when the last one — a slender man in a tweed suit with more hair growing from his ears than on his head — was in.

'You're disappointed because none of them is Jennie,' I said. I needed to say it aloud in order to believe it, I think.

'*Non, mon ami*. You are correct about the sentiment, but not about its cause. I feel the disappointment every time I think that, in a city as *énorme* as London, I am unlikely ever to see Jennie again. And yet . . . I hope.'

'For all your talk of scientific method, you're a bit of a dreamer, aren't you?'

'You believe hope to be the enemy of science and not its driving force? If so, I disagree, just as I disagree with you about the cufflink. It is a significant difference in the case of Richard Negus from the other two, the women. The difference of the position of the cufflink in Mr Negus's mouth cannot be explained by the killer hearing the voices of people in the corridor and wanting to avoid them,' Poirot spoke over me. 'Therefore there must be another explanation. Until we know what it is, we cannot be certain that it does not also apply to the open window, the key hidden in the room and the door locked from the inside.'

There comes a point in most cases — and by no means only those in which Hercule Poirot has involved himself — when one starts to feel that it would be a greater comfort, and actually no less effective, to talk only to oneself, and dispense with all attempts to communicate with the outside world.

In my head, to a sensible and appreciative

audience of one, I silently made the following point: the cufflink being in a slightly different part of Richard Negus's mouth was of absolutely no consequence. A mouth is a mouth, and that was all there was to it. In the murderer's mind, he had done the same thing to each of his three victims: he had opened their mouths and placed a monogrammed gold cufflink inside each one.

I could not think of any explanation for the hiding of the key behind the loose fireplace tile. It would have been quicker and easier for the murderer to take it with him, or drop it on the carpet after wiping it clean of his fingerprints.

Behind us, the mother and daughter had exhausted the topic of pastry and moved on to suet.

'We ought to think about returning to the hotel,' said Poirot.

'But we've only just got on the bus!' I protested.

'*Oui, c'est vrai*, but we do not want to stray too far from the Bloxham. We will soon be needed in the dining room.'

I exhaled slowly, knowing it would be pointless to ask why, in that case, he had felt it necessary to leave the hotel in the first place.

'We must get off this bus and catch another,' he said. 'Perhaps there will be better views from the next one.'

There were. Poirot saw no sign of Jennie, much to his consternation, but I saw some amusing sights that made me realize all over again why I loved London: a man dressed in a clown costume, juggling about as badly as I had ever seen a person juggle. Still, passers-by were throwing coins into the hat by his feet. Other highlights were a poodle that had a face exactly like a prominent politician, and a vagrant sitting on the pavement with an open suitcase beside him, eating food out of it as if it were his very own mobile tuck shop. 'Look, Poirot,' I said. 'That chap doesn't care about the cold — he's as happy as the cat that got the cream. The tramp that got the cream, I should say. Poirot, look at that poodle — does it remind you of anyone? Somebody famous. Go on, look, you can't fail to see it.'

'Catchpool,' Poirot said severely. 'Stand up, or we will miss our stop. Always you look away, seeking the diversion.'

I rose to my feet. As soon as we were off the bus, I said, 'You're the one who took me on a pointless sightseeing tour of London. You can hardly blame me for taking an interest in the sights.'

Poirot stopped walking. 'Tell me something. Why will you not look at the three bodies in the hotel? What is it that you cannot bear to observe?'

'Nothing. I've looked at the bodies as much as you have — I did quite a lot of my looking before you turned up, as a matter of fact.'

'If you do not wish to discuss it with me, you only need to say so, *mon ami*.'

'There is nothing to discuss. I don't know anybody who would stare at a deceased person for any longer than necessary. That's all there is to it.'

'*Non*,' said Poirot quietly. 'It is not all.'

I dare say I ought to have told him, and I still

don't know why I didn't. My grandfather died when I was five. He was dying for a long time, in a room in our house. I didn't like going to visit him in his room every day, but my parents insisted that it was important to him, and so I did it to please them, and for his sake also. I watched his skin turn gradually yellower, and listened as his breathing became more shallow and his eyes less focused. I didn't think of it then as fear, but I remember, every day, counting the seconds that I had to spend in that room, knowing that eventually I would be able to leave, close the door behind me and stop counting.

When he died, I felt as if I had been released from prison and could be fully alive again. He would be taken away, and there would be no more death in the house. And then my mother told me that I must go and see Grandfather one last time, in his room. She would come with me, she said. It would be all right.

The doctor had laid him out. My mother explained to me about the laying out of the dead. I counted the seconds in silence. More seconds than usual. A hundred and thirty at least, standing by my mother's side, looking at Grandpa's still, shrunken body. 'Hold his hand, Edward,' my mother said. When I said I didn't want to, she started to weep as if she would never stop.

So I held Grandpa's dead, bony hand. I wanted more than anything to drop it and run away, but I clung to it until my mother stopped crying and said we could go back downstairs.

Hold his hand, Edward. Hold his hand.

5

Ask a Hundred People

I barely noticed the large crowd gathered in the Bloxham Hotel's dining room as Poirot and I walked in. The room itself was so striking that I couldn't help but be diverted by its grandeur. I stopped in the doorway and stared up at the high, lavishly ornamented ceiling with its many emblems and carvings. It was strange to think of people eating ordinary things like toast and marmalade at the tables below a work of art such as this — not even looking up, perhaps, as they sliced the tops off their boiled eggs.

I was trying to make sense of the complete design, and how the different parts of the ceiling related to one another, when a disconsolate Luca Lazzari rushed towards me, interrupting my admiration of the artistic symmetry above my head with his loud lament. 'Mr Catchpool, Monsieur Poirot, I must apologize to you most profusely! I have hurried to assist you in your important work, and, in doing so, I have put forward a falsehood! It was simply, you see, that I heard many accounts, and my first attempt to collate them was not successful. My own foolishness was responsible! No one else was at fault. Ah — '

Lazzari broke off and looked over his shoulder at the hundred or so men and women in the room. Then he moved to his left, so that he was standing directly in front of Poirot, and stuck out his chest in a funny sort of way. He put his hands on his hips. I think he was hoping to hide his entire staff from Poirot's disapproving eye, on the principle that if they couldn't be seen, they couldn't be blamed for anything.

'What was your mistake, Signor Lazzari?' Poirot asked.

'It was a grave error! You observed that it was surely not possible, and you were right. But I want you to understand that my excellent staff, whom you see here before you, told me the truth of what took place, and it was I who twisted that truth to mislead — but I did not do it deliberately!'

'*Je comprends*. Now, to correct the mistake . . . ?' said Poirot hopefully.

The 'excellent' staff, meanwhile, sat silently at large round tables, listening carefully to every word. The mood was sombre. I made a quick survey of the faces and saw not a single smile.

'I told you that the three deceased guests asked to have dinner served in their rooms at a quarter past seven yesterday evening — each separately,' Lazzari said. 'This is not true! The three were together! They dined as a group! All in one room, Ida Gransbury's room, number 317. One waiter, not three, saw them alive and well at a quarter past seven. Do you see, Monsieur Poirot? It is not the great coincidence that I conveyed to you, but, instead, a commonplace occurrence: three guests taking dinner together in the room of one!'

'*Bon.*' Poirot sounded satisfied. 'That makes sense of that. And who was this one waiter?'

A stout, bald man seated at one of the tables rose to his feet. He looked to be around fifty, and had the jowlish tendency and mournful eyes of a Basset Hound. 'It was I, sir,' he said.

'What is your name, monsieur?'

'Rafal Bobak, sir.'

'You served dinner to Harriet Sippel, Ida Gransbury and Richard Negus in Room 317 at fifteen minutes past seven yesterday evening?' Poirot asked him.

'Not dinner, sir,' said Bobak. 'Afternoon tea — that was what Mr Negus ordered. Afternoon tea at dinner time. He asked if that was all right or if I was going to force them to have what he called 'a dinner sort of dinner'. Told me that he and his friends were of one mind as not being in the mood for one of those. Said they'd rather have afternoon tea. I told him he could have whatever he wanted, sir. He asked for sandwiches — ham, cheese, salmon and cucumber — and an assortment of cakes. And scones, sir, with jam and cream.'

'And beverages?' Poirot asked.

'Tea, sir. For all three of them.'

'*D'accord.* And the sherry for Richard Negus?'

Rafal Bobak shook his head. 'No, sir. No sherry. Mr Negus didn't ask me for a sherry. I didn't take a glass of sherry up to Room 317.'

'You are certain of this?'

'Absolutely, sir.'

Being on display in front of all those pairs of eyes was making me feel a touch awkward. I was

69

painfully aware that I had not yet asked a question. Letting Poirot run the show was all very well, but if I didn't participate at all, I would look feeble. I cleared my throat and addressed the room: 'Did any of you take a cup of tea to Harriet Sippel's room, number 121, at any point? Or a sherry to Richard Negus's room? Either yesterday or Wednesday, the day before?'

Heads began to shake. Unless someone was lying, it seemed that the only delivery to any of the three victims' rooms was the one of afternoon-tea-for-dinner made by Rafal Bobak to Room 317 at 7.15 p.m. on Thursday.

I tried to sort it out in my mind: the teacup in Harriet Sippel's room wasn't a problem. That must have been one of the three brought by Bobak, since only two cups were found in Ida Gransbury's room after the murders. But how did the sherry glass make its way to Richard Negus's room unless transported there by a waiter?

Did the killer arrive at the Bloxham with a glass of Harvey's Bristol Cream in his hand, as well as a pocket full of mongrammed cufflinks and poison? It seemed far-fetched.

Poirot appeared to have fixed on the same problem. 'To be absolutely clear: not one of you gave a glass of sherry to Mr Richard Negus, either in his room or anywhere else in the hotel?'

There was more head-shaking.

'Signor Lazzari, can you tell me please, was the glass found in Mr Negus's room one that belonged to the Bloxham Hotel?'

'Yes, it was, Monsieur Poirot. This is all very

perplexing. I would suggest that perhaps a waiter who is absent today gave the glass of sherry to Mr Negus on Thursday or Wednesday, but everybody is here now who was here then.'

'It is, as you say, perplexing,' Poirot agreed. 'Mr Bobak, perhaps you could tell us what happened when you took the evening-afternoon-tea to Ida Gransbury's room.'

'I set it out on the table and then I left them to it, sir.'

'They were all three in the room? Mrs Sippel, Miss Gransbury and Mr Negus?'

'They were, yes, sir.'

'Describe to us the scene.'

'The scene, sir?'

Seeing that Rafal Bobak was at a loss, I chipped in with: 'Which one of them opened the door?'

'Mr Negus opened the door, sir.'

'And where were the two women?' I asked.

'Oh, they were sitting in the two chairs over by the fireplace. Talking to each other. I had no dealings with them. I spoke only to Mr Negus. Laid everything out on the table by the window, and then I left, sir.'

'Can you recall what the two ladies talked about?' asked Poirot.

Bobak lowered his eyes. 'Well, sir . . . '

'It is important, monsieur. Every detail that you can tell me about these three people is important.'

'Well . . . they were being a bit cattish, sir. Laughing about it, too.'

'You mean they were being spiteful? How so?'

'One of them was, yes. And Mr Negus, he seemed to find it entertaining. It was something about an older woman and a younger man. It wasn't my business so I didn't listen.'

'Do you remember what precisely was said? At whom was the cattishness directed?'

'I couldn't tell you, sir, I'm sorry. An old woman that might be pining for the love of a young man, that was the sense I got. It sounded like gossip to me.'

'Monsieur,' said Poirot in his most authoritative voice. 'If you should happen to remember anything else about this conversation, anything at all, please inform me without delay.'

'I shall, sir. Now that I think about it, the young man might have deserted the older woman and eloped with another woman. Idle gossip, that's all it was.'

'So . . . ' Poirot started to pace the length of the room. It was strange to see more than a hundred heads turn slowly, then turn back as he retraced his steps. 'We have Richard Negus, Harriet Sippel and Ida Gransbury — one man and two women — in Room 317, talking cattishly about one man and two women!'

'But what's the significance of that, Poirot?' I asked.

'It might not be significant. It is interesting, however. And the idle gossip, the laughter, the afternoon tea for dinner . . . This tells us that our three murder victims were not strangers but acquaintances on friendly terms, unaware of the fate that would shortly befall them.'

A sudden movement startled me. At the table

immediately in front of where Poirot and I were standing, a black-haired, pale-faced young man had bounced out of his seat as if propelled from underneath. I would have assumed he was eager to say something were it not for the terror-frozen expression on his face.

'This is one of our junior clerks, Mr Thomas Brignell,' said Lazzari, presenting the man with a flourish of his hand.

'They were more than on friendly terms, sir,' Brignell breathed after a protracted silence. No one sitting behind him could have heard what he said, his voice was so quiet. 'They were good friends. They knew each other well.'

'Of course they were good friends!' Lazzari announced to the room. 'They ate a meal together!'

'Many people eat meals every day with those they dislike profoundly,' said Poirot. 'Please continue, Mr Brignell.'

'When I met Mr Negus last night, he was concerned for the two ladies as only a good friend would be,' Thomas Brignell whispered at us.

'You met him?' I said. 'When? Where?'

'Half past seven, sir.' He pointed towards the dining room's double doors. I noticed that his arm was shaking. 'Right outside here. I walked out and saw him going towards the lift. He saw me and stopped, called me over. I assumed he was making his way back to his room.'

'What did he say to you?' Poirot asked.

'He . . . he asked me to make sure that the meal was charged to him and not to either of the ladies. He could afford it, he said, but Mrs Sippel and Miss Gransbury could not.'

'Was that all he said, monsieur?'

'Yes.' Brignell looked as if he might faint if he was required to produce one more word.

'Thank you, Mr Brignell,' I said as warmly as I could. 'You've been very helpful.' Immediately I felt guilty for not having thanked Rafal Bobak in a similar manner, so I added, 'As have you, Mr Bobak. As have you all.'

'Catchpool,' Poirot murmured. 'Most people in this room have said nothing.'

'They have listened attentively and applied their minds to the problems presented to them. I think they deserve credit for that.'

'You have faith in their minds, yes? Perhaps these are the hundred people you call upon when we disagree? *Bien*, if we were to ask *these* hundred people . . . ' Poirot turned back to the crowd. 'Ladies and gentlemen, we have heard that Richard Negus, Harriet Sippel and Ida Gransbury were friends, and that their food was delivered to Room 317 at fifteen minutes past seven. Yet at half past seven, Mr Brignell saw Richard Negus on *this* floor of the hotel, walking towards the lift. Mr Negus must have been returning, *n'est-ce pas*, either to his own room, 238, or to Room 317 to join his two friends? But returning from where? His sandwiches and cakes were delivered only fifteen minutes earlier! Did he abandon them immediately and set off somewhere? Or did he eat his share of the food in only three or four minutes before rushing off? And to where did he rush? What was the

74

important errand for which he left Room 317? Was it to ensure that the food should not end up on the bill of Harriet Sippel or Ida Gransbury? He could not wait twenty or thirty minutes, or an hour, before setting off to attend to this matter?'

A sturdily built woman with curly brown hair and severe eyebrows sprang to her feet at the back of the room. 'You keep asking all these questions as if I might know the answer, as if we all might know the answers, and we don't know nothing!' Her eyes darted around the room as she spoke, settling on one person after another, though her words were addressed to Poirot. 'I want to go home, Mr Lazzari,' she wailed. 'I want to look in on my kiddies and see that they're safe!'

A younger woman sitting beside her put a hand on her arm and tried to calm her. 'Sit down, Tessie,' she said. 'The gentleman's only trying to help. Your bairns won't have come to any harm, not if they've been nowhere near the Bloxham.'

At this remark, intended as a comfort, both Luca Lazzari and Sturdy Tessie made anguished noises.

'We won't keep you much longer, madam,' I said. 'And I'm sure Mr Lazzari will allow you to pay a visit to your children afterwards, if that is what you feel you need to do.'

Lazzari indicated that this would be permissible, and Tessie sat down, slightly mollified.

I turned to Poirot and said, 'Richard Negus did not leave Room 317 in order to clear up the matter of the bill. He ran into Thomas Brignell on his way *back* from somewhere, so he had already done whatever it was that he set out to do by that point. He then happened to spot Mr Brignell and decided to clear up the matter of the bill.' I hoped, with this little speech, to demonstrate to all present that we had answers as well as questions. Perhaps not *all* the answers, yet, but some, and some was better than none.

'Monsieur Brignell, did you have the impression that Mr Negus *happened* to see you and take his opportunity, as Mr Catchpool describes? He was not looking for you? It was you who attended to him when he arrived at the hotel on Wednesday, yes?

'That's right, sir. No, he wasn't looking for me.' Brignell seemed happier about speaking while seated. 'He chanced upon me and thought, "Oh, there's that chap again", if you know what I mean, sir.'

'Indeed. Ladies and gentlemen,' Poirot raised his voice. 'After committing three murders in this hotel yesterday evening, the killer, or somebody who knows the identity of the killer and conspired with him, left a note on the front desk: "MAY THEY NEVER REST IN PEACE. 121. 238. 317." Did anybody happen to observe the leaving of this note that I show to you now?' Poirot produced the small white card from his pocket and held it up in the air. 'It was found by the clerk, Mr John Goode, at ten minutes past eight. Did any of you, perhaps, notice a person or persons near the desk who seemed to be conducting themselves in an unusual way? Think hard! Someone must have seen something!'

Sturdy Tessie had screwed her eyes shut and was leaning against her friend. The room had filled with whispers and gasps, but it was only the shock and excitement of seeing the handwriting of a killer — a souvenir that made the three deaths seem more vividly real.

Nobody had anything more to tell us. It turned out that if you asked a hundred people, you were likely to be disappointed.

6

The Sherry Conundrum

Half an hour later, Poirot and I sat drinking coffee in front of a roaring fire in what Lazzari had called 'our hidden lounge', a room that was behind the dining room and not accessible from any public corridor. The walls were covered with portraits which I tried to ignore. Give me a sunny landscape any day of the week, or even a cloudy one. It's the eyes that bother me when people are depicted; it doesn't seem to matter who the artist is. I've yet to see a portrait and not be convinced that its subject is regarding me with searing scorn.

After his exuberant performance as master of ceremonies in the dining room, Poirot had lapsed once more into quiet gloom. 'You're fretting about Jennie again, aren't you?' I asked him.

He admitted that he was. 'I do not want to hear that she has been found with a cufflink in her mouth, with the monogram PIJ. That is the news I dread.'

'Since there is nothing you can do about Jennie for the time being, I suggest you think about something else,' I advised.

'How practical you are, Catchpool. Very well. Let us think about teacups.'

'Teacups?'

'Yes. What do you make of them?'

After some consideration, I said, 'I believe I have no opinions whatever on the subject of teacups.'

Poirot made an impatient noise. 'Three teacups are brought to Ida Gransbury's room by the waiter Rafal Bobak. Three teacups for three people, as one would expect. But when the bodies of the three are found, there are only two teacups in the room.'

'The other one is in Harriet Sippel's room with Harriet Sippel's dead body,' I said.

'*Exactement*. And this is most curious, is it not? Did Mrs Sippel carry her teacup and saucer back to her room before or after the poison was put into it? In either scenario, who would carry a cup of tea along a hotel corridor, and then take it into a lift or walk down two flights of stairs with it in their hands? Either it is full and there is a risk of spillage, or it is half full or almost empty, and hardly worth transporting. Usually one drinks a cup of tea in the room in which one pours the cup of tea, *n'est-ce pas?*'

'Usually, yes. This killer strikes me as being as far from usual as it's possible to be,' I said with some vehemence.

'And his victims? Are they not ordinary people? What about their behaviour? Do you ask me to believe that Harriet Sippel carries her tea down to her room, sits in a chair to drink it, and then almost immediately the murderer knocks on her door, finds an opportunity to put cyanide in her drink? And Richard Negus, remember, has also left Ida Gransbury's room for some

79

unknown reason, but he arranges to be back in his own room soon afterwards, with a glass of sherry that nobody at the hotel gave him.'

'I suppose when you put it like that . . . ' I said.

Poirot carried on as if I had not just conceded the point. 'Ah, yes, Richard Negus too, he is sitting alone with his drink when the killer pays him a visit. He too says, 'By all means, drop your poison into my sherry.' And Ida Gransbury, she is all the while waiting patiently in Room 317, alone, for the murderer to come calling? She sips her tea *very slowly*. It would be inconsiderate of her to finish it before the killer arrives, of course — how then would he poison her? Where would he put his cyanide?'

'Damn it, Poirot — what do you want me to say? I don't understand it any more than you do! Look, it seems to me that the three murder victims must have had some kind of altercation. Why else would they plan to dine together and then all go their separate ways?'

'I do not think a woman leaving a room in anger would take a half-finished cup of tea with her,' said Poirot. 'Would it not in any case be cold by the time it reached Room 121?'

'I often drink tea cold,' I said. 'I quite like it.'

Poirot raised his eyebrows. 'If I did not know you to be an honest man, I should not believe it possible. Cold tea! *Déguelasse!*'

'Well, I should say I've *grown* to like it,' I added in my defence. 'There's no hurry, with cold tea. You can drink it at a time to suit you, and nothing bad's going to happen to it if you take a while. There's no time constraint and no pressure. That counts for a lot, in my book.'

There was a knock at the door. 'That will be Lazzari, coming to check that no one has disturbed us during our important conversation,' I said.

'Enter, please,' Poirot called out.

It was not Luca Lazzari but Thomas Brignell, the junior clerk who had spoken up about having seen Richard Negus by the lift at half past seven. 'Ah, Monsieur Brignell,' said Poirot. 'Do join us. Your account of yesterday evening was most helpful. Mr Catchpool and I are grateful.'

'Yes, very much so,' I said heartily. I'd have said almost anything to make it easier for Brignell to cough up whatever was bothering him. It was obvious that something was. The poor chap looked no more confident now than he had in the dining room. He rubbed the palms of his hands together, sliding them up and down. I could see sweat on his forehead, and he looked paler than he had before.

'I've let you down,' he said. 'I've let Mr Lazzari down, and he's been so good to me, he has. I didn't . . . in the dining room before, I didn't . . . ' He broke off and rubbed his palms together some more.

'You did not tell us the truth?' Poirot suggested.

'Every word I spoke was the truth, sir!' said Thomas Brignell indignantly. 'I'd be no better than the murderer myself if I lied to the police on a matter as important as this.'

'I do not think that you would be quite as

81

guilty as him, monsieur.'

'There were two things I neglected to mention. I can't tell you how sorry I am, sir. You see, speaking in front of a room full of people isn't something as comes easy to me. I've always been that way. And what made it harder in there, before' — he nodded in the direction of the dining room — 'was that I'd have been reluctant to say the other thing Mr Negus said to me because he paid me a compliment.

'What compliment?'

'It wasn't one I'd done anything to deserve, sir, I'm sure. I'm just an ordinary man. There's nothing notable about me at all. I do my job, as I'm paid to, and I try to do my best but there's no reason for anyone to single me out for special praise.'

'And Mr Negus did this?' asked Poirot. 'He singled you out for praise?'

Brignell winced. 'Yes, sir. Like I said: I didn't ask for it and I'm sure I'd done nothing to earn it. But when I saw him and he saw me, he said, 'Ah, Mr Brignell, you seem a most efficient fellow. I know I can trust you with this.' Then he proceeded to discuss the matter I mentioned before, sir — about the bill, and him wanting to pay it.'

'And you did not want to repeat the compliment you had received in front of everybody else, is that right?' I said. 'You feared it might sound boastful?'

'Yes, I did, sir. I did indeed. There's something else, too. Once we'd agreed the matter of the bill, Mr Negus asked me to fetch him a sherry. I was the person that did that. I offered to take it up to his room, but he said he was happy to wait. I brought it to him, and then up he went with it, in the lift.'

Poirot sat forward in his chair. 'Yet you said nothing when I asked if anyone in the room had given Richard Negus a glass of sherry?'

Brignell looked confused and frustrated — as if the right answer was on the tip of his tongue, but still, somehow, eluded him. 'I ought to have done, sir. I ought to have offered a full account of the incident as soon as you asked. I deeply regret that I failed in my duty to you and to the three deceased guests, God rest their souls. I can only hope that by coming to you now I've made a small amends.'

'Indeed, indeed. But, monsieur, I am curious about why you did not speak up in the dining room. When I asked, 'Who here took Richard Negus a glass of sherry?', what was it that caused you to remain silent?'

The poor clerk had started to tremble. 'I swear on my dear late mother's grave, Mr Poirot, I've now told you every particular of my encounter with Mr Negus yesterday evening. Every last particular. You couldn't have a more complete knowledge of what transpired — of that you may rest assured.'

Poirot opened his mouth to ask another question, but I leapt in before him and said, 'Thank you very much, Mr Brignell. Please don't worry about not having told us sooner. I understand how hard it is to stand up and speak in front of a crowd. I don't much like it myself.'

Once dismissed, Brignell hurried to the door like a fox fleeing from hounds.

'I believe him,' I said when he had gone. 'He's told us everything he knows.'

'About his meeting with Richard Negus beside the hotel lift, yes. The detail he conceals relates to himself. Why did he not speak up in the dining room about the sherry? I asked him that question twice, and still he did not answer. Instead, he elaborated upon his remorse, which was sincere. He would not lie, but he cannot bring himself to speak the truth. Ah, how he withholds! It is a form of lying — a very effective one, for there is no spoken lie to be contested.'

Poirot chuckled suddenly. 'And, you, Catchpool, you seek to protect him from Hercule Poirot, who would press him again and again, eh, for the information?'

'He looked as if he had reached his limit. And, frankly, if he is keeping quiet about anything, it's something that he thinks is of no consequence to us and yet it's a cause of great embarrassment to him. He's a fretful, conscientious sort. His sense of duty would oblige him to tell us if he thought it mattered.'

'And because you sent him away, I did not have the chance to explain to him that the information he withholds might be *vital*.' Having raised his voice, Poirot glared at me, to make sure I noted his annoyance. 'Even I, Hercule Poirot, do not yet know what matters and what is irrelevant. This is why I must know everything.' He stood up. 'And now, I will return to Pleasant's,' he said abruptly. 'The coffee there is far better than Signor Lazzari's.'

'But Richard Negus's brother Henry is on his way,' I protested. 'I thought you would want to speak to him.'

'I need a change of scenery, Catchpool. I must revitalize my little grey cells. They will begin to stagnate if I do not take them elsewhere.'

'Poppycock! You're hoping to bump into Jennie, or hear news of her,' I said. 'Poirot, I do think you're on a desperate goose chase with this Jennie business. You know it too, or else you would admit you're going to Pleasant's in the hope of finding her.'

'Maybe so. But if there is a goose killer at large, what else is one to do? Bring Mr Henry Negus to Pleasant's. I will talk to him there.'

'What? He's coming all the way from Devon. He's not going to want to arrive and then leave at once for — '

'But does he want the dead goose?' Poirot demanded. 'Ask him that!'

I resolved to ask Henry Negus no such thing, for fear he might turn on his heel and go straight back whence he came, having decided that Scotland Yard had been taken over by madmen.

7

Two Keys

Poirot arrived at the coffee house to find it very busy and smelling of a mixture of smoke and something sweet like pancake syrup. 'I need a table, but they are all taken,' he complained to Fee Spring, who had only just arrived herself and was standing by the wooden coat stand with her coat draped over her arm. When she pulled off her hat, her flyaway hair crackled and hung in the air for a few seconds before succumbing to gravity. The effect was rather comical, thought Poirot.

'Your need's in trouble, then, isn't it?' she said cheerfully. 'I can't shoo paying patrons out on to the street, not even for a famous detective.' She lowered her voice to a whisper. 'Mr and Mrs Ossessil will be on their way before too long. You can sit where they're sat.'

'Mr and Mrs Ossessil? That is an unusual name.'

Fee laughed at him, then whispered again. ''Oh, Cecil' — that's what she says all day long, the wife. The husband, poor soul, he can't get as much as two words out of his mouth without her setting him straight. He says he'd like scrambled eggs and toast? Right away she pipes up, 'Oh, Cecil, not eggs and toast!' And don't think he has to speak to set her off! He sits down at the first table he comes to and she says, 'Oh, Cecil, not this table!' 'Course, he ought to say he wants what he don't want, and don't want what he wants. That's what I'd do. I keep waiting for him to tumble to it but he's a useless old lump, truth be told. Brain like a mouldy cabbage. I expect that's what started her Oh-Cecil-ing.'

'If he does not leave soon I shall say 'Oh, Cecil' to him myself,' said Poirot, whose legs were already aching from a combination of standing and the thwarted desire to be seated.

'They'll be gone before your coffee's ready,' Fee said. 'She's finished her meal, see. She'll Oh-Cecil him out of here in no time. What you doing here lunchtime anyway? Wait, I know what you're up to! Looking for Jennie, aren't you? I heard you were in first thing this morning too.'

'How did you hear it?' Poirot asked. 'You have only just arrived, *n'est-ce pas?*'

'I'm never far away,' said Fee enigmatically. 'No one's seen hide nor hair of Jennie, but d'you know, Mr Poirot, I've got her stuck in my mind same as she's stuck in yours.'

'You too are worried?'

'Oh, not about her being in danger. It's not up to me to save her.'

'*Non.*'

'Nor's it up to you.'

'Ah, but Hercule Poirot, he has saved lives. He has saved innocent men from the gallows.'

'A good half of them's probably guilty,' said Fee cheerfully, as if the idea amused her.

'*Non, mademoiselle. Vous êtes misanthrope.*'

'If you say so. All's I know is, if I worried

about everyone as comes in here needing to be worried about, I'd not have a moment's peace. It's one sorry predicament after another and most of it's coming from their own heads, not real problems.'

'If something is in a person's head then it is real,' Poirot said.

'Not if it's daft nonsense dreamed up out of nowhere, which it often is,' said Fee. 'No, what I meant about Jennie is, I noticed something last night . . . except I can't think what it might be. I remember thinking, 'It's funny Jennie doing that, or saying that . . . ' Only trouble is, I can't remember what set me off thinking it — what she did, or what she said. I've tried and tried till it's made my head spin! Ah, look, they're going, Mr and Mrs Oh-Cecil. You go and sit yourself down. Coffee?'

'Yes, please. Mademoiselle, will you please continue in your efforts to remember what Jennie did or said? It matters more than I can express.'

'More than straight shelves?' Fee asked with sudden sharpness. 'More than cutlery laid out square on the table?'

'Ah. You think these things are the dreamed-up nonsense?' Poirot asked.

Fee's face reddened. 'Sorry if I spoke out of turn,' she said. 'It's only . . . well, you'd be a good deal happier, wouldn't you, if you stopped fussing about how a fork sits on a tablecloth?'

Poirot gave her the benefit of his best polite smile. 'I would be very much happier if you were to remember what it was about Mademoiselle Jennie that has stuck in your mind.' With that, he made a dignified exit from the conversation and sat down at his table.

He waited for an hour and a half, during which time he ate a good lunch, but saw no sign of Jennie.

It was nearly two o'clock when I arrived at Pleasant's with a man in tow whom Poirot at first took to be Henry Negus, Richard's brother. There was some confusion as I explained that I had left Constable Stanley Beer to wait for Negus and bring him along when he arrived, and that I had done so because the only person I could think about at the moment was the man standing beside me.

I introduced him — Mr Samuel Kidd, a boiler-maker — and watched with amusement as Poirot recoiled from the dirt-marked shirt with the missing button, and the partly unshaven face. Mr Kidd had nothing as ordinary as a beard or a moustache, but he plainly had trouble using a razor. The evidence suggested that he had started to shave, cut himself badly, and abandoned the enterprise. As a consequence, one side of his face was smooth and hairless but wounded, while the other was injury-free and covered with dark bristles. Which side looked worse was not an easy question to settle. 'Mr Kidd has a very interesting story to tell us,' I said. 'I was standing outside the Bloxham waiting for Henry Negus, when — '

'Ah!' Poirot interrupted me. 'You and Mr Kidd have come now from the Bloxham Hotel?'

'Yes.' Where did he think I had come from? Timbuktu?

'How did you travel?'

'Lazzari let me have one of the hotel's cars.'

'How long did the journey take?'

'Thirty minutes on the nose.'

'How were the roads? Were there many cars?'

'No. Hardly anyone about, as a matter of fact.'

'Do you think that in different conditions you could have made the journey in less time?' Poirot asked.

'Not unless I grew wings. Thirty minutes is jolly good going, I'd say.'

'*Bon*. Mr Kidd, please sit down and tell Poirot your very interesting story.'

To my astonishment, instead of sitting, Samuel Kidd laughed and repeated the very words Poirot had spoken in an exaggerated French accent, or Belgian accent, or however it is that Poirot speaks: '*Meester Keedd, please sit down and tell Poirr-oh your very interesting storrie.*'

Poirot looked affronted to have his voice mocked. I felt a pang of sympathy for him, until he said, 'Mr Kidd pronounces my name better than you do, Catchpool.'

'*Meester Keedd,*' the dishevelled man guffawed. 'Oh, don't mind me, sir. I'm only entertaining meself. *Meester Keedd!*'

'We are not here to entertain ourselves,' I told him, tired of his antics already. 'Please repeat what you told me outside the hotel.'

Kidd took ten minutes to tell a story that could have been distilled into three, but it was worth it. Walking past the Bloxham shortly after eight o'clock the previous evening, he had seen a

90

woman run out of the hotel, down the steps and on to the street. She was panting and looked frightful. He had started to make his way towards her to ask if she needed help, but she was too fast for him and ran away before he could get to her. As she ran, she dropped something on the floor: two gold-coloured keys. Realizing she had dropped them, she turned round and hurried back to retrieve them. Then, clutching them in her gloved hand, she had disappeared into the night.

'I said to meself, that's strange, that is, her hooking it like that,' Samuel Kidd mused. 'And then this morning I seen police everywhere and I asked one of 'em what was the big to-do. When I heard about these murders, I thought to meself, 'That could have been a murderer that you saw, Sammy.' She looked frightful, did the lady — frightful!'

Poirot was staring at one of the many stains on the man's shirt. 'Frightful,' he murmured. 'Your story is most intriguing, Mr Kidd. Two keys, you say?'

'That's right, sir. Two gold keys.'

'You were close enough to see, yes?'

'Oh, yes, sir — the street's nicely lit up outside the Bloxham. It was no trouble seeing.'

'Can you tell me anything else about these keys apart from their gold colour?'

'Yes. They had numbers on 'em.'

'Numbers?' I said. This was a detail that Samuel Kidd had not revealed to me in his first telling of the story outside the hotel, nor in his second, on the way here in the car. And . . . dash

91

it all, I should have thought to ask him. I had seen Richard Negus's key, the one that Poirot had found behind the loose fireplace tile. It had the number 238 on it.

'Yes, sir, numbers. Like, you know, one hundred, two hundred . . . '

'I know what numbers are,' I said brusquely.

'Were those, in fact, the numbers you saw on the keys, Mr Kidd?' Poirot asked. 'One hundred and two hundred?'

'No, sir. One of them was a hundred and summat, if I'm not mistaking. The other . . . ' Kidd scratched his head vigorously. Poirot averted his eyes. 'It was three hundred and summat, I think, sir. Though I couldn't swear to it, you understand. But that's what I'm seeing now in my mind's eye: one hundred and summat, three hundred and summat.'

Room 121, Harriet Sippel's room. And Ida Gransbury's, Room 317.

I felt a hollow space open up in my stomach. I recognized the sensation: it was how I had felt when I first saw the three dead bodies and was told by the police doctor that a gold monogrammed cufflink had been found in each of their mouths.

It now seemed likely that Samuel Kidd had been within inches of the murderer last night. *A frightful-looking lady*. I shivered.

'This woman that you saw,' said Poirot, 'did she have fair hair and a brown hat and coat?'

He was, of course, thinking of Jennie. I still believed there was no link, but I could see Poirot's reasoning: Jennie had been running around London last night in a state of great agitation and so had this other lady. It was just about possible they were one and the same person.

'No, sir. She had a hat on but it were pale blue, and her hair were dark. Curled and dark.'

'How old was she?'

'Wouldn't like to guess a lady's age, sir. Between young and old, I'd say.'

'Apart from the blue hat, what was she wearing?'

'Can't say I took that in, sir. I was too busy looking at her face when I could.'

'Was she pretty?' I asked.

'Yes, but I wasn't looking for that reason, sir. I was looking because I know her, see. I took one look and I thought to meself, 'Sammy, you know that lady.''

Poirot shifted in his chair. He looked at me, then back at Kidd. 'If you know her, Mr Kidd, please tell us who she is.'

'I can't, sir. That's what I was trying to get straight in my head when she ran away. I don't know *how* I know her, or her name, or nothing like that. It's not from making boilers I know her, I can say that much. She looked refined. A proper lady. I don't know anybody like that, but I *do* know her. That face — it's not a face I saw last night for the first time. No, sir.' Samuel Kidd shook his head. 'It's a puzzle all right. I might have asked her, if she'd not run away.'

I wondered, out of all the people that ever ran away, how many did so for that very reason: because they would rather not be asked, whatever the question might be.

Shortly after I had sent Samuel Kidd packing with orders to search his memory for the name of this mysterious woman and details of where and when he might have made her acquaintance, Constable Stanley Beer delivered Henry Negus to Pleasant's.

Mr Negus was considerably more pleasing to the eye than Samuel Kidd: a handsome man of around fifty with iron-grey hair and a wise face. He was smartly dressed and soft spoken. I liked him instantly. His grief at the loss of his brother was palpable, though he was a model of self-control throughout our conversation.

'Please accept my condolences, Mr Negus,' said Poirot. 'I am so sorry. It is a terrible thing to lose one so close as a brother.'

Negus nodded his gratitude. 'Anything I can do to help — anything at all — I will gladly do. Mr Catchpool says that you have questions for me?'

'Yes, monsieur. The names Harriet Sippel and Ida Gransbury — they are familiar to you?'

'Were they the other two who were ... ?' Henry Negus stopped talking as Fee Spring approached with the cup of tea he had asked for on arrival.

Once she had retreated, Poirot said, 'Yes. Harriet Sippel and Ida Gransbury were also murdered at the Bloxham Hotel yesterday evening.'

'The name Harriet Sippel means nothing to me. Ida Gransbury and my brother were engaged to be married years ago.'

'So you knew Mademoiselle Gransbury?' I heard the flare of excitement in Poirot's voice.

'No, I never met her,' said Henry Negus. 'I knew her name, of course, from Richard's letters. He and I rarely saw one another while he lived in Great Holling. We wrote instead.'

I felt another piece of the puzzle slide into position with a satisfying click. 'Richard lived in Great Holling?' I asked, struggling to keep my voice even. If Poirot shared my surprise at this discovery, he did not show it.

One village, linking all three murder victims. I repeated its name several times in my mind: *Great Holling, Great Holling, Great Holling.* Everything seemed to point in its direction.

'Yes, Richard lived there until 1913,' said Negus. 'He had a law practice in the Culver Valley. It's where he and I grew up — in Silsford. Then in 1913 he came to live in Devon with me, where he's lived ever since. I mean . . . where he lived,' he corrected himself. His face looked suddenly haggard, as if the knowledge of his brother's death had landed violently upon him once again, crushing him.

'Did Richard ever mention to you anyone from the Culver Valley by the name of Jennie?' asked Poirot. 'Or anyone at all with that name, perhaps from Great Holling or perhaps not?'

There was a pause that stretched forward. Then Henry Negus said, 'No.'

'What about a person with the initials PIJ?'

'No. The only one from the village that he ever mentioned was Ida, his fiancée.'

95

'If I may ask a delicate question, monsieur: why did your brother's engagement not result in a marriage?'

'I'm afraid I don't know. Richard and I were close but we tended to discuss ideas more than anything else. Philosophy, politics, theology ... We did not generally enquire into one another's private business. All he told me about Ida was that he was engaged to be married to her, and then, in 1913, that they were no longer engaged.'

'*Attendez.* In 1913, his engagement to Ida Gransbury ends, and also he leaves Great Holling to move to Devon and live with you?'

'And my wife and children, yes.'

'Did he leave Great Holling in order to put more distance between himself and Miss Gransbury?'

Henry Negus considered the question. 'I think that was part of it, but it wasn't the whole story. Richard hated Great Holling by the time he left it, and that can't have been only Ida Gransbury's doing. He loathed every inch of the place, he said. He didn't tell me why and I didn't ask. Richard had a way of letting you know when he had said all he wanted to say. His verdict on the village was delivered very much in the spirit of 'That's all there is to it', as I recall. Perhaps if I had tried to find out more — ' Negus broke off, an anguished expression on his face.

'You must not blame yourself, Mr Negus,' said Poirot. 'You did not cause your brother's death.'

'I couldn't help thinking that ... well, that something dreadful must have happened to him in that village. And one doesn't like to speak or think about things of that nature if one can help it.' Henry Negus sighed. 'Richard certainly didn't want to talk about it, whatever it was, so I took the view that it was better not talked about. He was the one with the authority, you see — the older brother. Everybody deferred to him. He had a brilliant mind, you know.'

'Indeed?' Poirot smiled kindly.

'Oh, no one paid attention to detail like Richard, before his decline. Meticulous, he was, in everything he did. You would entrust anything to him — anybody would. That was why he was so successful as a lawyer, before things went badly wrong. I always believed that he would right himself one day. When he seemed to perk up a few months ago, I thought, 'Finally, he has regained his appetite for life.' I hoped he might have been thinking about working again, before every last penny of his money ran out — '

'Mr Negus, if you would please slow down a little,' said Poirot, polite but insistent. 'Your brother did not at first work when he moved into your home?'

'No. As well as Great Holling and Ida Gransbury, Richard left behind his profession when he came to Devon. Instead of practising the law, he shut himself away in his room and practised drinking heavily.'

'Ah. The decline you mentioned?'

'Yes,' said Negus. 'It was a very different Richard that arrived at my house from the one I had last encountered. He was so withdrawn and dour. It was as if he had built a wall around himself. He never left the house — saw no one, wrote to no one, received no letters. All he did was read books and stare into space. He refused to accompany us to church and would not relent even to please my wife. One day, after he had been with us for about a year, I found a Bible outside his door, on the landing floor. It had been in a drawer in the bedroom we had given him. I tried to put it back there, but Richard made it clear that he wished to banish it from the room. I must confess that after that incident, I asked my wife whether . . . well, whether we ought to ask him to find a home elsewhere. It was rather disconcerting to have him around. But Clara — that's my wife — she wouldn't hear of it. 'Family's family,' she said. 'We're all Richard has. You don't turn family out onto the street.' She was quite right, of course.'

'You referred to your brother spending money excessively?' I said.

'Yes. He and I were both left very comfortably off.' Henry Negus shook his head. 'The idea that my responsible older brother Richard would tear through his fortune with no care for the future . . . and yet that's what he did. He seemed intent on converting what our father had left him into liquor and pouring it down his throat. He was heading for penury and serious illness, I feared. Some nights I lay awake worrying about the terrible end that might lie in store for him. Not murder, though. I never thought for a moment that Richard would be murdered, though perhaps I should have wondered.'

Poirot looked up, instantly alert. 'Why would

you wonder such a thing, monsieur? Most of us assume that our relations will not be murdered. It is a reasonable assumption, in almost all cases.'

Henry Negus thought for a while before answering. Finally he said, 'It would be fanciful to say that Richard seemed to know that he would be murdered, for who can know? But from the day that he moved into my home, he had the morose, doom-laden comportment of a man whose life had already ended. That is the only way I can describe it.'

'You say, however, that he, ah, *perked up* in the months preceding his death?'

'Yes. My wife noticed it too. She wanted me to ask him about it — women always do, don't they? — but I knew Richard well enough to know he would not welcome the intrusion.'

'He seemed happier?' Poirot asked.

'I wish I could say yes to that, Monsieur Poirot. If I could believe that Richard was happier than he had been for years on the day that he died, that would be a significant consolation to me. But no, it wasn't happiness. It was more as if he was planning something. He seemed to have a purpose again, after years without one. That was my impression, though, as I say, I know nothing of what that purpose might have been.'

'Yet you are certain you did not imagine this change?'

'Yes, I am. It manifested itself in several ways. Richard got up and came down to breakfast more often. He had more vim and energy about him. His personal hygiene improved. Most noticeable of all was that he stopped drinking. I cannot tell you how grateful I was for that alone. My wife and I prayed that he would succeed, whatever his venture — that finally the curse of Great Holling would release its grip on him and let him enjoy a fruitful life.'

'The curse, monsieur? You believe the village to be cursed?'

Henry Negus's face reddened. 'Not really, no. Of course, there's no such thing, is there? It's my wife's phrase. Deprived of a good yarn to get her teeth into, she dreamed up the notion of a curse, based on Richard fleeing the place, and his broken engagement, and the only other fact she knows about Great Holling.'

'What other fact?' I asked.

'Oh.' Henry Negus looked surprised. Then he said, 'No, I don't suppose you would know about it. Why should you? The terrible tragedy of the young vicar of the parish and his wife. Richard wrote and told us about it a few months before he left the village,' said Henry. 'They died within hours of one another.'

'Did they indeed? What was the cause of their deaths?' asked Poirot.

'I don't know. Richard didn't include that detail in his letter, assuming he knew it. He wrote only that it was a terrible tragedy. As a matter of fact I asked him about it later, but I'm afraid he rather growled at me, which left me none the wiser. I think he was too caught up in his own misfortunes to care to discuss anybody else's.'

8

Assembling Our Thoughts

'Or else,' said Poirot as he and I walked briskly from Pleasant's in the direction of our lodging house half an hour later, 'all these unhappy events sixteen years ago are connected: the tragic fate of the vicar and his wife, Richard Negus suddenly ending his engagement to Ida Gransbury, Richard Negus deciding that he loathes Great Holling and must flee to Devon — to become an idle spendthrift who drinks himself to death in his brother's house!'

'You think Richard Negus took to the bottle because the vicar died?' I said. 'Tempting as it is to make everything tie up, isn't it more likely that the one has nothing to do with the other?'

'I would not say so, no.' Poirot threw me a sharp look. 'Ingest the fresh air of this fine winter's day, Catchpool. It will perhaps help to introduce oxygen to your little grey cells. Take a deep breath, my friend.'

I humoured him by doing as he asked. I was, of course, breathing anyway, so it was rather silly.

'*Bon.* Now think of this: it is not merely that the young vicar died tragically, it is that he died only hours after his wife dying. This is most unusual. Richard Negus mentions the incident in a letter to his brother Henry. Several months later, he is no longer engaged to be married to

101

Ida Gransbury. He makes his escape to Devon, where he embarks upon a decline. *He refuses to admit a Bible to his room, and will not attend church even to placate the lady of the house.'*

'Why do you say that as though it has special significance?' I asked.

'Ah! The oxygen, it takes much time to make its way to the grey cells! Never mind: it will arrive eventually where it is most needed, in that pincushion of a brain of yours. Church, Catchpool! A vicar and his wife die tragically in Great Holling. Shortly afterwards, Richard Negus develops an aversion to the village, to church and to the Bible.'

'Oh, I see what you're driving at.'

'*Bon. Alors*, Richard Negus then takes himself to Devon where for many years he pursues the decline, during which time his brother does not make any unwelcome intrusion that might save him from the devastation he wreaks upon himself — '

'You think Henry Negus was negligent in that respect?'

'It is not his fault,' said Poirot with a wave of his hand. 'He is English. You English would sit by in polite silence while every species of avoidable disaster takes place in front of your eyes rather than make the social lapse of being seen to interfere!'

'I'm not sure that's quite fair.' I raised my voice to make myself heard against the bluster of the wind and the voices of other people on the busy London street.

Poirot ignored my complaint. 'For many years, Henry Negus worries in silence about his brother. He hopes, and no doubt also he prays, and when he has almost given up hope it appears that his prayers are answered: Richard Negus has the visible *upward perking* a few months ago. He seems to be planning something. Perhaps the plan involved booking three rooms at the Bloxham Hotel in London for himself and two women he knew from his days in Great Holling, since we know that this is what he did. And then last night he is found dead at the Bloxham Hotel with a mongrammed cufflink in his mouth, in close proximity to his former fiancée, Ida Gransbury, and to Harriet Sippel, another villager who was once his neighbour. Both women have been murdered in the same way.'

Poirot came to a standstill. He had been walking too fast and was out of breath. 'Catchpool,' he gasped, mopping his brow with a neatly folded handkerchief that he had pulled from his waistcoat pocket. 'Ask yourself what is the first event in this chain of events that I have presented to you. Is it not the tragic deaths of the vicar and his wife?'

'Well, yes, but only if we allow that they're part of the same story as the three Bloxham murders. There's no evidence of that, Poirot. I still contend that this poor vicar chap might be neither here nor there.'

'Just as *la pauvre* Jennie may be neither there nor here?'

'Exactly.'

We continued along the street.

'Have you ever tried to do a crossword puzzle, Poirot? Because . . . well, you know I'm trying to knock one together at the moment, one of my own?'

'It would be impossible to reside in such proximity to you as I do and not know, *mon ami*.'

'Yes. Right. Well, I've noticed something that happens when you're trying to puzzle out a crossword clue. It's interesting. Let's say you have the clue 'Kitchen utensil, three letters', and you have the letter 'P' as the first letter. It's very easy to think, 'Well, it has to be 'pot' because that has three letters and begins with 'P', and a pot is a kitchen utensil.' So you tell yourself it must be true, when all the while the right answer is 'pan' — also three letters, also a kitchen utensil beginning with P. Do you see?'

'That example does not serve you well, Catchpool. In the situation you describe, I would think of both 'pot' and 'pan' as being equally likely to be correct. Only a fool would consider one and not the other when both fit perfectly.'

'All right, if you want something equally likely to be correct, how about this theory: Richard Negus refused to go to church or have a Bible in his room because whatever misfortune had afflicted him in Great Holling had dented his faith a little? Doesn't that sound as if it could also be a perfect fit? And it might have nothing to do with the deaths of the vicar and his wife. Richard Negus wouldn't be the first to find himself in sore straits and wonder if God loved him quite as much as He seems to love everyone else!' That came out more vehemently than I had intended.

104

'Have you wondered this yourself, Catchpool?' Poirot laid his hand on my sleeve to stop me marching along. I sometimes forget that my legs are much longer than his.

'As a matter of fact, I have. It didn't stop me going to church, but I can see how it would with some people.' For instance, those who would object rather than silently concur if told their brains were pin-cushions, I thought. To Poirot I said, 'I suppose it all depends whether you hold yourself or God responsible for your problems.'

'Did your predicament involve a woman?'

'Several fine specimens, all of whom my parents fervently hoped I would marry. I stood firm and inflicted myself upon none of them.' I started to walk again, briskly.

Poirot hurried to catch me up. 'So according to your wisdom, we must forget about the tragically deceased vicar and his wife? We must pretend we do not know about this event, in case we are led by it to a mistaken conclusion? And we must forget about Jennie for the same reason?'

'Well, no, I wouldn't say that's the right course of action. I'm not suggesting we *forget* anything, only that — '

'I will tell you the right action! You must go to Great Holling. Harriet Sippel, Ida Gransbury and Richard Negus, they are not simply three pieces of a puzzle. They are not merely objects we move around in an attempt to fit them into a pattern. Before their deaths, they were people, with lives and emotions: the foolish predispositions, perhaps the moments of great wisdom and insight. You must go to the village where they all lived and find out who they *are*, Catchpool.'

'Me? You mean us?'

'*Non, mon ami*. Poirot, he will stay in London. I need only to move my mind, not my body, in order to make progress. No, you will go, and you will bring back to me the fullest account of your travels. That will be sufficient. Take with you two lists of names: guests at the Bloxham Hotel on Wednesday and Thursday nights, and employees of the Bloxham Hotel. Find out if anyone in this cursed village recognizes any of the names. Ask about Jennie and PIJ. Make sure not to return until you have discovered the story about this vicar and his wife and their tragic deaths in 1913.'

'Poirot, you've got to come with me,' I said rather desperately. 'I'm out of my depth with this Bloxham business. I am relying on you.'

'You may continue to do so, *mon ami*. We will go to the house of Mrs Blanche Unsworth and there we will assemble our thoughts so that you do not arrive in Great Holling unprepared.'

He always called it 'the house of Mrs Blanche Unsworth'. Every time he did, it reminded me that I too had once thought of it in those terms, before I started to call it 'home'.

★ ★ ★

'Assembling our thoughts' turned out to mean Poirot standing by the fire in the excessively lavender-fringed drawing room and dictating to me, while I sat in a chair nearby and wrote down

106

every word he said. I have never, before or since, heard anyone speak in such a perfectly orderly way. I tried to protest that he was making me write down many things of which I was already fully aware, and I got the benefit of his long and earnest disquisition on the subject of 'the importance of the method'. Apparently my pin-cushion brain cannot be expected to remember anything, and so I needed a written record to refer to.

After dictating a list of everything we knew, Poirot followed the same procedure for every-thing we didn't know but were hoping to find out. (I considered reproducing these two lists here, but do not wish to bore or infuriate others as I was bored and infuriated.)

To be fair to Poirot, once I had scribbled it all down and looked over what I had written, I did feel that I had a clearer view of things: clear, and inordinately discouraging. I put down my pen and said with a sigh, 'I'm not sure I want to carry around with me an endless list of questions I can't answer and probably have no hope of ever answering.'

'You lack the confidence, Catchpool.'

'Yes. What does one do about that?'

'I do not know. It is not a problem that I suffer from. I do not worry that I will meet a problem for which I will be unable to find the solution.'

'Do you think you'll be able to find the solution for this one?'

Poirot smiled. 'You wish me to encourage you to have confidence in me, since you have none in yourself? *Mon ami*, you know more than you are aware of knowing. Do you remember you made a joke, at the hotel, about all three victims arriving on Wednesday, the day before the murders? You said, 'It's almost as if they had an invitation to present themselves for slaughter, one that said, 'Please come to the day before, so that Thursday can be devoted entirely to your getting murdered'.''

'Well, what about it?'

'Your joke relied on the idea that getting murdered is more than enough activity for one day — to travel across the country by train and get murdered *on the same day*, that would be too much for anyone! And the killer does not want his victims to have to exert themselves unduly! This is funny!'

Poirot smoothed his moustaches, as if he imagined that laughing might have shaken them out of shape.

'Your words made me wonder, my friend: since getting murdered is really no effort for the victim, and since no killer is so considerate of those he intends to poison, *why does he not kill the three victims on the Wednesday night?*'

'He might have been busy on Wednesday night,' I said.

'Then why not arrange for the three victims to arrive at the hotel on Thursday morning and afternoon instead of Wednesday morning and afternoon? The killer would still have been able to kill them when he did, *n'est-ce pas?* On Thursday evening, between a quarter past seven and ten past eight?'

I did my best to look patient. 'You're

overcomplicating things, Poirot. If the victims all knew each other, which we know they did, maybe they had a reason for all being in London for two nights, a reason that had nothing to do with the killer. He chose to kill them on the second night because it was more convenient for him. He didn't invite them to the Bloxham; he simply knew that they would be there, and when. Also . . . ' I stopped. 'No, never mind. It's silly.'

'Tell me the thing that is silly,' Poirot ordered.

'Well, it's possible that if the murderer is a meticulous planner by nature, he would not plan the murders for the same day that he knew his victims would be travelling to London, in case their trains were delayed.'

'Perhaps the killer also had to travel to London, from Great Holling or somewhere else. It is possible that he — or she, for it might be a woman — did not want to make a long, tiring journey and commit three murders on the same day.'

'Even if that's so, the victims could still have arrived on the Thursday, couldn't they?'

'They did not,' said Poirot simply. 'We know that they arrived the day before, on Wednesday. So, I begin to wonder: did something need to happen that involved the murderer and all three victims *before the murders could be committed?* If so, then perhaps the murderer did not travel from far to come here, but lives here in London.'

'Could be,' I said. 'All of which is a long-winded way of saying that we have not the faintest idea of what happened or why. I seem to remember that being my original assessment of the situation. Oh, and Poirot . . . ?'

'Yes, *mon ami?*'

'I haven't had the heart to tell you before now, and I know you're not going to like it. The monogrammed cufflinks . . . '

'*Oui?*'

'You asked Henry Negus about PIJ. I don't think those are the chap's initials, whoever he is — the owner of the cufflinks. I think his initials are PJI. Look.' I reproduced the monogram on the back of one of my pieces of paper. As closely as I could from memory, I replicated the way the letters appeared on the cufflinks. 'Do you see that the 'I' is larger and the 'P' and the 'J' on either side are considerably smaller? That's a popular style of monogram. The larger initial signifies the surname and is in the middle.'

Poirot was frowning and shaking his head. 'The initials in the monogram are in *the wrong order*, deliberately? I have never heard of this. Who would have such an idea? It is nonsensical!'

'Common practice, I'm afraid. Trust me on this one. Chaps at work have monogrammed cufflinks of this sort.'

'*Incroyable*. The English have no sense of the proper order of things.'

'Yes, well, be that as it may . . . It's PJI we'll need to be asking about when we go to Great Holling, not PIJ.'

It was a feeble effort, and one that Poirot saw through straight away. '*You*, my friend, will go to Great Holling,' he said. 'Poirot will stay in London.'

110

9

A Visit to Great Holling

The following Monday morning, I set off to
Great Holling as instructed. My impression
upon arrival was that it was similar to many
other English villages I had visited, and that
there was not much more to say about it than
that. There is, I think, more difference between
cities than between villages, as well as more to
say about cities. I could certainly talk at length
about the intricacies of London. Perhaps it is
simply that I am not as finely attuned to places
such as Great Holling. They make me feel out of
my element — if I have an element, that is. I'm
not convinced that I do.

I had been told that I could not fail to spot the
King's Head Inn, where I would be staying, but
fail I did. Luckily, a bespectacled young man
with a boomerang-shaped scattering of freckles
across the bridge of his nose and a newspaper
tucked under his arm was on hand to help me.
He appeared at first behind me, startling me.
'Lost, are you?' he said.

'I believe I am, yes. I'm looking for the King's
Head.'

'Ah!' He grinned. 'Thought so, with your case
and all. You're not a native, then? King's Head
looks like a house from the street, so you'd not
notice it, not unless you went along the lane

there — see? Go down there, turn right and you'll see the sign and the way in.'

I thanked him, and was about to follow his advice when he called me back with, 'So where are you from, then?'

I told him, and he said, 'I've never been to London. What brings you to our neck of the woods, then?'

'Work,' I said. 'Listen, I hope this doesn't sound rude, and I'd be glad to talk to you later, but I'd like to get myself settled in first.'

'Well, don't let me keep you, then,' he said. 'What kind of work is it you do? Oh — there I go again, asking another question. Maybe I'll ask you later.' He waved and set off down the street.

I tried again to proceed to the King's Head and he shouted after me, 'Down the lane and turn right!' More jovial waving followed.

He was trying to be friendly and helpful, and I should have been grateful. Normally I would have been, except . . .

Well, I'll admit it: I don't like villages. I didn't say so to Poirot before I left, but I said it to myself many times during the train journey, and then again when I got off at the pretty little station. I didn't like this charming narrow street in which I stood, that curved in the exact shape of a letter S and had tiny cottages on both sides that looked more suitable for whiskery woodland creatures than for human beings.

I didn't like being asked presumptuous questions by complete strangers on the street, though I was fully aware of my own hypocrisy, since I was here in Great Holling to interrogate strangers myself.

Now that the bespectacled man had gone on his way, there was not a sound to be heard apart from the occasional bird and my own breathing. Beyond the houses I saw empty fields and hills in the distance that, combined with the silence, made me feel immediately lonely. Cities, of course, can also make a person feel alone. In London, you look at those who pass you by and you have no idea what is going on in their minds. Each one looks utterly closed to you and mysterious. In villages the same rule applies, except that you suspect it is the same thing going on in every mind.

The owner of the King's Head turned out to be a Mr Victor Meakin, who looked to be between fifty and sixty and had thin grey hair through which the tops of his ears poked pinkly on both sides. He too seemed eager to discuss London. 'Were you born there, if you don't mind my asking, Mr Catchpool? How many people live there now? What's the size of the population? Is it very dirty there? My aunt went there once — said it was very dirty. Still, I've always thought I'd like to go one day. I never said so to my aunt, though — I'd have had an argument from her, God rest her soul. Does everybody in London have a car of their own?'

I was relieved that his stream of chatter allowed me no time to answer. My luck ran out when he got to the question that really interested him: 'What brings you to Great Holling, Mr Catchpool? I can't think what business you might have here.'

At that point he stopped, and I had no choice

but to answer. 'I'm a policeman,' I told him. 'From Scotland Yard.'

'Policeman?' He maintained a determined smile, but he looked at me now with very different eyes: hard, probing and disdainful — as if he was speculating about me and drawing conclusions that were to my disadvantage. 'A policeman,' he said, more to himself than me. 'Now, why would a policeman be here? An important policeman from London, too.' Since he seemed not to be asking me directly, I neglected to reply.

As he carried my cases up the winding wooden stairs, he stopped three times and turned to peer at me for no discernible reason.

The room he had allocated to me was agreeably sparse and chilly — a welcome change from Blanche Unsworth's frilly, fringed extravagance. Here, thankfully, no hot-water bottle with a knitted cover had been laid out for my use. I can't bear the things; even the sight of them irks me. The warmest thing in any bed should always be a person, in my opinion.

Meakin pointed out some features of the room that I might have spotted myself, such as the bed and the large wooden cupboard. I tried to respond with the appropriate mixture of surprise and delight. Then, because I knew I would have to do so at some point, I told him the nature of my business in Great Holling, hoping this would satisfy his curiosity and allow him to look at me henceforth in a less penetrating way. I told him about the Bloxham Hotel murders.

His mouth twitched as he listened. It looked

114

rather as if he was trying not to laugh, though I might have been mistaken. 'Murdered, you say? In a fancy London hotel? Now, there's a thing! Mrs Sippel and Miss Gransbury, murdered? And Mr Negus?'

'You knew them, then?' I said, removing my coat and hanging it up in the cupboard.

'Oh, yes, I knew them.'

'They weren't friends of yours, I take it?'

'Weren't friends, weren't enemies,' said Meakin. 'That's the best way, when you've got an inn to run. Friends and enemies gets you into trouble. Looks like it got Mrs Sippel and Miss Gransbury into trouble. Mr Negus too.'

What was it that I could hear in his voice — that strange emphasis? Was it relish?

'Forgive me, Mr Meakin, but . . . does it please you to learn of these three deaths, or am I imagining it?'

'You are, Mr Catchpool. Indeed you are.' He delivered the denial with utmost confidence.

We stared at one another for a moment or two. I saw eyes that gleamed with suspicion, devoid now of all warmth.

'You told me some news and I took an interest, is all I did,' said Meakin. 'Just as I'd take an interest in the tellings of any visitor. It's only right and proper, when you've got an inn to run. Fancy that, though — murder!'

I turned away from him and said firmly, 'Thank you for showing me to my room. You've been very helpful.'

'I expect you'll want to ask me a fair share of questions, won't you? The King's Head's been

115

mine since 1911. You'll find no one better to ask.'

'Oh — yes, of course. Once I've unpacked and eaten, stretched my legs a little.' I didn't relish the prospect of speaking to this man at length, but it was going to be necessary. 'One more thing, Mr Meakin, and it's very important: if you would be kind enough not to pass on what I've told you to anyone else, I'd be grateful.'

'Secret, is it?'

'Not at all, no. It's simply that I would rather tell people myself.'

'You'll be asking questions, will you? There's not a body in Great Holling who'll tell you anything worth knowing.'

'I'm sure that's not true,' I said. 'You've already offered to talk to me, after all.'

Meakin shook his head. 'I don't believe I have, Mr Catchpool. I said you'll be wanting to ask me, not that I'd be wanting to answer. I will say this, though . . . ' He pointed a bony, swollen-knuckled index finger at me. 'If you've stumbled upon three murders in your fancy London hotel, and keeping in mind that you're a London policeman, you'd be better off asking your questions there and not here.'

'Are you insinuating that you would like me to leave, Mr Meakin?'

'Not at all. Your itinerary is entirely your own affair. You'll be welcome at this establishment for as long as you choose to remain. It's no concern of mine.' With that, he turned and left.

I shook my head in puzzlement. It was hard to reconcile Victor Meakin as he was now with the

116

man who had greeted me when I first walked into the King's Head, who had babbled away merrily about London and his dirt-averse aunt.

I sat down on the bed, then immediately stood up, feeling the need of fresh air. If only there had been somewhere else to stay in Great Holling apart from the King's Head.

I put on the coat I had taken off a few minutes earlier, locked my room and descended the stairs. Victor Meakin was drying beer glasses behind the bar. He bowed as I entered the room.

In the corner, on either side of a table that was covered in glasses both full and empty, sat two men who were intent upon becoming as intoxicated as possible. Both had perfected the art of swaying while seated. One of these determined drinkers was a decrepit old gnome of a chap with a white beard that brought to mind Father Christmas. The other was well-built and square-jawed and could not have been older than twenty. He was trying to speak to the old man, but his mouth was too slack from the liquor and he couldn't make himself understood. Fortunately, his drinking companion was in no fit state to listen, so it was perhaps lucky that it was unintelligible nonsense that was going to waste and not the finest repartee.

The sight of the young man disturbed me. How had he ended up at such a low ebb? He looked as if he was trying on a face that, if he didn't change his habits, he would soon be doomed to wear for ever.

'Would you care for a drink, Mr Catchpool?' Meakin asked.

'Perhaps later, thank you.' I smiled warmly. I try to make a point of being as good-humoured as I can with those I dislike or don't trust. It doesn't always work, but sometimes they respond in kind. 'First, time to stretch the old legs.'

The inebriated young man rose unsteadily to his feet. He seemed suddenly angry and said something that began with the word 'No'. The rest was unintelligible. He staggered past me and out on to the street. The old man raised his arm — a process which took him nearly ten seconds — until his finger was pointing straight at me. 'You,' he said.

I had been in the village of Great Holling for less than an hour, and already two men had pointed rudely straight at my face. Perhaps among the local folk this was a sign of welcome, though I doubted it. 'I beg your pardon?' I said.

Father Christmas made sounds that I translated as: 'Yes, you, good fellow. Come and sit down here. In this chair here. Next to me, here. The chair that the unfortunate young ne'er-do-well no longer has the need of, here.'

Under normal circumstances the repetition might have grated, but since I was engaged in a translation exercise, I rather welcomed it.

'Actually, I was about to take a stroll around the village . . . ' I started to say, but the old man had made his mind up that I should do no such thing.

'There's plenty of time for that later!' he barked. 'Now, you'll come and sit down, and we'll have ourselves a talk.' To my alarm, he began to sing:

'Come and sit down,
Come and sit down,
Mr Policeman from London Town.'

I looked at Meakin, who kept his eyes on his beer glasses. Anger emboldened me and I said to him, 'I seem to remember asking you only ten minutes ago not to discuss my business with anybody.'

'I haven't said a word.' He did not even have the good grace to look at me.

'Mr Meakin, how has this gentleman found out that I'm a policeman from London if not from your telling him? Nobody else in the village knows who I am.'

'You mustn't go leaping to conclusions, Mr Catchpool. That'll get you nowhere, I expect. I've said not a word about you to a single body. Not a word.'

He was lying. He knew that I knew, and he didn't care.

* * *

Defeated, I went and sat with the old gnome-like man in his corner of the inn. There were hops and brasses on the dark beams all around him, and for a second he struck me as a strange white-haired creature in an even stranger nest.

He started to talk as if our conversation were already in full swing: ' . . . not a gentleman but a ne'er-do-well, and his parents are the same way. They can't read, or write their own names, and nor can he. No Latin to speak of! Twenty years

119

of age and look at him! When I was his age — ah, but that was long ago. Time immemorial! I made the best of myself as a young man, but some take the blessings the Lord bestowed and squander them all. They don't realize that greatness is within the grasp of every man, so they don't try to achieve it.'

'Latin, eh?' was all I could manage by way of reply. Greatness? I counted myself as lucky every time I avoided a humiliating failure. There was nothing coarse about the old man's voice, in spite of his lumpy claret-coloured nose and ale-soaked beard. Undistorted by drink, his was a voice one might be pleased to listen to, I thought.

'So, have you done great things, then?' I asked him.

'I've tried, and I've succeeded beyond my wildest dreams.'

'Have you really?'

'Ah, but that was long ago. It doesn't pay a man to dream, and the dreams that matter most can never come true. I didn't know that when I was young. I'm glad I didn't.' He sighed. 'What about you, my good fellow? What will be your great achievement? Solving the murders of Harriet Sippel, Ida Gransbury and Richard Negus?'

He spoke as if this were an unworthy goal.

'I never knew Negus, though I saw him once or twice,' he went on. 'Shortly after I arrived in the village, he left it. One man comes, another man goes, and both for the very same reason. Both with the heaviest of hearts.'

'What reason?'

The old gnome poured an almost impossible amount of ale down his throat in one swift motion. 'She never got over it!' he said.

'Who never got over what? Do you mean that Ida Gransbury never got over Richard Negus leaving Great Holling?'

'The loss of her husband. Or so they say. Harriet Sippel. They say it was losing him so young that made her what she was. I say that's a poor excuse. Not much older than the kid that was sitting where you're sitting before you were sitting there. Too young to die. There's no end to them.'

'When you say 'made her what she was' — I wonder what you meant by that, Mr . . . um . . . ? Can you explain?'

'What, my good fellow? Oh, yes. It doesn't pay a man or a woman to dream. I'm glad I was old by the time I tumbled to that.'

'Forgive me, but I'd like to check I've got this right,' I said, wishing he would stick to the point. 'Are you saying that Harriet Sippel lost her husband at a young age, and that being widowed was what made her become . . . what?'

To my horror, the old man started to cry. 'Why did she have to come here? She could have had a husband, children, a home of her own, a happy life.'

'Who could have had those things?' I asked rather desperately. 'Harriet Sippel?'

'If she hadn't told an unforgivable lie . . . That was what started all the trouble.' As if an invisible participant in the conversation had

121

suddenly asked him another question, the old man frowned and said, 'No, no. Harriet Sippel had a husband. George. He died. Young. A terrible illness. He wasn't much older than the kid, the ne'er-do-well that was sitting before where you're sitting now. Stoakley.'

'The ne'er-do-well's name is Stoakley, is it?'

'No, my good fellow. *My* name is Stoakley. Walter Stoakley. I don't know his name.' The old gnome combed his fingers through his beard, then said, 'She devoted her *life* to him. Oh, I know why, I've always understood why. He was a substantial man, whatever his sins. She sacrificed everything for him.'

'For . . . the young man who was here just now?' No, that seemed unlikely; the ne'er-do-well had not looked substantial.

It was lucky that Poirot wasn't party to this conversation, I thought. Walter Stoakley's disorganized ramblings would have given him a seizure.

'No, no. He's only twenty, you know.'

'Yes, you told me a few moments ago.'

'No point devoting your life to a wastrel who spends his days drinking.'

'I agree, but — '

'She couldn't marry some kid, not once she'd fallen in love with a man of substance. So she left him behind.'

I had an idea, inspired by what the waiter Rafal Bobak had said in the dining room of the Bloxham Hotel. 'Is she many years older than him?' I asked.

'Who?' Stoakley looked puzzled.

122

'The woman you're talking about. How old is she?'

'A good ten years older than you. Forty-two, forty-three at an estimate.'

'I see.' I couldn't help being impressed that he had guessed my age accurately. If he was able to do that, I reasoned, then surely I would eventually manage to draw some coherent sense from him.

Back into the discursive chaos I went: 'So the woman you're talking about is *older* than the ne'er-do-well who was sitting here in this chair a few minutes ago?'

Stoakley frowned. 'Why, my good fellow, she's more than twenty years older than him! You policemen ask peculiar questions.'

An older woman and a younger man: the very pairing that Harriet Sippel, Ida Gransbury and Richard Negus had been overheard gossiping about at the Bloxham Hotel. I was definitely making progress. 'So she was supposed to marry the ne'er-do-well, but then chose a more substantial man instead?'

'No, not the ne'er-do-well,' said Stoakley impatiently. Then his eyelids flickered. He smiled and said, 'Ah, but Patrick! He had greatness within his grasp. She saw it. She understood. If you want women to fall in love with you, Mr Catchpool, show them you have greatness within your grasp.'

'I don't want women to fall in love with me, Mr Stoakley.'

'Why ever not?'

I took a deep breath.

'Mr Stoakley, could you please tell me the name of the woman you were talking about — the one you wish hadn't come here, who fell in love with a more substantial man and who told the unforgivable lie?'

'Unforgivable,' the old gnome agreed.

'Who is Patrick? What is the rest of his name? Are his initials PJI? And is there, or was there ever, a woman by the name of Jennie in Great Holling?'

'Greatness in his grasp,' said Stoakley sadly.

'Yes, quite. But — '

'She sacrificed everything for him, and I don't think she would say she regretted it, if you asked her today. What else could she do? She loved him, you see. There's no arguing with love.' He clutched at his shirt and twisted it. 'You might as well try to rip out your heart.'

Which was rather how I felt after a further half hour of trying to extract some logic from Walter Stoakley. I applied myself until I could bear it no longer, and then gave up.

10

Slander's Mark

I stepped out of the King's Head Inn with great relief. A light rain had started to fall. In front of me, a man wearing a long coat and a cap broke into a trot, no doubt hoping to reach his house and get himself inside before the weather worsened. I gazed out across the field that was opposite the pub, beyond a low hedge: a sizeable expanse of green, bordered by rows of trees on three sides. Again, that silence. Nothing to hear but the rain on the leaves; nothing to see but green.

A country village was the wrong place to live for anyone who wanted to be distracted from their own thoughts, that was for sure. In London, there was always a car or a bus or a face or a dog whizzing past, making some sort of commotion. How I longed for commotion now; anything but this stillness.

Two women passed me, also apparently in a hurry. They ignored my friendly greeting and scuttled away without looking up. It was only when I heard over my shoulder the words 'policeman' and 'Harriet' that I wondered if I had blamed the perfectly innocent rain for a phenomenon of my own making. Were these people running from the weather or from the London policeman?

While I had been applying my little grey cells, as Poirot would call them, to Walter Stoakley's disjointed proclamations, had Victor Meakin left his inn by the back door and stopped passers-by on the street to inform them of my presence in the village, against my clearly stated wishes? I could imagine that might be his idea of sport. What a strange and unpleasant man he was.

I continued along the S-shaped street. Ahead of me, a young man emerged from one of the houses. I was pleased to see that it was the man with the glasses and freckles whom I had met when I first got off the train. When he saw me strolling towards him, he stopped as if the soles of his shoes had been glued to the pavement. 'Hello!' I called out. 'I found the King's Head, thanks to your help!'

The young man's eyes widened as I approached. He looked as if he wanted to hook it; evidently he was too polite to do so. If it hadn't been for that distinctive boomerang of freckles across his nose, I might have concluded that this could not be the same person I met before. His manner had totally altered — exactly as Victor Meakin's had.

'I don't know anything about who killed them, sir,' he stammered before I had an opportunity to aim a question at him. 'I don't know anything. I've never been to London, like I told you.'

Well, that put the matter beyond doubt: my identity and reason for being in Great Holling were common knowledge. Silently, I cursed Meakin. 'It isn't London that I'm here to find out about,' I said. 'Did you know Harriet Sippel,

126

Ida Gransbury and Richard Negus?'

'I can't stop, sir, I'm afraid. I have an errand.' He was calling me 'sir' all over the place. He had not done so the first time we spoke, before he knew I was a policeman.

'Oh,' I said. 'Well, might we speak later today?'

'No, sir, I don't think I'll be able to spare the time.'

'How about tomorrow?'

'No, sir.' He chewed his bottom lip.

'I see. And if I force the issue, I dare say you would only clam up or lie, wouldn't you?' I sighed. 'Thank you for exchanging these few words with me, at any rate. Most people see me coming and hare off in the opposite direction.'

'It's no reflection on you, sir. People are scared.'

'Of what?'

'Three are dead. No one wants to be next.'

I don't know what answer I was expecting, but it wasn't that one. Before I could reply, the young man darted past me and marched off down the street. What, I wondered, made him believe that there was likely to be a 'next'? I thought about Poirot's mention of a fourth cufflink, waiting in the murderer's pocket to be placed in a future victim's mouth, and my throat tightened involuntarily. I could not allow the possibility of another laid-out body. *Palms facing downwards . . .*

No. That was absolutely not going to happen. Announcing this to myself made me feel better.

I walked up and down the street for a while, hoping to catch sight of someone else, but nobody appeared. I was not yet ready to return to the King's Head, so I walked to the very end of the village where the railway station was. I stood on the platform for the London trains, frustrated that I could not board one and return home immediately. I wondered what Blanche Unsworth would cook for dinner tonight, and whether Poirot would judge it to be satisfactory. Then I forced my thoughts back in the direction of Great Holling.

What could I do if everybody in the village had resolved to avoid and ignore me?

The church! I had strode past its graveyard several times without noticing it properly — without thinking about the tragic story of the vicar and his wife who had died within hours of each other. How could I have been so oblivious?

I walked back into the village and made straight for the church. It was called Holy Saints and was a smallish building of the same honey-coloured stone as the railway station. The grass in the churchyard was well tended. Most of the graves had flowers by them that appeared newly laid.

Behind the church, on the other side of a low wall into which a gate had been fitted, I saw two houses. One, set back, looked as if it must be the vicarage. The other, much smaller, was a long, low cottage, the back of which was almost pressed up against the wall. It had no back door but I counted four windows — large ones for a cottage — that would have afforded views of nothing but rows of gravestones. One would have to be made of strong stuff to live there, I thought.

I opened the iron gates and walked from the street into the churchyard. Many of the headstones were so old that the names were illegible. Just as I was thinking this, a new and rather handsome one caught my eye. It was one of the few by which no flowers were laid, and the names carved upon it made my breath catch in my throat.

It couldn't be . . . But surely it *had* to be!

Patrick James Ive, vicar of this parish, and Frances Maria Ive, his beloved wife.

PJI. It was as I had explained to Poirot: the larger initial in the middle of the monogram was the first letter of the surname. And Patrick Ive was once the vicar of Great Holling.

I looked again at the birth and death dates to check I had not made a mistake. No, Patrick and Frances Ive had both died in 1913, he at the age of twenty-nine and she at twenty-eight.

A vicar and his wife who had died tragically, within hours of one another . . . His initials on three cufflinks that ended up in three murder victims' mouths at the Bloxham Hotel . . .

Confound it all! Poirot was right, loath though I was to admit it. There *was* a link. Did that mean he must also be right about this Jennie woman? Was she connected too?

Beneath the names and dates on the gravestone there was a poem. It was a sonnet, but not one I knew. I started to read:

That thou art blamed shall not be thy defect,
For slander's mark was ever yet the fair;

I had read only the first two lines when a voice spoke behind me and prevented me from getting any further. 'The author is William Shakespeare.'

I turned and saw a woman of fifty or thereabouts, with a long and somewhat bony face, hair the colour of horse chestnuts with the odd streak of grey here and there, and wise, watchful grey-green eyes. Pulling her dark coat tight around her body, she said, 'There was much debate about whether the name William Shakespeare ought to be included.'

'Pardon?'

'Beneath the sonnet. In the end, it was decided that the only names on the stone should be . . . ' She turned away suddenly, without finishing her sentence. When she turned back to me, her eyes were damp. 'Well, it was decided that . . . by which I mean that my late husband Charles and I decided . . . Oh, it was me, really. But Charles was my loyal supporter in everything I did. We agreed that William Shakespeare's name received plenty of attention one way and another, and did not need to be carved there too.' She nodded at the stone. 'Though when I saw you looking, I felt obliged to steal up on you and tell you who wrote the poem.'

'I thought I was alone,' I said, wondering how I could have missed her arrival, facing towards the street as I had been.

'I entered through the other gate,' she said, pointing over her shoulder with her thumb. 'I live in the cottage. I saw you through my window.'

My face must have betrayed my thoughts on the unfortunate situation of her home, because she smiled and said, 'Do I mind the view? Not at all. I took the cottage so that I could watch the graveyard.'

She said this as though it were a perfectly normal thing to say. She must have been reading my mind, for she went on to explain: 'There is only one reason that Patrick Ive's gravestone has not been dug out of the ground, Mr Catchpool, and it is this: everybody knows I am watching.' She advanced upon me without warning and held out her hand. I shook it. 'Margaret Ernst,' she said. 'You may call me Margaret.'

'Do you mean . . . Are you saying that there are people in the village who would wish to disturb Patrick and Frances Ive's grave?'

'Yes. I used to lay flowers by it, but it soon became apparent that there was little point. Flowers are easy to destroy, easier than a slab of stone. When I stopped leaving the flowers, there was nothing for them to destroy apart from the gravestone itself, but I was in the cottage by then. Watching.'

'How appalling that anybody would do such a thing to another person's resting place,' I said.

'Well, people *are* appalling, aren't they? Did you read the poem?'

'I started to and then you appeared.'

'Read it now,' she ordered.

I turned back to the stone and read the sonnet in its entirety.

That thou art blamed shall not be thy defect,
For slander's mark was ever yet the fair;
The ornament of beauty is suspect,

131

A crow that flies in heaven's sweetest air.
So thou be good, slander doth but approve
Thy worth the greater, being wooed of time;
For canker vice the sweetest buds doth love,
And thou present'st a pure unstained prime.
Thou hast passed by the ambush of young
  days
Either not assailed, or victor being charged;
Yet this thy praise cannot be so thy praise,
To tie up envy, evermore enlarged,
If some suspect of ill masked not thy show,
Then thou alone kingdoms of hearts shouldst
  owe.

'Well, Mr Catchpool?'

'It's a peculiar poem to fetch up on a gravestone.'

'Do you think so?'

'Slander's a strong word. The poem suggests that — well, unless I'm mistaken — that there were attacks upon Patrick and Frances Ive's characters?'

'There were. Hence the sonnet. I chose it. I was advised that it would prove too costly to engrave the whole poem, and that I should content myself with the first two lines — as if cost were the most important consideration. People are such brutes!' Margaret Ernst gave a disgusted snort. She rested the palm of her hand on the stone, as if it were the top of a beloved child's head instead of a grave. 'Patrick and Frances Ive were kind people who would never willingly have hurt anybody. About how many can one say that, truly?'

'Oh. Well — '

'I didn't know them myself — Charles and I only took over the parish after their deaths — but that's what the village doctor says, Dr Flowerday, and he is the only person in Great Holling with an opinion worth listening to.'

Wanting to check I had not misunderstood her, I said, 'So your husband was the vicar here, after Patrick Ive?'

'Until he died three years ago, yes. There is a new vicar now: a bookish chap without a wife who keeps himself to himself.'

'And this Dr Flowerday . . . ?'

'Forget about him,' Margaret Ernst said quickly, which did an excellent job of fixing the name Dr Flowerday firmly in my mind.

'All right,' I said dishonestly. Having known Margaret Ernst for less than a quarter of an hour, I suspected that all-embracing obedience was the tactic most likely to serve me well.

'Why did the inscription on the gravestone fall to you?' I asked her. 'Did the Ives not have family?'

'None who were both interested and capable, sadly.'

'Mrs Ernst,' I said. 'Margaret, I mean . . . I can't tell you how much more welcome in the village you have made me feel. It's plain that you know who I am, so you must also know why I'm here. No one else will speak to me, apart from an old chap at the King's Head Inn who made little sense.'

'I'm not sure my intention was to make you feel welcome, Mr Catchpool.'

'Less unwelcome, then. At least you don't flee from me as from a monstrous apparition.'

She laughed. 'You? Monstrous? Oh, dear.'

I didn't know what to say to that.

'This man who made little sense at the King's Head — did he have a white beard?'

'Yes.'

'He spoke to you because he is not afraid.'

'Because he's too furiously drunk to fear a thing?'

'No. Because he was not . . . ' Margaret stopped and changed course. 'He is in no danger from the murderer of Harriet, Ida and Richard.'

'And you?' I asked.

'I would speak to you as I have, and as I am, whatever the danger.'

'I see. Are you unusually brave?'

'I am unusually pig-headed. I say what I believe needs to be said, and I do what I believe needs to be done. And if I happen to catch a suggestion that others would prefer me to remain silent, then I do the opposite.'

'That's commendable, I suppose.'

'Do you find me too direct, Mr Catchpool?'

'Not at all. It makes life easier, to speak one's mind.'

'And is that one of the reasons *your* life has never been easy?' Margaret Ernst smiled. 'Ah — I see you would prefer not to talk about yourself. Very well then. What is your impression of my character? If you don't object to the question.'

'I have only just met you.' Heavens above! I thought. Unprepared as I was for an exchange of this nature, the best I could muster was, 'I'd say you come over as a good egg, all in all.'

'That's a rather abstract description of a person, wouldn't you say? Also rather brief. Besides, what is goodness? Morally, the best thing I have ever done was unquestionably wrong.'

'Was it really?' What an extraordinary woman she was. I decided to take a chance. 'What you said before about doing the opposite of what people would like you to do . . . Victor Meakin told me nobody would speak to me. He would be delighted if you neglected to invite me to your cottage for a cup of tea, so that we can talk at greater length, out of the rain. What do you say?'

Margaret Ernst smiled. She seemed to appreciate my boldness, as I had hoped she would. I noticed, however, that her eyes grew more wary. 'Mr Meakin would be similarly delighted if you followed the example of most in the village and refused to cross my threshold,' she said. 'He is joyous about any misfortune to anyone. We could displease him on two accounts, if you are mutinously inclined?'

'Well, then,' I said. 'It sounds to me as if that settles the matter!'

* * *

'Tell me what happened to Patrick and Frances Ive,' I said once the tea was made and we were sitting by the fire in Margaret Ernst's long, narrow parlour. That was what she called the room we were in, though it contained so many

135

books that 'library' would have done just as well. On one wall hung three portraits, two painted and one photographic, of a man with a high forehead and unruly eyebrows. I assumed that he was Margaret's late husband, Charles. It was disconcerting to have three of him staring at me, so I turned to the window instead. My chair afforded an excellent view of the Ives' gravestone, and I decided it must be where Margaret usually sat in order to conduct her vigil.

From this distance, the sonnet was unreadable. I had forgotten all of it apart from the line 'For slander's mark was ever yet the fair', which had lodged itself in my mind.

'No,' said Margaret Ernst.

'No? You won't tell me about Patrick and Frances Ive?'

'Not today. Maybe I will tomorrow. Do you have other questions for me in the meantime?'

'Yes, but . . . do you mind if I ask what is likely to change between now and tomorrow?'

'I would like some time to consider.'

'The thing is — '

'You're going to remind me that you're a policeman working on a murder case, and it is my duty to tell you everything I know. But what have Patrick and Frances Ive to do with your case?'

I ought to have done some delaying and considering of my own, but I was eager to see what response I would get if I presented her with a fact I had not told Victor Meakin, and that therefore she couldn't possibly already know.

'Each of the three victims was found with a

gold cufflink in his or her mouth,' I said. 'All three cufflinks were monogrammed with Patrick Ive's initials: PIJ.' I explained, as I had to Poirot, about the surname's initial being the largest of the three, and in the middle. Unlike my Belgian friend, Margaret Ernst showed no sign of believing civilization to be imperilled by such an arrangement of letters. She also did not appear shocked or surprised by what I had told her, which I found unusual.

'Now do you see why Patrick Ive is of interest to me?' I said.

'Yes.'

'Then will you tell me about him?'

'As I said: perhaps tomorrow. Would you like some more tea, Mr Catchpool?'

I told her that I would, and she left the room. Alone in the parlour, I ruminated over whether I had left it too late to ask her to call me Edward, and, if not, whether I ought to do so. I pondered this while knowing that I would say nothing, and would allow her to continue with 'Mr Catchpool'. It is among the more pointless of my habits: wondering what I ought to do when there is no doubt about what I am going to do.

When Margaret returned with the tea, I thanked her and asked her if she could tell me about Harriet Sippel, Ida Gransbury and Richard Negus. The transformation was incredible. She made no attempt to dissemble, and, in a most efficient fashion, told me enough about two of the three murder victims to fill several pages. Infuriatingly, the notebook I had brought with me to Great Holling lay in one of my cases

137

in my room at the King's Head Inn. This would be a test for my memory.

'Harriet used to have a sweet nature, according to the overflowing archive of village legend,' said Margaret. 'Kind, generous, always a smile on her face, forever laughing and offering to help friends and neighbours, never once thinking of herself — positively saintly. Determined to think well of all she met, to see everything in the best possible light. Naïvely trusting, some said. I'm not sure if I believe all of it. No one could be as perfect as Harriet-Before-She-Changed is painted as being. I wonder if it's the contrast with what she became . . . ' Margaret frowned. 'Perhaps it wasn't, in strictest truth, a case of her going from one extreme to the other, but when one is telling a story, one always wants to make it as dramatic as possible, doesn't one? And I suppose losing a husband so young could turn even the sunniest nature. Harriet was devoted to her George, so they say, and he to her. He died in 1911 at the age of twenty-seven — dropped down dead one day in the street, having always been the picture of health. A blood clot in his brain. Harriet was a widow at twenty-five.'

'What a blow that must have been for her,' I said.

'Yes,' Margaret agreed. 'A loss of that magnitude might have a terrible effect upon a person. It's interesting that some describe her as having been naive.'

'Why do you say that?'

'"Naïve" suggests a falsely rosy conception of

life. If one believed in a wholly benign world and then tragedy of the worst kind struck, one might feel anger and resentment as well as sadness, as if one had been duped. And of course, when we suffer greatly ourselves, it becomes so much easier to blame and persecute others.'

I was attempting to conceal my strenuous disagreement when she added, 'For *some*, I should say. Not for all. I expect you find it easier to persecute yourself, don't you, Mr Catchpool?'

'I hope I don't persecute anybody,' I said, bemused. 'So am I to take it that the loss of her husband had an unfortunate effect upon Harriet Sippel's character?'

'Yes. I never knew sweet, kind Harriet. The Harriet Sippel I knew was spiteful and sanctimonious. She treated the world and nearly everyone in it as an enemy, deserving of her suspicion. Instead of seeing only the good, she saw the threat of evil everywhere, and behaved as if she had been charged with unearthing and defeating it. If there was a newcomer to the village, she would start out with the belief that he or she was bound to be heinous in some respect. She would tell others of her suspicions, as many as would listen, and encourage them to look out for signs. Put a person in front of her and she would search for wickedness in that person. If she found none, she would invent it. Her only pleasure after George died was condemning others as wicked, as if doing so made her a better person somehow. The way her eyes would shine whenever she'd sniffed out some new wrong-doing . . . '

Margaret shuddered. 'It was as if, in the absence of her husband, she had found something else that could ignite her passion and so she clung to it. But it was a dark, destructive passion that sprang from hatred, not love. The worst part was that people flocked around her, readily agreeing with all her unpleasant accusations.'

'Why did they?' I asked.

'They didn't want to be next. They knew Harriet was never without prey. I don't think she could have survived for as long as a week without a focus for her righteous spite.'

I thought of the bespectacled young man who had said, 'No one wants to be next.'

Margaret said: 'They were happy to condemn whichever pour soul she had fixed upon if it diverted her attention from them and whatever they might be up to. That was Harriet's idea of a friend: someone who joined her in vilifying those she deemed to be guilty of a sin, minor or major.'

'You're describing, if I may say so, the sort of person who is likely to end up getting murdered.'

'Am I? I think people like Harriet Sippel aren't murdered nearly often enough.' Margaret raised her eyebrows. 'I see I've shocked you again, Mr Catchpool. As a vicar's wife, I shouldn't say these things, I dare say. I try to be a good Christian, but I have my weaknesses, as we all do. Mine is the inability to forgive the inability to forgive. Does that sound contradictory?'

'It sounds like a tongue-twister. Do you mind if I ask you where you were last Thursday evening?'

140

Margaret sighed and looked out of the window. 'I was where I always am: sitting where you're sitting now, watching the graveyard.'

'Alone?'

'Yes.'

'Thank you.'

'Would you like me to tell you about Ida Gransbury now?'

I nodded, with some trepidation. I wondered how I would feel if it turned out that all three of the murder victims were vindictive monsters while alive. The words 'MAY THEY NEVER REST IN PEACE' passed through my mind, swiftly followed by Poirot's account of his meeting with Jennie, her insistence that justice would finally be done once she was dead . . .

'Ida was a dreadful prig,' said Margaret. 'She was every inch as sanctimonious as Harriet in her outward behaviour, but she was driven by fear, and faith in the rules we are all supposed to obey rather than the thrill of persecution. Denouncing the sins of others wasn't a pleasure for Ida as it was for Harriet. She saw it as her moral duty as a good Christian.'

'When you say fear, do you mean fear of divine retribution?'

'Oh, that, certainly, but not only that,' said Margaret. 'Different people regard rules differently, no matter what those rules happen to be. Mutinous characters like me always resent constraints, even perfectly sensible ones, but there are some who welcome their existence and enforcement because it makes them feel safer. Protected.'

'And Ida Gransbury was the second sort?'

'I think so, yes. She would not have said so. She was always careful to present herself as a woman driven by strong principle and nothing else. No shameful human weaknesses for Ida! I am sorry she is dead, though she did untold harm while alive. Unlike Harriet, Ida believed in redemption. She wanted to save sinners, while Harriet wanted only to revile them and feel elevated by comparison. I think Ida would have forgiven a demonstrably repentant sinner. She was reassured by contrition of the standard Christian sort. It bolstered her view of the world.'

'What untold harm did Ida do?' I asked. 'To whom?'

'Come back and ask me that question tomorrow.' Her tone was generous but firm.

'To Patrick and Frances Ive?'

'Tomorrow, Mr Catchpool.'

'What can you tell me about Richard Negus?' I asked.

'Precious little, I'm afraid. He left Great Holling soon after Charles and I arrived. I think he was an authoritative presence in the village — a man people listened to and took advice from. Everybody speaks of him with the greatest respect, apart from Ida Gransbury. She never spoke of him at all after he left both her and Great Holling behind.'

'Was it his decision or hers to call off the marriage plans?' I asked.

'His.'

'How do you know that she never spoke of him afterwards? Perhaps to others she did, even if not to you?'

'Oh, Ida wouldn't have spoken to me about Richard Negus or anything else. I know only what I have been told by Ambrose Flowerday, the village doctor, but there is no more reliable man on earth. Ambrose gets to hear about most things that go on, as long as he remembers to leave the door to his waiting room ajar.'

'Is this the same Dr Flowerday that I am supposed to forget about? I had better forget his Christian name too, I dare say.'

Margaret ignored my mischievous remark. 'I have it on good authority that after Richard Negus abandoned her, Ida resolved never to speak or think of him again,' she said. 'She showed no outward signs of upset. People remarked upon it: how strong and resolute she was. She announced her intention to reserve all her love for God thenceforth. She found him to be more reliable than mortal men.'

'Would it surprise you to learn that Richard Negus and Ida Gransbury took afternoon tea together in her hotel room in London last Thursday evening?'

Margaret's eyes widened. 'To hear that the two of them took tea *alone* together — yes, it would surprise me greatly. Ida was the sort who drew firm lines and did not cross them. By all accounts so was Richard Negus. Having decided he didn't want Ida as a wife, he is unlikely to have changed his mind, and I cannot think that anything short of prostrate penitence and a renewed declaration of love would have persuaded Ida to agree to a meeting with him in private.'

After a pause, Margaret went on, 'But since Harriet Sippel was at the same London hotel, I assume that she too was present at this afternoon tea ceremony?'

I nodded.

'Well, then. The three of them obviously had something to discuss that was more important than the lines any of them had drawn in the past.'

'You have an idea about what that thing might be, don't you?'

Margaret looked out of the window towards the rows of graves. 'Perhaps I shall have some ideas by the time you visit me tomorrow,' she said.

11

Two Recollections

While I struggled in vain to persuade Margaret
Ernst to tell me the story of Patrick and Frances
Ive before she was ready to do so, Hercule Poirot
was at Pleasant's Coffee House in London,
engaged in an effort of equal futility: that of
trying to persuade the waitress Fee Spring to tell
him what she could not remember.

'All I can tell you's what I've already told you,'
she said several times, with increasing weariness.
'I noticed something not right about Jennie that
night. I tucked it away to fret about later, and
now it's buried somewhere and won't come out.
You pestering me won't change that, if anything
will. Chances are you've scared it away for good.
You've no patience about you, that's for sure.'

'Please continue to try to retrieve the memory,
mademoiselle. It might be important.'

Fee Spring looked over Poirot's shoulder
towards the door. 'If it's memories you're after,
there'll be a man bringing one in for you soon.
He was in round about an hour ago. Shown the
way here by a policeman, he was — escorted,
like royalty. Must be someone important, I
thought. You weren't here, so I told him to come
back now.' She was looking up at the clock that
was wedged in between two teapots on a bowed
shelf above her head. 'I knew you'd be in again at

145

least once today, looking for Jennie when I've told you you won't find her.'

'Did this gentleman tell you his name?'

'No. He was nice and polite, though. Respectful. Not like the one who was all mucky looking and spoke with your voice. He had no right doing that, however clever it was.'

'*Pardon*, mademoiselle. The man to whom you refer — Mr Samuel Kidd — he did not speak with my voice. He attempted to replicate it, but no person can replicate the voice of another.'

Fee laughed. 'He did yours pretty darn good! I'd not know the difference, with my eyes closed.'

'Then you do not pay attention when people talk,' said Poirot irritably. 'Each of us has a speaking voice that is unique, a cadence that belongs to that individual alone.' To illustrate his point, Poirot held up his cup. 'As unique as the tremendous coffee of Pleasant's Coffee House.'

'You're drinking far too much of it,' said Fee. 'It's not good for you.'

'From where did you get this idea?'

'You can't see your eyes, Mr Poirot. I can. You should try drinking a cup of tea once in a while. Tea doesn't taste like mud, and there's no such thing as too much of it. Tea's only ever good for a person.' Having delivered her speech, Fee smoothed down the front of her apron. 'And I *do* listen when people talk — to the words, not the accent. It's what people say that counts, not whether they say it Belgian-sounding or English-sounding.'

At that moment, the coffee-house door opened and a man walked in. He had the drooping eyes of a basset hound.

Fee nudged Poirot. 'Here he is, without the police fellow,' she whispered.

The man was Rafal Bobak, the waiter from the Bloxham Hotel who had served afternoon tea to Harriet Sippel, Ida Gransbury and Richard Negus at a quarter past seven on the night of the murders. Bobak apologized for the intrusion, and explained that Luca Lazzari had told his whole staff that if any of them wanted to speak to the famous detective Hercule Poirot, Pleasant's Coffee House in St Gregory's Alley was the place to find him.

Once they had settled themselves at a table, Poirot asked, 'What is it that you wish to tell me? You have remembered something?'

'I've remembered as much as I'm likely to remember, sir, and I thought it would be as well to tell you while it's fresh in my mind. Some of it you've heard already, but I've been going over and over it, and it's remarkable how much comes back to you once you apply yourself.'

'Indeed, monsieur. It is necessary only to sit still and employ the little grey cells.'

'Mr Negus was the one who took delivery of the meal, as I've told you, sir. The two ladies were discussing a woman and a man, like I said at the hotel. It sounded as if she'd been abandoned by him for being too old, or he'd lost interest in her for some other reason. At least, that was my understanding, sir, but I've managed to remember a bit of what they said, so

147

you can judge for yourself.'

'Ah! Most helpful!'

'Well, sir, the first thing I've managed to remember is Mrs Harriet Sippel saying, 'She had no choice, did she? She's no longer the one he confides in. He'd hardly be interested in her now — she's let herself go, and she's old enough to be his mother. No, if she wanted to find out what's going on in his mind, she had no choice but to receive the woman he *does* confide in, and talk to her.' After saying all this, Mrs Sippel broke into peals of laughter, and it wasn't *nice* laughter. Cattish, as I said at the hotel.'

'Please go on, Mr Bobak.'

'Well, Mr Negus heard what she said, because he turned away from me — he and I had been exchanging pleasantries, you see — and he said, 'Oh, Harriet, that's hardly fair. Ida's easily shocked. Go easy on her.' And then either Harriet Sippel or the other one, Ida Gransbury, said *something*. I can't for the life of me remember what it was, sir, for which I'm sorry.'

'There is no need to apologize,' said Poirot. 'Your recollection, incomplete as it is, will prove invaluable, I am sure.'

'I hope so, sir,' said Bobak doubtfully. 'The next bit I remember word by word was many minutes later, as I laid everything out on the table for the three guests. Mr Negus said to Mrs Sippel, 'His mind? I'd argue he has no mind. And I dispute your old-enough-to-be-his-mother claim. I dispute it utterly.' Mrs Sippel laughed at this and said, 'Well, neither of us can prove we're right, so let's agree to disagree!' That was the last thing I heard before I left the room, sir.'

''I would argue he has no mind',' Poirot murmured.

'What they were saying, sir — none of it was friendly. This woman they were talking about, they harboured nothing but ill will for her.'

'I cannot thank you enough, Mr Bobak,' said Poirot warmly. 'Your account is inordinately helpful. To know the very words that were spoken, and so many of them, is more than I could have hoped for.'

'I only wish I could remember the rest, sir.'

Poirot tried to persuade Bobak to stay and drink a cup of something, but the waiter was determined to return to the Bloxham Hotel as soon as he could, and not take advantage of Luca Lazzari's good nature.

Refused another cup of coffee by Fee Spring, who cited his health in her defence, Poirot decided to return to Blanche Unsworth's lodging house. He moved slowly, ambling through the busy London streets, while his mind raced ahead. As he walked, he turned over in his mind the words Rafal Bobak had repeated to him: 'He'd hardly be interested in her now . . . She's old enough to be his mother . . . His mind? I'd argue he has no mind . . . I dispute your old-enough-to-be-his-mother claim . . . Well, neither of us can prove we're right . . . '

He was still murmuring these phrases to himself when he arrived at his temporary accommodation. Blanche Unsworth rushed towards him as he entered. 'What are you saying to yourself, Mr Poirot?' she asked cheerily. 'It's

149

like having two of you!'

Poirot looked down at his body, the shape of which inclined towards rotundity. 'I hope I have not eaten so much that I have doubled in size, madame,' he said.

'No, I meant two of you *talking*.' Blanche Unsworth lowered her voice to a whisper and came so close to Poirot that he felt obliged to pin himself against the wall in order to avoid physical contact with her. 'There's a chap come to call on you, and *his voice is just like yours*. He's waiting in the drawing room. A visitor from your native Belgium, he must be. Raggedy fellow, but I let him in, since there was no bad smell coming from him, and . . . well, I didn't want to turn away a relation of yours, Mr Poirot. I expect customs with regard to clothing are different in every country. 'Course, it's the *French* who likes to dress smart, isn't it?'

'He is no relative of mine,' said Poirot stiffly. 'His name is Samuel Kidd and he is as English as you are, madame.'

'He's got cuts all over his face,' said Blanche Unsworth. 'From shaving, he said. I don't think he must know how to do it properly, poor lamb. I told him I'd something to put on the cuts to help them heal, but all he did was laugh!'

'All over his face?' Poirot frowned. 'The Mr Kidd I met last Friday at Pleasant's Coffee House had only one cut on his face, on a patch of skin that he had shaved. Tell me, does this man in the drawing room have a beard?'

'Oh, no. There's not a hair on his face apart from his eyebrows. Not as much skin on his face

150

as there should be either! I wish you'd teach him how to shave without causing himself lacerations, Mr Poirot. Oh, I'm sorry.' Blanche clapped her hands over her mouth. 'You did say he was no relation, didn't you. I still have him down in my head as Belgian. He sounded *exactly* like you, the way he spoke. I thought he might be a younger brother. About forty, isn't he?'

Affronted that anyone might take raggedy Samuel Kidd to be his kin, Poirot cut short his exchange with Blanche Unsworth somewhat abruptly, and proceeded to the drawing room.

Inside it, he found what he had been told he would find: a man — the same man he had met at Pleasant's the previous Friday — who had removed all his facial hair and cut himself extensively in the process.

'Good afternoon, Mr *Poirr-oh*.' Samuel Kidd rose to his feet. 'I bet I fooled her, didn't I, her what let me in? Did she think I was a native of your country?'

'Good afternoon, Mr Kidd. I see that you have suffered much misfortune since the last time we met.'

'Misfortune?'

'The injuries to your face.'

'Ah, you're right there, sir. Truth is, I don't like thinking about a sharp blade so close to me eyes. I think about it cutting clean through the eyeball, and it gives me a shaky hand. I'm funny about eyes. I've tried telling meself to think about something different, but it don't work. Always end up sliced to ribbons, I do.'

'So I see. May I ask: how did you know that

you would find me at this address?'

'Mr Lazzari at the hotel said that Constable Stanley Beer said that Mr Catchpool lived here and you did too, sir. I'm sorry about disturbing you at home, but I've got good news for you and I thought you'd want to know it straight away.'

'What is the news?'

'The lady that dropped the two keys, the one I saw running from the hotel after the murders . . . I've remembered who she is! It came to me when I looked at a newspaper this morning. I don't often look at a newspaper.'

'Who is the woman you saw, monsieur? You are right. Poirot, he would like to know her name straight away.'

Samuel Kidd traced an angry red ridge of scab on his left cheek with the tip of his finger as he mused, 'Seems to me there's not much time to read about other people's lives and live your own while you're at it. If I have to choose, and I reckon I do, I'll choose living my own life over reading summat about someone else's. But as I say, I *did* look at the newspaper this morning, because I wanted to see if there was anything about the Bloxham Hotel murders.'

'*Oui*,' said Poirot, struggling to remain patient. 'And what did you see?'

'Oh, there was plenty about the murders, most of it saying the police aren't getting very far and asking for anyone who saw summat to come forward. Well, I did, as you know, Mr Poirot, and forward I came. But, like I said the other day, at first I couldn't put a name to a face. Well, now I can!'

152

'That is excellent news, Mr Kidd. It will be more excellent still if you can put that name into the next sentence that you speak, so that I may hear it.'

'That's where I've seen her, you see: her photograph, in the newspaper. That's why looking at a newspaper made me think of her. She's a famous lady, sir. Her name's Nancy Ducane.'

Poirot's eyes widened. 'Nancy Ducane the artist?'

'Yes, sir. She's the one, and no other. I'd swear to it. Paints portraits, she does. And got a face worth painting of her own, which is probably why I remembered it. I said to meself, 'Sammy, that was Nancy Ducane you saw running from the Bloxham Hotel on the night of the murders.' And now I'm here saying it to you.'

12

A Grievous Wound

The following day, immediately after breakfast, I set out for Margaret Ernst's cottage next to Holy Saints churchyard in Great Holling. I found the front door ajar and knocked as lightly as I could, taking care not to push it open any further.

There was no answer, so I knocked again, more volubly. 'Mrs Ernst?' I called out. 'Margaret?'

Silence.

I don't know why, but I turned, sensing some kind of movement behind me, but perhaps it was only the wind in the trees.

I pushed the door gently and it swung open with a creak. The first thing I saw was a scarf on the kitchen's flagstone floor: blue and green silk, elaborately patterned. What was it doing there? I took a deep breath and was steeling myself to enter when a voice called out, 'Come in, Mr Catchpool.' I nearly jumped out of my skin.

Margaret Ernst appeared in the kitchen. 'Oh, I was looking for that,' she said with a smile, bending to retrieve the scarf. 'I knew it would be you. I left the door open. In fact, I expected you to arrive five minutes ago, but I suppose nine o'clock on the dot would have looked too eager, wouldn't it?' She ushered me inside, draping the scarf around her neck.

Something about her teasing — though I knew

154

it was not intended to offend — emboldened me to be more direct than I might otherwise have been. 'I am eager to discover the truth, and I don't mind looking it,' I said. 'Who might have wished to murder Harriet Sippel, Ida Gransbury and Richard Negus? I believe you have an idea about that, and I'd like to know it.'

'What are those papers?'

'What? Oh!' I had forgotten I was holding them. 'Lists. Guests at the Bloxham Hotel around the time of the murders, and people employed by the Bloxham. I was wondering if you might take a look and let me know if you see a name you recognize — after you've answered my question about who might have wanted to murder — '

'Nancy Ducane,' said Margaret. She took the two lists from my hand and studied them, frowning.

I said the very same words to her that Poirot had said to Samuel Kidd the day before, though I did not know then that he had said them. 'Nancy Ducane the artist?'

'Wait a moment.' We stood in silence while Margaret read the two lists. 'None of these names is familiar to me, I'm afraid.'

'Are you saying that Nancy Ducane — the same Nancy Ducane I'm thinking of, the society portrait painter — had a motive for killing Harriet Sippel, Ida Gransbury and Richard Negus?'

Margaret folded the two pieces of paper, handed them back to me, then beckoned me to follow her into the parlour. Once we were sitting

155

comfortably in the same chairs as the previous day, she said, 'Yes. Nancy Ducane the famous artist. She is the only person I can think of who would have had both the desire to kill Harriet, Ida and Richard and the ability to do it and get away with it. Don't look so surprised, Mr Catchpool. Famous people aren't exempt from evil. Though I must say I can't believe that Nancy would do such a thing. She was a civilized woman when I knew her, and no one ever changes all that much. She was a *brave* woman.'

I said nothing. The trouble is, I thought, that some killers *are* civilized for the most part, and only break from their routine of civility once, to commit murder.

Margaret said, 'I lay awake all of last night wondering if Walter Stoakley might have done it, but, no, it's impossible. He can't stand up without help, let alone get himself to London. To commit three murders would be quite beyond him.'

'Walter Stoakley?' I sat forward in my chair. 'The drunken old cove at the King's Head that I spoke to yesterday? Why should he want to murder Harriet Sippel, Ida Gransbury and Richard Negus?'

'Because Frances Ive was his daughter,' said Margaret. She turned to look out of the window at the Ives' gravestone, and once again the line from the Shakespeare sonnet came into my mind: *For slander's mark was ever yet the fair.*

'I would be glad if Walter had committed the murders,' said Margaret. 'Isn't that dreadful of me? I would be relieved that Nancy hadn't done

156

it. Walter's old, and there's not much life left in him, I don't think. Oh, I don't want it to be Nancy! I've read in the papers about how well Nancy is doing as an artist. She left here and really made a name for herself. That was a source of comfort to me. I was happy to think of her prospering in London.'

'Left here?' I said. 'So Nancy Ducane also lived in Great Holling at one time?'

Margaret Ernst was still staring out of the window. 'Yes. Until 1913.'

'The same year that Patrick and Frances Ive died. The same year that Richard Negus also left the village.'

'Yes.'

'Margaret . . . ' I leaned forward in an attempt to draw her attention away from the Ives' gravestone. 'I'm hoping for all I'm worth that you have decided to tell me the story of Patrick and Frances Ive. I'm certain that once I have heard it, I will understand many things that are a mystery to me at present.'

She turned her serious eyes towards me. 'I *have* decided to tell you the story, on one condition. You must promise not to repeat it to anybody in the village. What I say to you in this room must go no further until you arrive in London. There, you may tell whomever you wish.'

'No need to worry on that score,' I said. 'My opportunities for conversation in Great Holling are limited. Everyone scarpers as soon as they see me coming.' It had happened twice on the way to Margaret Ernst's cottage that morning.

One of the gaspers was a boy of no more than ten years old: a child, and yet he knew who I was and that he should avert his eyes and hurry past me to safety. He would, I felt sure, have known my Christian name, my surname, and the nature of my business in Great Holling. Small villages have at least one talent that London lacks: they know how to ignore a chap in a way that makes him feel terribly important.

'I am asking for a solemn promise, Mr Catchpool — not an evasion.'

'Why is there a need for secrecy? Don't all the villagers know about the Ives and whatever it was that happened to them?'

What Margaret said next revealed that her concern was for one villager in particular. 'Once you have heard what I have to say, you will doubtless want to speak to Dr Ambrose Flowerday.'

'The man you urge me to forget, yet remind me of time and time again?'

She blushed. 'You must promise not to seek him out and, if you do happen to encounter him, not to raise the subject of Patrick and Frances Ive. Unless you can give me such an under-taking, I shan't be able to tell you anything.'

'I'm not sure I can. What would I tell my boss at Scotland Yard? He sent me here to ask questions.'

'Well, then. We're in a bind.' Margaret Ernst folded her arms.

'Supposing I find this Dr Flowerday and ask him to tell me the story instead? He knew the Ives, didn't he? Yesterday you said that, unlike

158

you, he lived in Great Holling while they were still alive.'

'No!' The fear in her eyes was unmistakable. 'Please don't speak to Ambrose! You don't understand. You *can't* understand.'

'What are you so afraid of, Margaret? You seem to me to be a woman of integrity, but . . . well, I can't help wondering if you intend to give me only a partial account.'

'Oh, my account will be thorough. It will lack nothing.'

For some reason, I believed her. 'Then, if you're not intending to withhold a portion of the truth, why must I not talk to anybody else about Patrick and Frances Ive?'

Margaret rose to her feet, walked over to the window and stood with her forehead touching the glass and her body blocking my view of the Ives' gravestone. 'What happened here in 1913 inflicted a grievous wound upon this village,' she said quietly. 'No one living here escaped it. Nancy Ducane moved to London afterwards, and Richard Negus to Devon, but neither of them escaped. They carried the wound with them. It wasn't visible on their skin or on any part of their bodies, but it was there. The wounds you can't see are the worst. And those who stayed, like Ambrose Flowerday — well, it was terrible for them too. I don't know if Great Holling can recover. I know that it hasn't yet.'

She turned to face me. 'The tragedy is never spoken of, Mr Catchpool. Not by anybody here, never directly. Sometimes silence is the only way. Silence and forgetting, if only one *could* forget.'

She clasped and unclasped her hands.

'Are you worried about the effect my question might have upon Dr Flowerday? Is he trying to forget?'

'As I said: forgetting is impossible.'

'Nevertheless . . . it would be a distressing subject for him to discuss?'

'Yes. Very.'

'Is he a good friend of yours?'

'This has nothing to do with *me*,' came her sharp retort. 'Ambrose is a good man and I don't want him bothered. Why can you not agree to what I'm asking?'

'All right, you have my word,' I said reluctantly. 'I will discuss what you tell me with no one in the village.' Having made this pledge, I found myself hoping that the residents of Great Holling would continue to ignore me as assiduously as they had thus far, and not put temptation in my way. It would be just my luck to leave Margaret Ernst's cottage and run into a garrulous Dr Flowerday, keen to have a good old chinwag.

From his three portraits on the wall, the late Charles Ernst bestowed three warning glances upon me: 'Break your promise to my wife and you will regret it, you scoundrel,' his eyes seemed to say.

'What about your own peace of mind?' I asked. 'You don't want me to talk to Dr Flowerday in case it upsets him, but I'm worried I might upset you. I don't want to cause you any distress.'

'Good.' Margaret sighed with relief. 'The truth is, I would welcome the chance to tell the story to another outsider like myself.'

160

'Then please do,' I said.

She nodded, returned to her chair, and proceeded to tell me the story of Patrick and Frances Ive, to which I listened without interruption. I shall now set it down here.

★ ★ ★

The rumour that started all the trouble sixteen years ago came from a servant girl who worked in the home of Reverend Patrick Ive, the young vicar of Great Holling, and his wife Frances. Having said that, the servant was not solely or even mainly responsible for the tragedy that resulted. She told a spiteful lie, but she told it to one person only, and had no part in spreading it more widely throughout the village. Indeed, once the unpleasantness began, she withdrew almost completely and was scarcely seen. Some speculated that she was ashamed, as she should have been, of what she had set in motion. Later, she regretted her part in the affair and did her best to make amends, though by then it was too late.

Of course, she was wicked to tell a lie of such magnitude even to one person. Perhaps she was frustrated after a particularly hard day's work at the vicarage, or it could be that, as a servant with ideas above her station, she resented the Ives. Maybe she wished to perk up her dreary life with a little malicious gossip, and was naive enough to imagine that no serious harm would be done.

Unfortunately, the person she chose as audience for her heinous lie was Harriet Sippel. Again, maybe her choice was easy to understand.

161

Harriet, embittered and vindictive as she was since the death of her husband, could be relied upon to receive the lie with great excitement and to believe it, because, of course, she would want it to be true. Someone in the village was doing something gravely wrong, and, even worse (or, from Harriet's point of view, even better) that someone was the vicar! How her eyes must have flashed with glee! Yes, Harriet was the perfect audience for the servant girl's slanderous story, and no doubt that was why she was chosen.

The servant told Harriet Sippel that Patrick Ive was a swindler of the most cruel and sacrilegious kind: he was, she claimed, luring villagers to the vicarage late at night whenever his wife Frances was elsewhere helping parishioners, as she often was, and taking their money in exchange for passing on communications from their deceased loved ones — messages from the afterlife that these departed souls had entrusted to him, Patrick Ive, to deliver.

Harriet Sippel told anybody who would listen that Patrick was practising his charlatan trickery upon several villagers, but this might have been her attempt to enlarge his wrongdoing in order to make a more shocking story. The servant girl insisted later that she had only ever mentioned one name to Harriet: that of Nancy Ducane.

Nancy was at that time not a famous portrait painter but an ordinary young woman. She had moved to Great Holling in 1910 with her husband William when he took a job as headmaster of the village school. William was much older than Nancy. She was eighteen when they married and he was almost fifty, and in 1912 he died of a respiratory illness.

According to the wicked rumours that Harriet Sippel began to circulate in the snow-beleaguered January of 1913, Nancy had been seen several times entering and leaving the vicarage at night or in the evening, always when it was dark; always looking furtive, and only on nights when Frances Ive wasn't at home.

Anyone with a grain of sense would have doubted the story. It is surely impossible to observe a furtive expression, or indeed any expression, on a person's face in the pitch-darkness. It would have been hard to ascertain the identity of a woman leaving the vicarage in the dead of night unless she had a particularly distinctive gait, and Nancy Ducane did not; indeed, it is more likely that whoever saw her on these several occasions followed her home and found out who she was that way.

It is easier to accept the account of a person more zealous than yourself than to challenge it, and that is what most people in Great Holling did. They were content to trust the rumour, and join Harriet in accusing Patrick Ive of blasphemy and extortion. Most believed (or, to avoid Harriet's vitriolic scorn, pretended to believe) that Patrick Ive was secretly acting as a conduit for exchanges between the living and the souls of the dead, and taking substantial sums of money from gullible parishioners as recompense. It struck the villagers of Great Holling as eminently plausible that Nancy Ducane would be unable to resist if offered a means of receiving messages from her late husband William, especially if the offer came from the vicar of the parish. And, yes, she might well pay handsomely for such an arrangement.

The villagers forgot that they knew, liked and trusted Patrick Ive. They ignored what they knew of his decency and kindness, and disregarded Harriet Sippel's relish for sniffing out sinners. They fell in with her campaign of spite because they were afraid to attract her wrath, but that was not the only thing that persuaded them. More influential still was the knowledge that Harriet had two substantial allies: Richard Negus and Ida Gransbury had lent their support to her cause.

Ida was known to be the most pious woman in Great Holling. Her faith never wavered, and she rarely opened her mouth to speak without quoting from the New Testament. She was admired and revered by all, even if she was not the sort of woman you would seek out if you wanted to have a riot of a time. She was far from being gay company, but she was the closest thing the village had to a saint all of its own. And she was engaged to be married to Richard Negus, a lawyer who was said to have a brilliant mind.

Richard's considerable intellect and air of quiet authority had earned him the respect of the whole village. He believed the lie when Harriet presented it to him because it tallied with the evidence of his own eyes. He too had seen Nancy Ducane — or at least a woman who might have been Nancy Ducane — leaving the vicarage in the middle of the night on more than one

164

occasion when the vicar's wife was known to be away visiting her father, or staying in the home of one of her parishioners.

Richard Negus believed the rumour, and so Ida Gransbury believed it too. She was shocked to her core to think that Patrick Ive, a man of the cloth, had been carrying on in such an unchristian fashion. She, Harriet and Richard made it their mission to remove Patrick Ive from his position as vicar of Great Holling, and to see him expelled from the church. They demanded that he appear in public and admit to his sinful behaviour. He declined to do so, since the rumours were untrue.

The villagers' hatred of Patrick Ive soon expanded to include his wife Frances, whom people said must have known about the heretical and fraudulent activities of her husband. Frances swore that she did not. At first she tried to say that Patrick would never do such a thing, but when person after person insisted that he had, she stopped saying anything at all.

Only two people in Great Holling declined to participate in the hounding of the Ives: Nancy Ducane (for obvious reasons, some said) and Dr Ambrose Flowerday, who was particularly vociferous in his defence of Frances Ive. If Frances knew about the unsavoury activities that were taking place at the vicarage, he argued, why did they only happen when she was elsewhere? Surely that suggested she was entirely innocent? It was Dr Flowerday who pointed out that it is impossible to see a guilty expression on a person's face in the pitch dark, Dr Flowerday who declared that he intended to believe his friend Patrick Ive unless and until someone produced undeniable evidence of his wrongdoing, Dr Flowerday who told Harriet Sippel (one day on the street, in front of several witnesses) that she had very likely packed more wickedness into the last half hour than Patrick Ive had committed in his entire life.

Ambrose Flowerday did not make himself popular by taking this view, but he is one of those rare people who does not care what the world thinks of him. He defended Patrick Ive to the Church authorities and told them that, in his opinion, there was not a grain of truth in the rumours. He was dreadfully worried about Frances Ive, who by now was in a pitiful condition. She had stopped eating, hardly slept, and could not under any circumstances be persuaded to leave the vicarage. Patrick Ive was frantic. His position as vicar and his reputation no longer mattered to him, he said. His only wish was to restore his wife to good health.

Nancy Ducane, meanwhile, had said nothing at all, neither confirming nor denying the rumours. The more Harriet Sippel goaded her, the more determined she seemed to remain silent. Then one day, she changed her mind. She told Victor Meakin that she had something important to say, to put a stop to the foolishness that had gone on for long enough. Victor Meakin chuckled, rubbed his hands together, and quietly slipped out of the back door of the King's Head. Very shortly afterwards, everybody in Great Holling knew that Nancy Ducane wished to make an announcement.

Patrick and Frances Ive were the only people in the village who did not appear in response to the summons. Everybody else — even the servant girl who had started the rumour and whom no one had seen for weeks — assembled at the King's Head, eager for the next phase of the drama to begin.

After a brief, warm smile at Ambrose Flowerday, Nancy Ducane assumed a cool and forthright manner to address the crowd. She told them that the story about Patrick Ive taking her money in exchange for communications from her late husband was completely untrue. However, she said, not all of what was being said was a lie. She had, she admitted, visited Patrick Ive in the vicarage at night more than once when his wife was not present. She had done this because she and Patrick Ive were in love.

The villagers gasped in shock. Some started to whisper. Some people covered their mouths with their hands, or clutched the arm of whoever was next to them.

Nancy waited for the hubbub to subside before she continued. 'We were wrong to meet in secret and put ourselves in temptation's way,' she said, 'but we could not stay apart. When we met at the vicarage, all we ever did was talk — about our feelings for one another, and how impossible they were. We would agree that we must never be alone together again, but then Frances would go somewhere and . . . well, the strength of our love was such that we could not resist.'

Someone shouted out, 'All you did was talk,

was it? My eye and Betty Martin!' Once again, Nancy assured the crowd that nothing of a physical nature had taken place between herself and Patrick Ive.

'I have now told you the truth,' she said. 'It is a truth I would rather not have told, but it was the only way to put a stop to the vile lies. Those of you who know what it means to feel deep, all-consuming love for another person — you will find yourselves unable to condemn me and unable to condemn Patrick. Those with condemnation in your hearts — you are ignorant of love, and I pity you.'

Then Nancy looked straight at Harriet Sippel and said, 'Harriet, I believe you *did* know true love once, but when you lost George, you chose to forget what you knew. You made an adversary of love and an ally of hate.'

As if determined to prove her right, Harriet Sippel rose to her feet and, after a swift dismissal of Nancy as a lying harlot, began to denounce Patrick Ive more vociferously than ever before: not only did he profit from selling fraudulent encounters with the souls of the dead, but he also consorted with women of loose morals while his wife was away. He was a heretic and an adulterer! He was even worse than she, Harriet, had suspected! It was an outrage, she said, that a man so steeped in sin should be allowed to call himself vicar of Great Holling.

Nancy Ducane left the King's Head halfway through Harriet's rousing speech, unable to bear it. A few seconds later, the Ives' servant girl ran for the door, red-faced and in floods of tears.

168

Most of the villagers did not know what to think. They were confused by what they had heard. And then Ida Gransbury spoke up in support of Harriet. Though it was unclear what was rumour and what was true, she said, it was surely beyond doubt that Patrick Ive was a sinner of some description and that he could not be allowed to remain in his post as vicar of Great Holling.

Yes, agreed most of the villagers. Yes, that was true.

Richard Negus said nothing, even when called upon to speak by Ida, his fiancée. He told Dr Ambrose Flowerday later that day that he was worried by the turn events had taken. 'A sinner of some description', while apparently good enough for Ida, was not, he said, good enough for him. He declared himself disgusted by Harriet Sippel's opportunistic attempt to portray Patrick Ive as guilty twice over, of two sins instead of one. She had taken Nancy Ducane's 'not this but that' and turned it into 'this *and* that', without evidence or justification.

Ida had used the words 'beyond doubt' at the King's Head; what now seemed to Richard Negus to be beyond doubt, he told Ambrose Flowerday, was that people (including himself, to his shame) had been telling lies about Patrick Ive. What if Nancy Ducane had also lied? What if her love for Patrick Ive was unrequited, and he had met her in secret at her insistence, only to try to explain to her that she must desist from harbouring these feelings for him?

Dr Flowerday agreed: no one knew for certain

that Patrick Ive had done anything wrong, which had been his opinion of the matter from the start. He was the only person the Ives would admit to the vicarage, and on his next visit, he told Patrick what Nancy Ducane had said at the King's Head. Patrick simply shook his head. He made no comment on the truth or falsehood of Nancy's story. Frances Ive, meanwhile, was physically and mentally deteriorating.

Richard Negus failed to persuade Ida Gransbury to see things the way he saw them, and relations between them became strained. The villagers, led by Harriet, continued to persecute Patrick and Frances Ive, shouting accusations outside the vicarage all day and night. Ida continued to petition the Church to remove the Ives from the vicarage, the church and the village of Great Holling, for their own sakes.

And then tragedy struck: Frances Ive, unable to bear the ignominy any longer, swallowed poison and put an end to her unhappy life. Her husband found her and knew straight away that it was too late. There was no point summoning Dr Flowerday; Frances could not be saved. Patrick Ive knew, also, that he could not live with the guilt and the pain, and so he too took his own life.

Ida Gransbury advised the villagers to pray for mercy for the sinful souls of Patrick and Frances Ive, however unlikely it was that the Lord would forgive them.

Harriet Sippel saw no need to allow the Lord any discretion in the matter; the Ives would burn in Hell for ever, she told her flock of righteous persecutors, and it would be no more than they deserved.

Within a few months of the Ives' deaths, Richard Negus had ended his engagement to Ida Gransbury and left Great Holling. Nancy Ducane left for London, and the servant girl who told the horrible lie was never seen again in the village.

In the meantime, Charles and Margaret Ernst had arrived and taken over at the vicarage. They quickly became friendly with Dr Ambrose Flowerday, who forced himself to relate the whole tragic tale. He told them that Patrick Ive, whether or not he had made the mistake of harbouring a secret passion for Nancy Ducane, had been one of the most generous and benign men he had ever known, and the least deserving of slander.

It was his mention of slander that gave Margaret Ernst the idea for the poem on the gravestone. Charles Ernst was against the idea, not wishing to provoke the villagers, but Margaret stood her ground, determined that Holy Saints Church should display its support for Patrick and Frances Ive. 'I would like to do considerably more to Harriet Sippel and Ida Gransbury than provoke them,' she said. And yes, when she uttered those words, murder was what she had in mind, though only as a fantasy, not as a crime she intended to commit.

★ ★ ★

After she had told me the story, Margaret Ernst fell silent. It was a while before either of us spoke.

171

Finally I said, 'I can see why you gave me the name of Nancy Ducane when I asked you who might have a motive. Would she have murdered Richard Negus, though? He withdrew his support for Harriet Sippel and Ida Gransbury as soon as doubt was cast upon the servant girl's lie.'

'I can only tell you how I would feel if I were Nancy,' said Margaret. 'Would I forgive Richard Negus? No, I would not. Without his early endorsement of the lies told by Harriet and that wretched servant girl, Ida Gransbury might not have believed the nonsense they were spouting. Three people drummed up hostility towards Patrick Ive in Great Holling. Those three people were Harriet Sippel, Ida Gransbury and Richard Negus.'

'What about the servant?'

'Ambrose Flowerday doesn't believe that she meant to start what she started. She was clearly unhappy as soon as the bad feeling towards the Ives took hold in the village.'

I frowned, dissatisfied. 'But from a murderous Nancy Ducane's point of view — purely for the sake of argument — if she can't forgive Richard Negus who later saw the error of his ways, why would she forgive the girl who told the lie in the first place?'

'Perhaps she didn't,' said Margaret. 'Perhaps she has murdered her too. I don't know where the servant ended up, but Nancy Ducane might have known. She could have hunted her down and killed her too. What's the matter? Your face has turned rather grey.'

'What . . . what was the name of the servant girl who told the lie?' I stammered, fearing I knew the answer. 'No, no, it can't be,' said a voice in my head, 'and yet how can it *not* be?'

'Jennie Hobbs. Mr Catchpool, are you all right? You don't look at all well.'

'He was right! She *is* in danger.'

'Who is 'He'?'

'Hercule Poirot. He's always right. How is that possible?'

'Why do you sound cross? Did you want him to be wrong?'

'No. No, I suppose not.' I sighed. 'Although I am now worried that Jennie Hobbs is not safe, assuming she's still alive.'

'I see. How strange.'

'What is strange?'

Margaret sighed. 'In spite of everything I have said, it's hard for me to think of anyone being in danger from Nancy. Motive or no motive, I don't see her committing murder. This will sound peculiar but . . . one cannot kill without immersing oneself in horror and unpleasantness — wouldn't you say?'

I nodded.

'Nancy liked fun and beauty and pleasure and love. All the happy things. She would want nothing to do with a business as ugly as murder.'

'So if not Nancy Ducane then who?' I asked. 'What about drunk old Walter Stoakley? As Frances Ive's father, he has a powerful motive. If he laid off the drink for a day or so, it might not be beyond him to kill three people.'

'It would be quite impossible for Walter to lay

off the drink even for an hour. I can assure you, Mr Catchpool, Walter Stoakley is not the man you're looking for. You see, unlike Nancy Ducane, he never blamed Harriet, Ida and Richard for what happened to Frances. He blamed himself.'

'Hence the drinking?'

'Yes. It is Walter Stoakley that Walter Stoakley set out to kill after he lost his daughter, and he shall very soon succeed, I imagine.'

'In what possible way could Frances's suicide have been his fault?'

'Walter didn't always live in Great Holling. He moved here to be closer to Patrick and Frances's resting place. You will find this difficult to believe, having seen him as he is now, but until Frances's death, Walter Stoakley was an eminent Classicist, and Master of the University of Cambridge's Saviour College. That is where Patrick Ive trained for the priesthood. Patrick had no parents. He was orphaned at a young age, and Walter made a sort of protege of him. Jennie Hobbs, then only seventeen years old, was a bed-maker at the college. She was the best bedder Saviour had, and so Walter Stoakley arranged for her to look after Patrick Ive's rooms. Then Patrick married Frances Stoakley, Walter's daughter, and when they moved to Holy Saints Vicarage in Great Holling, Jennie went with them. Do you see?'

I nodded. 'Walter Stoakley blames himself for putting Patrick Ive and Jennie Hobbs together. If Patrick and Frances had not taken Jennie with them to Great Holling, she would not have been in a position to tell the terrible lie that led to their deaths.'

'And I would not have to spend my life watching a gravestone to make sure nobody desecrates it.'

'Who would do such a thing?' I asked. 'Harriet Sippel? Before she was killed, I mean.'

'Oh, no, Harriet's weapon was her toxic tongue, not her hands. She would never defile a grave. No, it's the rowdy young men of the village who would do that, given half a chance. They were children when Patrick and Frances died, but they've heard their parents' stories. If you ask anyone around here, besides me and Ambrose Flowerday, they will tell you that Patrick Ive was a wicked man — that he and his wife practised black magic. I think most of them believe it more strongly as time goes on. They have to, don't they? It's either that or dislike themselves as heartily as I dislike them.'

There was something I wanted to clarify. 'Did Richard Negus sever ties with Ida Gransbury because she continued to denounce Patrick Ive after he had come to his senses? Was it following Nancy's announcement at the King's Head that he ended their engagement?'

A peculiar expression passed across Margaret's face. She started to say, 'That day at the King's Head was the beginning of . . . ', then stopped and changed course. 'Yes. He found her irrational insistence upon the virtue of her and Harriet's cause too galling to bear.'

Margaret's face had a shut-down look about it all of a sudden. I had the impression that there was something important she had chosen not to tell me.

'You mentioned that Frances Ive swallowed poison,' I said. 'How? Where did she get it from? And how did Patrick Ive die?'

'The same way: poison. I don't suppose you've heard of Abrin?'

'I can't say I have.'

'It comes from a plant called the rosary pea, common in the tropics. Frances Ive obtained several vials of the stuff from somewhere.'

'Forgive me, but if they both took the same poison and were found together, how was it established that Frances killed herself first and that Patrick only did so after finding her dead?'

Margaret looked wary. 'You will repeat what I tell you to no one in Great Holling? Only to Scotland Yard people in London?'

'Yes.' I decided that, for present purposes, Hercule Poirot counted as a Scotland Yard person.

'Frances Ive wrote a note to her husband before she took her own life,' said Margaret. 'It was plain that she expected him to survive her. Patrick also left a note that . . . ' She stopped.

I waited.

Eventually she said, 'The two notes told us the sequence of events.'

'What became of the notes?'

'I destroyed them. Ambrose Flowerday gave them to me, and I threw them on the fire.'

This struck me as most curious. 'Why on earth did you do that?' I asked.

'I . . . ' Margaret sniffed and turned away. 'I

176

don't know,' she said firmly.

She certainly did know, I thought to myself. It was clear from her clamped-shut mouth that she intended to say no more on the matter. Further interrogation from me would only consolidate her determination to withhold.

I stood to stretch my legs, which had grown stiff. 'You're right about one thing,' I said. 'Now that I know the story of Patrick and Frances Ive, I *do* want to speak to Dr Ambrose Flowerday. He was here in the village when it all happened. However faithful your account — '

'No. You made me a promise.'

'I should very much like to ask him about Jennie Hobbs, for example.'

'I can tell you about Jennie. What would you like to know? Both Patrick and Frances Ive seemed to think that she was indispensible. They were very fond of her. Everyone else found her to be quiet, polite — harmless enough, until she told a dangerous lie. Personally, I don't believe that someone who could produce a lie of that sort from thin air can be harmless the rest of the time. And she had ideas above her station. Her way of speaking changed.'

'How?'

'Ambrose said it was very sudden. One day she spoke as you would expect a domestic servant to speak. The next day she had a new, far more polished voice and was speaking very correctly.'

And using correct grammatical constructions, I thought to myself. *Oh, please let no one open their mouths.* Three mouths, each one with a monogrammed cufflink inside it: grammatically satisfactory. Confound it all, Poirot had probably been right about that too.

'Ambrose said that Jennie altered her voice in imitation of Patrick and Frances Ive. They were both educated, and spoke very well.'

'Margaret, please tell me the truth: why are you so determined that I should not speak to Ambrose Flowerday? Are you afraid of him telling me something you would rather I didn't know?'

'It would be of no help to you to speak to Ambrose, and it would be a great hindrance to him,' Margaret said firmly. 'You have my permission to terrify the life out of any other villagers you come across.' She smiled but her eyes were hard. 'They are scared already — the guilty are being picked off one by one, and deep down they must know they are all guilty — but they would be even more afraid if they heard you say that, in your expert opinion, the killer will not be content until all who helped to destroy Patrick and Frances Ive have been dispatched to the fiery pits of Hell.'

'That's rather extreme,' I said.

'I have an unorthodox sense of humour. Charles used to complain about it. I never told him this, but I don't believe in Heaven and Hell. Oh, I believe in God, but not the God we hear so much about.'

I must have looked nervous. I did not want to discuss theology; I wanted to return to London as soon as I could and tell Poirot what I had found out.

Margaret continued: 'There is only one God, of course, but I don't believe for a moment that He wants us to follow rules without questioning them, or be unkind to anybody who falls short.' She smiled then with more warmth and said, 'I think that God sees the world in the way that *I* see it, and not at all in the way that Ida Gransbury saw it. Would you agree?'

I gave a non-committal grunt.

'The Church teaches that only God can judge,' said Margaret. 'Why didn't pious Ida Gransbury point that out to Harriet Sippel and her baying flock? Why did she reserve all of her condemnation for Patrick Ive? If one is going to present oneself as a model of Christianity, one should strive to get the basic teachings right.'

'I see you are still angry about it.'

'I will be angry until my dying day, Mr Catchpool. Greater sinners persecuting lesser sinners in the name of morality — that's something worth raging about.'

'Hypocrisy is an ugly thing,' I concurred.

'Besides, one could argue that it cannot be wrong to be with the person you truly love.'

'I'm not sure about that. If a person is married — '

'Oh, fiddlesticks to marriage!' Margaret looked up at the paintings on the parlour wall, then addressed them directly: 'I'm sorry, Charles, dear, but if two people love one another, then however inconvenient it is for the Church and however against the rules it might be . . . well, love is love, isn't it? I know you don't like it when I say that.'

I can't say I liked it much either. 'Love can cause a whole heap of trouble,' I said. 'If Nancy Ducane had not loved Patrick Ive, I would not now have three murders to investigate.'

'What a nonsensical thing to say.' Margaret wrinkled her nose at me. 'It is hate that makes people kill, Mr Catchpool, not love. Never love. Please be rational.'

'I have always believed that the hardest rules to follow are the best tests of character,' I told her.

'Yes, but what aspect of our characters do they test? Our credulity, perhaps. Our cloth-headed idiocy. The Bible, with all its rules, is simply a book written by a person or people. It ought to carry a disclaimer, prominently displayed: 'The word of God, distorted and misrepresented by man'.'

'I must go,' I said, uncomfortable about the turn our discussion had taken. 'I have to get back to London. Thank you for your time and your help. It has been invaluable.'

'You must forgive me,' Margaret said as she followed me to her front door. 'I do not usually speak my mind quite so bluntly, apart from to Ambrose and Charles-on-the-wall.'

'I suppose I should feel honoured, in that case,' I said.

'I have spent my whole life following most of the rules in the dusty old Book, Mr Catchpool. That is how I know it's a foolish thing to do. Whenever lovers throw caution to the wind and meet when they ought not to . . . I admire them! And whoever murdered Harriet Sippel, I admire that person too. I can't help it. That doesn't mean that I condone murder. I don't. Now, go away before I become even more outspoken.'

As I walked back to the King's Head, I thought to myself that a conversation was a strange thing that could take you almost anywhere. Often you were left stranded miles from where you had started, with no idea about how to get back. Margaret Ernst's words rang in my ears as I walked: *However against the rules it might be, love is love, isn't it?*

At the King's Head, I strode past a snoring Walter Stoakley and a pruriently peering Victor Meakin, and went upstairs to pack my things.

I caught the next train to London and bade a joyous farewell to Great Holling as the train pulled out of the station. As happy as I was to be leaving the village, I wished I could have spoken to the doctor, Ambrose Flowerday. What would Poirot say when I told him about my promise to Margaret Ernst? He would disapprove, for sure, and say something about the English and their foolish sense of honour, and I would no doubt hang my head and mumble apologetically rather than voice my true opinion on the matter, which is that one always manages to extract more information from people in the end if one respects their wishes. Let people think that you have no wish to force them to tell you what they know, and it's surprising how often they approach you of their own accord in due course with the very answers you were looking for.

I knew Poirot would disapprove, and decided not to care. If Margaret Ernst could disagree

181

with God, then it was perfectly all right for me to disagree with Hercule Poirot occasionally. If he wished to interview Dr Flowerday, he could come to Great Holling and speak to the man himself.

I hoped that it would not be necessary. Nancy Ducane was the person we needed to concentrate on. That and saving the life of Jennie, assuming we were not too late. I was full of remorse on account of having dismissed the possible danger to her. If we did manage to save her, the credit would be all Poirot's. If we solved the three Bloxham Hotel murders satisfactorily, that would be down to Poirot too. Officially, at Scotland Yard, it would be noted as one of my successes, but everyone would know that it was Poirot's triumph and not mine. Indeed, it was thanks to my bosses' knowledge of Poirot's involvement in the case that they were content to leave me to my own — or rather, to my Belgian friend's — devices. It was the famous Hercule Poirot they trusted to do as he wished, not me.

I started to wonder if I might not prefer to fail alone and entirely on my own steam than succeed only thanks to Poirot's involvement, and I fell asleep before I had reached a conclusion.

I had a dream — my first on a train — about being condemned by everybody I knew for something I hadn't done. In it, I saw my own gravestone clearly, with my name instead of Patrick and Frances Ives' carved on it, and the 'slander's mark' sonnet beneath. In the earth beside the grave, there was a glint of metal, and I knew somehow that it was a cufflink bearing my initials that was partially buried there. I woke as the train pulled into London, bathed in sweat, my heart beating fit to burst from my chest.

13

Nancy Ducane

I didn't know, of course, that Poirot was already aware of the probable involvement of Nancy Ducane in our three murders. As I made my escape from Great Holling by train, Poirot was busy making arrangements, with the help of Scotland Yard, to visit Mrs Ducane in her London home.

This he managed to do later that same day, with Constable Stanley Beer as his escort. A young maid in a starched apron answered the door of the large white stucco townhouse in Belgravia. Poirot was expecting to be shown to a tasteful drawing room where he would wait to be seen, and was surprised to find Nancy Ducane herself standing in the hall at the foot of the stairs.

'Monsieur Poirot? Welcome. I see you have brought a policeman with you. This all seems rather unusual, I must say.'

Stanley Beer made a strange noise in his throat and turned beetroot red. Nancy Ducane was an unusually beautiful woman with a peaches-and-cream complexion, lustrous dark hair and deep blue eyes with long lashes. She looked to be somewhere in the region of forty and was stylishly dressed in peacock blues and deep greens. For once in his life, Poirot was not the

184

most elegantly attired person present.

'It is a pleasure to make your acquaintance, Madame Ducane.' He bowed. 'I am in awe of your artistic abilities. I have been fortunate enough to see one or two of your paintings in exhibitions in recent years. You have a talent most rare.'

'Thank you. That is kind of you. Now, if you will give your overcoats and hats to Tabitha here, we can find somewhere comfortable to sit and talk. Would you care for some tea or coffee?'

'*Non, merci.*'

'Very well. Follow me.'

They proceeded to a small sitting room that I was pleased only to hear about later and not to have to sit in myself, since Poirot reported it as being full of portraits. All those watchful eyes hanging on the wall . . .

Poirot asked if all of the paintings were by Nancy Ducane.

'Oh, no,' she said. 'Very few of these are mine. I buy as many as I sell, which is as it should be, I think. Art is my passion.'

'It is one of mine also,' Poirot told her.

'Looking at nothing but one's own pictures would be unbearably lonely. I always think when I hang a painting by another artist that it's like having a good friend on my wall.'

'*D'accord.* You put it succinctly, madame.'

Once they were all seated, Nancy said, 'May I get straight to the point and ask what has brought you here? You said on the telephone that you would like to search my house. You are welcome to do so, but why is there a need?'

185

'You might have read in the newspapers, madame, that three guests of the Bloxham Hotel were murdered last Thursday night.'

'At the Bloxham?' Nancy laughed. Then her face fell. 'Oh, heavens — you're serious, aren't you? *Three?* Are you sure? The Bloxham's a super place, I've always thought. I can't imagine murders happening there.'

'So you know the hotel?'

'Oh yes. I'm often there for afternoon tea. Lazzari, the manager — he's a *darling*. They're famous for their scones, you know — the best in London. I'm sorry . . . ' She broke off. 'I don't mean to babble about scones if three people have really been murdered. That's terrible. I don't see what it has to do with me, though.'

'Then you have not read about these deaths in the newspapers?' Poirot asked.

'No.' Nancy Ducane's mouth set in a line. 'I don't read newspapers and I won't have them in the house. They are full of misery. I avoid misery if I can.'

'So you do not know the names of the three murder victims?'

'No. Nor do I wish to.' Nancy shuddered.

'I am afraid I must tell you whether you wish it or not. Their names were Harriet Sippel, Ida Gransbury and Richard Negus.'

'Oh, no, no. Oh, Monsieur Poirot!' Nancy pressed her hand against her mouth. She was unable to speak for almost a full minute. Eventually she said, 'This is not some sort of joke, is it? Please say that it is.'

'It is not a joke. I am very sorry, madame. I

186

have distressed you.'

'Hearing those names has distressed me. Whether they're dead or alive, it doesn't matter to me, as long as I don't have to think about them. You see, one tries to avoid upsetting things, but one doesn't always succeed, and . . . I am more averse to unhappiness than most people.'

'You have suffered very much in your life?'

'I do not wish to discuss my private affairs.' Nancy turned away.

It would not have done Poirot any good whatever to state that his wishes were the precise opposite of hers in this respect. Nothing fascinated him more than the private passions of strangers he would probably never meet again.

Instead he said, 'Then let us return to the business of the police investigation that brings me here. You are familiar with the names of the three murder victims?'

Nancy nodded. 'I used to live in a village called Great Holling, in the Culver Valley. You won't know it. Nobody does. Harriet, Ida and Richard were neighbours of mine. I haven't seen or heard tell of them for years. Not since 1913, when I moved to London. Have they really been *murdered?*'

'*Oui*, madame.'

'At the Bloxham Hotel? But what were they doing there? Why had they come to London?'

'That is one of the many questions for which I do not yet have an answer,' Poirot told her.

'It makes no sense, them getting killed.' Nancy sprang up from her chair and started to walk

187

back and forth between the door and the far wall. 'The only person who would do it *didn't* do it!'

'Who is that person?'

'Oh, pay no attention to me.' Nancy returned to her chair and sat down again. 'I'm sorry. Your news has shocked me, as you see. I can't help you. And . . . I don't mean to be rude, but I think I should like you to leave now.'

'Were you referring to yourself, madame, as the only person who would commit these three murders? And yet you did not?'

'I did not . . . ' Nancy said slowly, her eyes flitting around the room. 'Ah, but now I see what you're about. You've heard some story or other and you think *I* killed them. And that is why you wish to search my house. Well, I didn't murder anybody. Search to your heart's content, Monsieur Poirot. Ask Tabitha to take you through every room — there are so many, you'll miss one if you don't have her as a guide.'

'Thank you, madame.'

'You will find nothing incriminating because there's nothing to find. I wish you would leave! I can't tell you how you have upset me.'

Stanley Beer rose to his feet. 'I'll make a start,' he said. 'Thank you for your cooperation, Mrs Ducane.' He left the room, closing the door behind him.

'You're clever, aren't you?' Nancy Ducane said to Poirot as if this counted as a point against him. 'As clever as people say you are. I can tell by your eyes.'

'I am thought to have a superior mind, *oui*.'

188

'How proud you sound. In my opinion, a superior mind counts for nothing unless accompanied by a superior heart.'

'*Naturellement*. As lovers of great art, we must believe this. Art speaks to the heart and soul more than to the mind.'

'I agree,' said Nancy quietly. 'You know, Monsieur Poirot, your eyes . . . they are more than clever. They're *wise*. They go back a long way. Oh, you won't know what I mean by that, but it's true. They would be wonderful in a painting, though I can never paint you, not now that you have brought those three dreaded names into my home.'

'That is unfortunate.'

'I blame you,' Nancy said bluntly. She clasped her hands together. 'Oh, I suppose I might as well tell you: I *was* talking about myself before. I am the person who would murder Harriet, Ida and Richard if anyone did, but, as you heard me say, I did not. So I don't understand what can have happened.'

'You disliked them?'

'Loathed them. Wished them dead many a time. Oh, my!' Nancy clapped her hands to her cheeks suddenly. 'Are they really dead? I suppose I should feel thrilled, or relieved. I want to be happy about it, but I can't be happy while thinking about Harriet, Richard and Ida. Isn't that a fine irony?'

'Why did you dislike them so?'

'I would rather not discuss it.'

'Madame, I would not ask if I did not judge it necessary.'

'Nevertheless, I am unwilling to answer.'

Poirot sighed. 'Where were you on Thursday evening of last week, between a quarter past seven and eight o'clock?'

Nancy frowned. 'I haven't the faintest idea. I have enough trouble remembering what I need to do *this* week. Oh, wait. Thursday, of course. I was across the road, at my friend Louisa's house. Louisa Wallace. I had finished my portrait of her, so I took it round there and stayed for dinner. I think I was there from about six until nearly ten. I might have even stayed longer if Louisa's husband St John had not been there too. He's an appalling snob. Louisa is such a darling, she's incapable of recognizing fault in anyone — you must know the type. She likes to believe that St John and I are desperately fond of one another because we're both artists, but I can't abide him. He's *certain* that his sort of art is superior to mine, and he takes every opportunity to tell me so. Plants and fish — that's what he paints. Dreary old leaves and chilly-eyed cods and haddocks!'

'He is a zoological and botanical artist?'

'I am not interested in any painter who never paints a human face,' said Nancy flatly. 'I'm sorry, but there it is. St John insists that you can't paint a face without telling a story, and once you start to impose a story, you inevitably distort the visual data, or some such nonsense! What is wrong with telling a story, for heaven's sake?'

'Will St John Wallace tell me the same story that you have told me about last Thursday evening?' asked Poirot. 'Will he confirm that you

190

were in his house between six and nearly ten o'clock?'

'Of course. This is absurd, Monsieur Poirot. You're asking me all the questions you would ask a murderer, and I'm not one. Who has told you that these murders must have been committed by me?'

'You were seen running from the Bloxham Hotel in a state of agitation shortly after eight o'clock. As you ran, you dropped two keys on the ground. You bent to pick them up, then ran away. The witness who saw you, he recognized your face from the newspapers and identified the famous artist Nancy Ducane.'

'That is simply impossible. Your witness is mistaken. Ask St John and Louisa Wallace.'

'I shall, madame. *Bon*, now I have another question for you: are the initials PIJ familiar to you, or perhaps PJI? It could be somebody else from Great Holling.'

All the colour drained from Nancy's face. 'Yes,' she whispered. 'Patrick James Ive. He was the vicar.'

'Ah! This vicar, he died tragically, did he not? His wife too?'

'Yes.'

'What happened to them?'

'I won't talk about it. I won't!'

'It is of the utmost importance. I must implore you to tell me.'

'I shan't!' cried Nancy. 'I couldn't if I tried. You don't understand. I haven't spoken of it for so long, I . . . ' Her mouth opened and closed for a few seconds, while no words came out. Then her face twisted in pain. 'What happened to Harriet, Ida and Richard?' she asked. 'How were they killed?'

'With poison.'

'Oh, how awful! But fitting.'

'How so, madame? Did Patrick Ive and his wife die as a result of poisoning?'

'I won't talk about them, I tell you!'

'Did you also know a Jennie in Great Holling?'

Nancy gasped and put her hand to her throat. 'Jennie Hobbs. I have nothing to say about her, nothing whatsoever. Do not ask me another question!' She blinked away tears. 'Why do people have to be so cruel, Monsieur Poirot? Do you understand it? No, don't answer! Let us talk about something else, something uplifting. We must talk about art, since we both love it.' Nancy stood and walked over to a large portrait that hung to the left of the window. It was of a man with unruly black hair, a wide mouth and a cleft chin. He was smiling. There was a suggestion of laughter.

'My father,' said Nancy. 'Albinus Johnson. You might know the name.'

'It is familiar, though I cannot immediately place it,' said Poirot.

'He died two years ago. I last saw him when I was nineteen. I am now forty-two.'

'Please accept my condolences.'

'I didn't paint it. I don't know who did, or when. It isn't signed or dated, so I don't think much of the artist, whoever he is — an amateur — but . . . it's my father smiling, and that's why it's up on the wall. If he had smiled more in real life . . . ' Nancy broke off and turned to face Poirot. 'You see?' she said. 'St John Wallace is wrong! It is the job of art to replace unhappy true stories with happier inventions.'

There was a loud knock at the door, followed by the reappearance of Constable Stanley Beer. Poirot knew what was coming from the way that Beer looked only at him and avoided Nancy's eye. 'I've found something, sir.'

'What is it?'

'Two keys. They were in a coat pocket, a dark blue coat with fur cuffs. The maid tells me it belongs to Mrs Ducane.'

'Which two keys?' asked Nancy. 'Let me see them. I don't keep keys in coat pockets, ever. I have a drawer for them.'

Beer still didn't look at her. Instead, he approached Poirot's chair. When he was standing beside him, he opened his closed fist.

'What has he got there?' said Nancy impatiently.

'Two keys with room numbers engraved upon them, belonging to the Bloxham Hotel,' said Poirot in a solemn voice. 'Room 121 and Room 317.'

'Should those numbers mean something to me?' Nancy asked.

'Two of the three murders were committed in those rooms, madame: 121 and 317. The witness who saw you run from the Bloxham Hotel on the night of the murders, he said that the two keys he saw you drop had numbers on them: one hundred and something, and three hundred and something.'

'Why, what an *extraordinary* coincidence! Oh, Monsieur Poirot!' Nancy laughed. 'Are you *sure* you're clever? Can't you see what's in front of your nose? Does that enormous moustache of yours impede your view? Someone has taken it upon himself to frame me for murder. It's almost intriguing! I might have some fun trying to work out who it is — as soon as we've agreed I'm not on my way to the gallows.'

'Who has had the opportunity to put keys into your coat pocket between last Thursday and now?' Poirot asked her.

'How should I know? Anyone who passed me in the street, I dare say. I wear that blue coat a lot. You know, it's ever so slightly irrational.'

'Please explain.'

For a few moments she appeared lost in a reverie. Then she came to and said, 'Anyone who disliked Harriet, Ida and Richard enough to kill them . . . well, they would almost certainly be favourably disposed towards me. And yet here they are trying to frame me for murder.'

'Shall I arrest her, sir?' Stanley Beer asked Poirot. 'Take her in?'

'Oh, don't be ridiculous,' said Nancy wearily. 'I say 'frame me for murder' and you immediately assume you must do it? Are you a policeman or a parrot? If you want to arrest somebody, arrest your witness. What if he's not only a liar but a murderer? Have you thought of that? You must go across the road at once and hear the truth from St John and Louisa Wallace. That's the only way to put a stop to this nonsense.'

Poirot lifted himself out of his chair with some difficulty; it was one of those armchairs that didn't make it easy for a person of his size and shape. 'We will do that *précisément*,' he said. Then, to Stanley Beer, 'No one is to be arrested at the present time, Constable. I do not believe, madame, that you would keep these two keys if you had indeed committed murder in rooms 121 and 317 of the Bloxham Hotel. Why would you not dispose of them?'

'Quite. I would have disposed of them at the first opportunity, wouldn't I?'

'I shall call upon Mr and Mrs Wallace immediately.'

'Actually,' said Nancy, 'it's Lord and Lady Wallace you'll be calling on. Louisa wouldn't care, but St John won't forgive you if you deprive him of his title.'

★ ★ ★

Not long afterwards, Poirot was standing by the side of Louisa Wallace as she stared, enraptured, at Nancy Ducane's portrait of her that hung on the wall of her drawing room. 'Isn't it perfect?' she breathed. 'Neither flattering nor insulting. With high colour and a round face like mine, there is always a danger I shall end up looking like a farmer's wife, but I don't. I don't look ravishing, but I do look quite nice, I think. St John used the word 'voluptuous', a word he has never used about me before — but the picture made him think of it.' She laughed. 'Isn't it wonderful that there are people in the world as

195

talented as Nancy?'

Poirot was having trouble concentrating on the painting. Louisa Wallace's equivalent of Nancy Ducane's smartly starched maid Tabitha was a clumsy girl named Dorcas who had dropped Poirot's coat twice so far, and once dropped and stood on his hat.

The Wallace home might have been beautiful under a different regime, but as Poirot found it that day it left a lot to be desired. Apart from the heavier items of furniture that stood sensibly against walls, everything in the house looked as if it had been blown about by a strong wind before falling in a random and inconvenient place. Poirot couldn't abide disorder; it prevented him from thinking clearly.

Eventually, having scooped up his coat and trodden-on hat, the maid Dorcas withdrew, and Poirot was left alone with Louisa Wallace. Stanley Beer had stayed at Nancy Ducane's house to complete his search of the rooms, and His Lordship was not at home; he had apparently set off for the family's country estate that morning. Poirot had spotted a few 'dreary old leaves and chilly-eyed cods and haddocks' on the walls, as Nancy had called them, and he wondered if those pictures were the work of St John Wallace.

'I'm so sorry about Dorcas,' Louisa said. 'She's very new and quite the most hopeless girl ever to inflict herself upon us, but I won't admit defeat. It has only been three days. She will learn, with time and patience. If only she wouldn't worry so! I know that's what it is: she tells herself that she absolutely mustn't drop the important gentleman's hat and coat, and that puts the idea of dropping them into her mind, and then it happens. It's maddening!'

'Quite so,' Poirot agreed. 'Lady Wallace, about last Thursday . . . '

'Oh, yes, that's where we'd got to — and then I brought you in here to show you the portrait. Yes, Nancy was here that evening.'

'From what time and until what time, madame?'

'I can't recall precisely. I know we agreed that she would come at six to bring the painting, and I don't remember noticing that she was late at all. I'm afraid I don't remember when she left. If I had to guess, I would say ten o'clock or shortly thereafter.'

'And she was here that whole time — that is to say, until she left? She did not, for instance, leave and then return?'

'No.' Louisa Wallace looked puzzled. 'She came at six with the picture, and then we were together until she left for good. What is this about?'

'Can you confirm that Mrs Ducane left here no earlier than half past eight?'

'Oh, gracious, yes. She left much later than that. At half past eight we were still at the table.'

'Who is 'we'?'

'Nancy, St John and me.'

'Your husband, if I were to speak to him, would confirm this?'

'Yes. I hope you're not suggesting that I'm not telling you the truth, Monsieur Poirot.'

'No, no. *Pas du tout.*'

'Good,' said Louisa Wallace decisively. She turned back to the picture of herself on the wall. 'Colour's her special talent, you know. Oh, she can capture personality in a face, but her greatest strength is her use of colour. Look at the way the light falls on my green dress.'

Poirot saw what she meant. The green seemed brighter one moment, then darker the next. There was not one consistent shade. The light seemed to change as one regarded the picture; such was Nancy Ducane's skill. The portrait depicted Louisa Wallace sitting in a chair, wearing a green low-necked dress, with a blue jug and bowl set behind her on a wooden table. Poirot walked up and down the room, inspecting the picture from different angles and positions.

'I wanted to pay Nancy her usual rate for a portrait, but she wouldn't hear of it,' said Louisa Wallace. 'I'm so lucky to have such a generous friend. You know, I think my husband is a little jealous of it — the painting, I mean. The whole house is full of his pictures — we've barely a free wall left. *Only* his pictures, until this one arrived. He and Nancy have this silly rivalry between them. I take no notice. They're both brilliant in their different ways.'

So Nancy Ducane had given the painting to Louisa Wallace as a gift, thought Poirot. Did she really want nothing in return, or did she perhaps hope for an alibi? Some loyal friends would be unable to resist if asked to tell one small, harmless lie after being given such a lavish present. Poirot wondered if he ought to tell

198

Louisa Wallace that he was here in connection with a murder case. He had not yet done so.

He was distracted from his train of thought by the sudden appearance of Dorcas the maid, who bounded into the room with an air of urgency and anxiety. 'Excuse me, sir!'

'What is the matter?' Poirot half expected her to say that she had accidentally set fire to his hat and coat.

'Would you like a cup of tea or coffee, sir?'

'This is what you have come to ask me?'

'Yes, sir.'

'There is nothing else? Nothing has happened?'

'No, sir.' Dorcas sounded confused.

'*Bon*. In that case, yes, please, I will take a coffee. Thank you.'

'Right you are, sir.'

'Did you see that?' Louisa Wallace grumbled as the girl lolloped out of the room. 'Can you credit it? I thought she was about to announce that she had to leave at once for her mother's deathbed! She really is the limit. I should dismiss her without further ado, but even help that's no help at all is better than none. It's impossible to find decent girls these days.'

Poirot made appropriate noises of concern. He did not wish to discuss domestic servants. He was far more interested in his own ideas, especially the one that had struck him while Louisa Wallace had been complaining about Dorcas and he had been staring at a blue painted jug and bowl set.

'Madame, if I might take a little more of your

time . . . these other pictures here on the walls, they are by your husband?'

'Yes.'

'As you say, he too is an excellent artist. I would be honoured, madame, if you would show me around your beautiful house. I would very much like to look at your husband's paintings. You said they are on every wall?'

'Yes. I'll happily give you the St John Wallace art tour and you will see that I wasn't exaggerating.' Louisa beamed and clapped her hands together. 'What fun! Though I do wish St John were here — he would be able to tell you so much more about the pictures than I can. Still, I shall do my best. You would be amazed, Monsieur Poirot, by the number of people who come to the house and don't look at the paintings or ask about them or anything. Dorcas is a case in point. There could be five hundred framed dishcloths hanging on the walls and she wouldn't notice the difference. Let's start in the hall, shall we?'

It was lucky, thought Poirot as he made the tour of the house and had many species of spider, plant and fish pointed out to him, that he was an appreciator of art. As far as the rivalry between St John Wallace and Nancy Ducane went, he knew what he thought about that. Wallace's pictures were meticulous and worthy, but they made one feel nothing. Nancy Ducane's was the greater talent. She had encapsulated the essence of Louisa Wallace and made her live on canvas as vividly as she lived in real life. Poirot found himself wanting to look at the portrait again before he left the house, and not only to check that he was not mistaken about the important detail he thought he had noticed.

Dorcas appeared on the upstairs landing. 'Your coffee, sir.' Poirot, who had been inside St John Wallace's study, stepped forward to take the cup from her hand. She lurched back as if she hadn't expected him to move towards her, and spilled most of the drink on her white apron. 'Oh, dear! I'm sorry, sir, I'm a right old butterfingers. I'll make you another cup.'

'No, no, please. There is no need.' Poirot seized what was left of his coffee and ingested it in one gulp, before any more of it could be spilled.

'This one is my favourite, I think,' said Louisa Wallace, still in the study. She was pointing at a painting that Poirot couldn't see. '*Blue Bindweed: Solanum Dulcamara*. The fourth of August last year, you see? This was my wedding anniversary present from St John. Thirty years. Beautiful, isn't it?'

'Are you sure you wouldn't like another cup of coffee, sir?' said Dorcas.

'The fourth of . . . *Sacré tonnerre*,' Poirot murmured to himself as a feeling of excitement started to grow inside him. He returned to the study and looked at the picture of blue bindweed.

'He has answered that question once, Dorcas. He does *not* want more coffee.'

'It's no trouble, ma'am, honest it isn't. He wanted coffee, and there was nothing left in the cup by the time he got it.'

201

'If nothing is there, one sees nothing,' mused Poirot cryptically. 'One thinks of nothing. To notice a nothing — that is a difficult thing, even for Poirot, until one sees, somewhere else, the thing that should have been there.' He took Dorcas's hand and kissed it. 'My dear young lady, what you have brought to me is more valuable than coffee!'

'Ooh.' Dorcas tilted her head and stared. 'Your eyes have gone all funny and green, sir.'.

'Whatever can you mean, Monsieur Poirot?' Louisa Wallace asked. 'Dorcas, go and get on with something useful.'

'Yes, madam.' The girl hurried away.

'I am indebted both to Dorcas and to you, madame,' said Poirot. 'When I arrived here only — what is it? — half an hour ago, I did not see clearly. I saw only confusion and puzzles. Now, I begin to put things together . . . It is very important that I should think without interruption.'

'Oh.' Louisa looked disappointed. 'Well, if you need to hurry off — '

'Oh, no, no, you misunderstand me. Pardon, madame. The fault is mine: I did not make myself clear. Of course we must finish the tour of the art. There is much still to explore! After that, I shall depart and do my thinking.'

'Are you sure?' Louisa regarded him with something akin to alarm. 'Well, all right, then, if it's not too much of a bore.' She recommenced her enthusiastic commentary on her husband's pictures as they moved from room to room.

In one of the guest bedrooms, the last upstairs

room that they came to, there was a white jug and bowl set with a red, green and white crest on it. There was also a wooden table, and a chair; Poirot recognized both from Nancy Ducane's painting of Louisa. He said, 'Pardon, madame, but where is the blue jug and bowl from the portrait?'

'The blue jug and bowl,' Louisa repeated, seemingly confused.

'I think you posed for Nancy Ducane's painting in this room, n'est-ce pas?'

'Yes, I did. And . . . wait a minute! This jug and bowl set is the one from the other guest bedroom!'

'And yet it is not there. It is here.'

'So it is. But . . . then where is the blue jug and bowl?'

'I do not know, madame.'

'Well, it must be in a different bedroom. Mine, perhaps. Dorcas must have swapped them around.' She set off at a brisk pace in search of the missing items.

Poirot followed. 'There is no other jug and bowl set in any of the bedrooms,' he said.

After a thorough check, Louisa Wallace said through gritted teeth, 'That useless girl! I'll tell you what's happened, Monsieur Poirot. Dorcas has broken it and she's too scared to tell me. Let us go and ask her, shall we? She will deny it, of course, but it's the only possible explanation. Jugs and bowls don't disappear, and they don't move from room to room on their own.'

'When did you last see the blue jug and bowl, madame?'

'I don't know. I haven't noticed them in a long while. I hardly ever go into the guest bedrooms.'

'Is it possible that Nancy Ducane removed the blue jug and bowl when she left here on Thursday night?'

'No. Why would she? That's silly! I stood at the door and said goodbye to her, and she was not holding anything apart from her house key. Besides, Nancy isn't a thief. Dorcas, on the other hand . . . That will be it! She hasn't broken it, she has stolen it, I'm sure — but how can I prove it? She's bound to deny it.'

'Madame, do me one favour: do not accuse Dorcas of stealing or of anything else. I do not think she is guilty.'

'Well, then where is my blue jug and bowl?'

'This is what I must think about,' said Poirot. 'I will leave you in peace in a moment, but first may I take a last look at Nancy Ducane's remarkable portrait of you?'

'Yes, with pleasure.'

Together, Louisa Wallace and Hercule Poirot made their way back down to the drawing room. They stood in front of the painting. 'Dratted girl,' muttered Louisa. 'All I can see when I look at it now is the blue jug and bowl.'

'*Oui.* It stands out, does it not?'

'It used to be in my house, and now it isn't, and all I can do is stare at a picture of it and wonder what became of it! Oh, dear, what an upsetting day this has turned out to be!'

★ ★ ★

Blanche Unsworth, as was her custom, asked Poirot the moment he returned to the lodging house if there was anything she could get for him.

'Indeed there is,' he told her. 'I should like a piece of paper and some pencils to draw with. Coloured pencils.'

Blanche's face fell. 'I can bring you paper, but as for coloured pencils, I can't say as I've got any, unless you're interested in the colour of ordinary pencil lead.'

'Ah! Grey: the best of all.'

'Are you having me on, Mr Poirot? Grey?'

'*Oui.*' Poirot tapped the side of his head. 'The colour of the little grey cells.'

'Oh, no. Give me a nice soft pink or lilac any day of the week.'

'Colours do not matter — a green dress, a blue jug and bowl set, a white one.'

'I'm not following you, Mr Poirot.'

'I do not ask you to follow me, Mrs Unsworth — only to bring me one of your ordinary pencils and a piece of paper, quickly. And an envelope. I have been talking at great length about art today. Hercule Poirot will attempt now to compose his own work of art!'

Twenty minutes later, seated at one of the tables in the dining room, Poirot called for Blanche Unsworth again. When she appeared, he handed her the envelope, which was sealed. 'Please telephone to Scotland Yard for me,' he said. 'Ask them to send somebody to collect this without delay and deliver it to Constable Stanley Beer. I have written his name on the envelope.

Please explain that this is important. It is in connection with the Bloxham Hotel murders.'

'I thought you were drawing a picture,' said Blanche.

'My picture is sealed inside the envelope, accompanied by a letter.'

'Oh. Well, then, I can't see the picture, can I?'

Poirot smiled. 'It is not necessary for you to see it, madame, unless you work for Scotland Yard — which, to my knowledge, you do not.'

'Oh.' Blanche Unsworth looked vexed. 'Well. I suppose I should make this call for you, then,' she said.

'*Merci, madame.*'

When she returned five minutes later, she had her hand over her mouth and pink spots on her cheeks. 'Oh, dear, Mr Poirot,' she said. 'Oh, this is bad news for all of us! I don't know what's wrong with people, I really don't.'

'What news?'

'I telephoned to Scotland Yard, like you asked — they said they'll send someone to collect your envelope. Then the phone rang again, right after I'd put it down. Oh, Mr Poirot, it's dreadful!'

'Calm yourself, madame. Tell me, please.'

'There's been another murder at the Bloxham! I don't know what's wrong with some of these fancy hotels, I really don't.'

14

The Mind in the Mirror

On arriving back in London, I proceeded to Pleasant's, thinking I might find Poirot there, but the only familiar face in the coffee house was that of the waitress with what Poirot calls 'the flyaway hair'. I had always found her to be a tonic, and enjoyed Pleasant's on account of her presence as much as anything else. What was her name? Poirot had told me. Oh yes: Fee Spring, short for Euphemia.

I liked her chiefly for her comforting habit of saying the same two things every time she saw me. She said them now. The first was about her long-standing ambition to change the name of Pleasant's from 'Coffee House' to 'Tea Rooms', to reflect the relative merits of the two beverages, and the second was: 'How's Scotland Yard treating you, then? I'd like to work there — only if I could be in charge, mind.'

'Oh, I'm sure you would be leading the troops in no time,' I told her. 'Just as I suspect that one day I shall arrive here to find 'Pleasant's Tea Rooms' on the sign outside.'

'Not likely. It's the only thing they won't let me change. Mr Poirot wouldn't like it, would he?'

'He would be aghast.'

'You're not to tell him, or anyone.' Fee's

proposed change of name for her place of work was something she professed to have told nobody but me.

'I shan't,' I assured her. 'I tell you what: come and work with me solving crimes and I'll ask my boss if we can change our name to Scotland Yard Tea Rooms. We do drink tea there, so it wouldn't be altogether unsuitable.'

'Hmph.' Fee wasn't impressed. 'I've heard women police aren't allowed to stay on if they marry. That's all right; I'd rather solve crimes with you than have a husband to look after.'

'There you are, then!'

'So don't go proposing to me.'

'No fear!'

'Charming, aren't you?'

To dig myself out of the hole, I said, 'I shan't be proposing to anybody, but if my parents ever put a gun to my head, I shall ask you before any other girl — how's that?'

'Better me than some dreamer with notions of romance in her head. She'd be disappointed, all right.'

I did not want to discuss romance. I said, 'As far as our crime-solving partnership goes . . . I don't suppose you're expecting Poirot, are you? I hoped he might be here waiting for Jennie Hobbs to reappear.'

'Jennie Hobbs, is it? So you've found a family name for her. Mr Poirot'll be pleased to know who he's been fretting over all this time. Maybe now he'll stop pestering me. Every time I turn round, there he is under my feet, asking me all the same questions about Jennie that he's already asked me. I never ask him where you are — never!'

I was rather stumped by this last statement. 'Why would you?' I said.

'I wouldn't and I don't. You've got to be careful what questions you ask the question-asking sort. Did you find out anything else about Jennie?'

'Nothing I can tell you, I'm afraid.'

'Then why don't I tell you something instead? Mr Poirot'll want to know.' Fee propelled me towards an unoccupied table. We sat down. She said, 'That night Jennie came in, when she was all sixes and sevens — last Thursday. I told Mr Poirot I noticed something, and then it escaped me. Well, I've remembered what it was. It was dark, and I hadn't pulled the curtains across. I never do. Might as well light up the alley, I always think. And folk who can see in are more likely to come in.'

'Especially if they catch sight of you in the window,' I teased her.

Her eyes widened. 'That's just it,' she said.

'What do you mean?'

'After I made her shut the door, Jennie darted over to the window and stared out. She was acting as if someone out there was after her. She stared and stared out of the window, but all she would have seen was herself, this room, and me — my reflection, I mean. And I saw her. That's how I knew who she was. You ask Mr Poirot, he'll tell you. I said, 'Oh, it's you, is it?' before she'd turned round. The window was like a mirror, see, with it being all lit up in here and dark outside. Now, you might say that maybe she was *trying* to see outside even if she wasn't having much luck, but that's not true.'

'What do you mean?'

'She wasn't looking out for anyone following her. She was watching me, like I was watching her. My eyes could see hers reflected, and hers could see mine — like with a mirror, if you know how that is?'

I nodded. 'Whenever you can see someone in a mirror, they can always see you too.'

'Right enough. And Jennie was watching me, I swear: waiting to see what I'd say or do about her coming in all of a pet. This'll sound funny, Mr Catchpool, but it was like I could see *more* than her eyes. I could see her mind, if that don't sound too fanciful. I'd swear she was waiting for me to take charge.'

'Anyone sensible would wait for you to take charge.' I smiled.

'*Tschk.*' Fee made a noise that suggested irritation. 'I don't know how I forgot it, if you must know. I want to grab hold of me and give me a good shaking for not remembering before now. I swear I didn't imagine it. Her reflection was staring mine right in the eyes, as if . . . ' Fee frowned. 'As if *I* was the danger and not nobody outside on the street. But why would she look at me that way? Can you make sense of it? I can't.'

★ ★ ★

After looking in on things at Scotland Yard, I returned to the lodging house to find Poirot endeavouring to leave it. He was standing by the open front door in his hat and coat, with high colour in his face and an unsettled air about him, as if he was having trouble keeping still. This was a problem that did not normally afflict him. Unusually for her, Blanche Unsworth showed no interest in my arrival, and was instead fussing about a car that was late. She too was pink-faced.

'We must leave at once for the Bloxham Hotel, Catchpool,' said Poirot, adjusting his moustache with gloved fingers. 'As soon as the car arrives.'

'It should have been here ten minutes ago,' said Blanche. 'I suppose the boon of it being late is you can take Mr Catchpool with you.'

'What is the emergency?' I asked.

'There has been another murder,' said Poirot. 'At the Bloxham Hotel.'

'Oh, dear.' For several seconds, abject panic coursed through my veins. On it went: the laying out of the dead. One, two, three, four . . .

Eight lifeless hands, palms facing down . . .

Hold his hand, Edward . . .

'Is it Jennie Hobbs?' I asked Poirot, as the blood pounded in my ears.

I should have listened to him about the danger. Why didn't I take him seriously?

'I do not know. Ah! So you too know her name. Signor Lazzari sent a summons by telephone, since when I have been unable to contact him. *Bon*, here at last is the car.'

As I moved towards it, I felt myself pulled back. Blanche Unsworth was tugging at my coat sleeve. 'Be careful at that hotel, won't you, Mr

Catchpool. I couldn't bear it if you were to come to any harm.'

'I shall, of course.'

Her face set in a ferocious grimace. 'You shouldn't have to go there, if you ask me. What was this fellow doing there anyway, the one that got himself killed this time? Three people have been murdered already at the Bloxham, and only last week! Why didn't he go and stay somewhere else if he didn't want the same to happen to him? It's not right, him ignoring the danger signs and putting you to all this bother.'

'I shall say so to his corpse in no uncertain terms.' I reasoned to myself that if I smiled and said all the right words, I might soon feel more settled.

'Say something to the other guests while you're about it,' Blanche advised. 'Tell them I've two spare rooms here. It might not be as grand as the Bloxham, but everybody's still alive when they wake up in the morning.'

'Catchpool, please hurry,' Poirot called from the car.

Hurriedly, I handed my cases to Blanche and did as I was told.

Once we were on our way, Poirot said, 'I hoped very much to prevent a fourth murder, mon ami. I have failed.'

'I wouldn't look at it that way,' I said.

'Non?'

'You did all you could. Just because the killer succeeded, it does not mean you failed.'

Poirot's face was a mask of contempt. 'If that is your opinion then you must be every murderer's favourite policeman. Of course I have failed!' He raised his hand to stop me speaking. 'Please, say no more absurd things. Tell me about your stay in Great Holling. What did you discover, apart from the surname of Jennie?'

I told him all about my trip, feeling gradually more like my normal self as I went on, making sure to leave out no detail that a thorough chap like Poirot might consider relevant. As I spoke, I noticed the strangest thing: his eyes were growing greener. It was as if someone was shining small torches on them from inside his head, to make them glow brighter.

When I had finished, he said, 'So, Jennie was a bed-maker for Patrick Ive at the University of Cambridge's Saviour College. That is most interesting.'

'Why?'

No answer was forthcoming, only another question.

'You did not lie in wait for Margaret Ernst and follow her, after your first visit to her cottage?'

'Follow her? No. I had no reason to think that she would go anywhere. She seems to spend all her time staring out of her window at the Ives' gravestone.'

'You had *every* reason to think she would go somewhere, or that someone would come to her,' said Poirot severely. 'Think, Catchpool. She would not tell you about Patrick and Frances Ive on the first day that you spoke to her, *n'est-ce pas?* 'Come back tomorrow,' she said. When you did, she told you the whole story. Did it not strike you that the reason for this postponement

213

might have been her desire to consult with another person?'

'No. As a matter of fact, it didn't. She struck me as a woman who would want to think carefully and not rush an important decision. Also as a woman determined to make up her own mind, not one who would rush to a friend for advice. Hence, I suspected nothing.'

'I, on the other hand, suspect,' said Poirot. 'I suspect that Margaret Ernst wished to discuss with Dr Ambrose Flowerday what she ought to say.'

'Well, it would likely be him if it were anyone,' I conceded. 'She certainly brought his name into the conversation plenty of times. She clearly admires him.'

'Yet you did not go in search of Dr Flowerday.' Poirot made a small snorting sound. 'You were too honourable to do so, having made your vow of silence. And is it your English sense of decorum that causes you to substitute the word 'admire' for the word 'love'? Margaret Ernst *loves* Ambrose Flowerday — this is clear from what you have told me! She is filled with passionate emotion when discussing this vicar and his wife *that she never once met?* No, her passion is for Dr Flowerday — she feels *his* feelings about the tragically deceased Reverend Ive and his wife — they were *his* dear friends. Do you see, Catchpool?'

I gave a non-committal grunt. Margaret Ernst had seemed to me to be passionate about the principles at stake as much as anything else — about the idea of the injustice that had been

214

done to the Ives — but I knew that to say so would be foolish. Poirot would only lecture me about my inability to recognize amorous feelings. To give him something to think about apart from my countless mistakes and inadequacies, I told him about my visit to Pleasant's, and what Fee Spring had told me. 'What do you think it means?' I asked as our car bumped over something bulky that must have been lying on the road.

Once more, Poirot ignored my question. He asked me if I had told him everything.

'Everything that took place in Great Holling, yes. The only other news is the inquest, which was today. The three victims were poisoned. Cyanide, as we thought. Here's a strange puzzle, though: no recently consumed food was found in their stomach contents. Harriet Sippel, Ida Gransbury and Richard Negus had not eaten for several hours before they were murdered. Which means we have a missing afternoon tea for three to account for.'

'Ah! That is one mystery solved.'

'Solved? I'd say it was a mystery created. Am I wrong?'

'Oh, Catchpool,' said Poirot sadly. 'If I tell you the answer, if I take pity on you, you will not hone your ability to think for yourself — and you must! I have a very good friend that I have not spoken of to you. Hastings is his name. Often I entreat him to use his little grey cells, but I know that they will never be a match for mine.'

I thought he was limbering up to give me a compliment — '*You*, on the other hand . . . '

215

— but then he said, 'Yours, too, will never match mine. It is not the intelligence that you lack, nor the sensitivity, nor even the originality. It is merely the confidence. Instead of looking for the answer, you look around for somebody to find it and tell it to you — *eh bien*, you find Hercule Poirot! But Poirot is not only a solver of puzzles, *mon ami*. He is also a guide, a teacher. He wishes you to learn to think for yourself, as he does. As does this woman that you describe, Margaret Ernst, who relies not upon the Bible but upon her own judgement.'

'Yes. I thought that rather arrogant of her,' I said pointedly. I would have liked to elaborate, but we had arrived at the Bloxham Hotel.

15

The Fourth Cufflink

In the lobby of the Bloxham, we nearly walked straight into Henry Negus, Richard Negus's brother. He was carrying a small briefcase in one hand. In the other, he carried a very large suitcase, which he dropped in order to speak to us. 'I wish I were a younger, stronger man,' he said, out of breath. 'How is the case progressing, if I might enquire?'

From his expression and tone of voice, I deduced that he was unaware there had been a fourth murder. I said nothing, interested to see what Poirot would do.

'We are confident of success,' said Poirot with deliberate vagueness. 'You have spent the night here, monsieur?'

'Night? Oh, the suitcase. No, I stayed at the Langham. Couldn't face this place, though Mr Lazzari was good enough to offer. I am here only to collect Richard's belongings.' Henry Negus inclined his head towards the suitcase, but kept his eyes averted, as if he didn't want to see it himself. I looked at the stiff card label attached to its handle: *Mr R. Negus*.

'Well, I had better make haste,' said Negus. 'Please keep me informed.'

'We will,' I said. 'Goodbye, Mr Negus. I am so very sorry about your brother.'

'Thank you, Mr Catchpool. Monsieur Poirot.' Negus looked embarrassed, perhaps even angry. I thought I understood why: in the face of tragedy, he had decided to be efficient, and did not wish to be reminded of his own sadness while he was trying to focus on the practicalities.

As he walked out on to the street, I saw Luca Lazzari rushing towards us, clutching at his hair. A sheen of sweat covered his face. 'Ah, Monsieur Poirot, Mr Catchpool! At last! You have heard the disastrous news? Unhappy days at the Bloxham Hotel! Oh, unhappy days!'

Was it my imagination, or had he styled his moustache to resemble Poirot's? It was a pale imitation, if imitation it was. I found it fascinating that a fourth murder in his hotel had produced in him such a mournful disposition. When only three guests had been murdered at the Bloxham, he had remained chipper. A thought occurred to me: maybe this time the victim was an employee of the hotel and not a guest. I asked who had been killed.

'I do not know who she is or where she is now,' said Lazzari. 'Come, follow me. You will see for yourselves.'

'You do not know where she is?' Poirot demanded as we followed the hotel manager to the lift. 'What do you mean? Is she not here, in the hotel?'

'Ah, but where in the hotel? She could be anywhere!' Lazzari wailed.

Rafal Bobak inclined his head in greeting as he came towards us, pushing a large cart on wheels full of what looked like sheets in need of laundering. 'Monsieur Poirot,' he said, stopping when he saw us. 'I have been going over and over it in my mind, to see if I can remember any more of what was said in Room 317 on the night of the murders.'

'*Oui?*' Poirot sounded hopeful.

'I haven't remembered anything else, sir. I'm sorry.'

'Never mind. Thank you for trying, Mr Bobak.'

'Look,' said Lazzari. 'Here comes the lift, and I am afraid to step into it! In my own hotel! I do not know, any more, what I will find, or not find. I am afraid to turn one more corner, to open one more door . . . I fear the shadows in the corridors, the creaks of the floorboards . . . '

As we went up in the lift, Poirot tried to get some sense out of the distraught hotel manager, but to no avail. Lazzari seemed unable to manage more than six linked words at a time: 'Miss Jennie Hobbs reserved the room . . . What? Yes, fair hair . . . But then where did she go? . . . Yes, brown hat . . . We have *lost* her! . . . She was without cases . . . I saw her myself, yes . . . I was too late to the room! . . . What? Yes, a coat. Pale brown . . . '

On the fourth floor, we followed Lazzari as he hurried ahead of us along the corridor. 'Harriet Sippel was on the first floor, remember?' I said to Poirot. 'Richard Negus was on the second and Ida Gransbury on the third. I wonder if it means anything.'

By the time we caught up with Lazzari, he had unlocked the door to Room 402. 'Gentlemen, you are about to see a most anomalous scene of ugliness in the beautiful Bloxham Hotel. Please prepare yourselves.' Having issued this warning, he flung open the door so that it banged against the wall inside the room.

'But . . . Where is the body?' I asked. It was not inside the room, laid out like the others. Immense relief suffused me.

'Nobody knows, Catchpool.' Poirot's voice was quiet but there was anger in it. Or it might have been fear.

Between a chair and a small occasional table — positioned exactly where the bodies had been in rooms 121, 238 and 317 — there was a pool of blood on the floor, with a long smear mark at one side, as if something had been dragged through part of it. Jennie Hobbs' body? An arm perhaps, from the shape of the smear. There were small lines breaking up the red that might have been fingermarks . . .

I turned away, sickened by the sight.

'Poirot, look.' In one corner of the room there was a dark brown hat, upturned. There was something inside it, a small metal object. Could it be . . . ?

'Jennie's hat,' said Poirot, a tremor in his voice. 'My worst fear, it has come to pass, Catchpool. And inside the hat . . . ' He walked over, very slowly. 'Yes, it is as I thought: a cufflink. The fourth cufflink, also with the monogram PIJ.'

His moustaches began to move with some energy, and I could only imagine the grimaces they concealed. 'Poirot, he has been a fool — a

220

contemptible fool — to allow this to happen!'

'Poirot, no one could possibly accuse you of — ' I began.

'*Non!* Do not try to console me! Always you want to turn away from pain and suffering, but I am not like you, Catchpool! I cannot countenance such . . . cowardice. I want to regret what I regret, without you trying to stop me. It is necessary!'

I stood as still as a statue. He had wanted to silence me, and he had succeeded.

'Catchpool,' he said my name abruptly, as if he thought my attention might have wandered far from the matter at hand. 'Observe the marks made by the blood here. The body was pulled through it to leave this . . . trail. Does that make sense to you?' he demanded.

'Well . . . yes, I'd say so.'

'Look at the direction of movement: not towards the window, but away from it.'

'Which means what?' I asked.

'Since Jennie's body is not here, it must have been removed from the room. The trail of blood is going *not towards the window but towards the corridor*, so . . . ' Poirot stared at me expectantly.

'So?' I said tentatively. Then, as clarity dawned, 'Oh, I see what you mean: the marks, the smears, were made when the killer pulled Jennie Hobbs' body from the pool of blood towards the door?'

'*Non.* Look at the width of the doorway, Catchpool. Look at it: it is *wide*. What does this tell you?'

'Not an awful lot,' I said, thinking it best to be

candid. 'A murderer wishing to remove his victim's body from a hotel room would hardly care whether the doorway of that room was wide or narrow.'

Poirot shook his head disconsolately, muttering under his breath.

He turned to Lazzari. 'Signor, please tell me everything you know, from the beginning.'

'Of course. Certainly.' Lazzari cleared his throat in preparation. 'A room was taken by a woman named Jennie Hobbs. Monsieur Poirot, she ran into the hotel as if a calamity had befallen her, and threw money down on the desk. She requested a room as if escaping from a pursuing demon! I showed her to the room myself, then went away to commence the consideration: what ought I to do? Should I inform the police that a woman with the name Jennie has arrived at the hotel? You had asked me about that name in particular, Monsieur Poirot, but there must be many women in London with the name Jennie, and more than one of those Jennies must have cause for great unhappiness that is nothing to do with a murder case. How am I to know if — '

'Please, signor, arrive at the point,' said Poirot, interrupting his flow. 'What did you do?'

'I waited about thirty minutes, then came up here to the fourth floor and knocked at the door. No answer! So I went back downstairs to get a key.'

As Lazzari spoke, I walked over to the window and looked out. Anything was preferable to the sight of the blood and the hat, and the wretched

222

monogrammed cufflink. Room 402, like Richard Negus's room, 238, was on the garden side of the hotel. I stared at the pleached limes, but soon had to look away, as even they looked sinister to me: a row of inanimate objects fused together, as if they had held hands for too long.

I was about to turn back to Poirot and Lazzari when I spotted two people in the garden beneath the window. They stood beside a brown wheelbarrow. I could see only the tops of their heads. One was a man and the other a woman, and they were locked together in an embrace. The woman seemed to stumble or slump, her head tilting to one side. Her companion grasped her more tightly. I took a step back, but I was not fast enough: the man had looked up and seen me. It was Thomas Brignell, the assistant clerk. His face instantly turned beetroot red. I took another step back so that I could no longer see the gardens at all. Poor Brignell, I thought; given his reluctance to stand up and speak in public, I could well imagine how painfully embarrassed he must be to be caught canoodling.

Lazzari continued with his account: 'When I returned with a master key, I knocked again, to make sure I was not about to intrude upon the young lady's privacy, and still she did not open the door! So I unlocked it myself . . . and this is what I found!'

'Did Jennie Hobbs specifically request a room on the fourth floor?' I asked.

'No, she did not. I assisted her myself, since my dear trusty clerk John Goode was otherwise occupied. Miss Hobbs said, 'Put me in any

223

room, but *quickly*! Quickly, I beg of you.''

'Was any sort of note left at the front desk to announce the fourth murder?' asked Poirot.

'No. This time, there was not the note,' said Lazzari.

'Were any food or beverages served to the room, or requested?'

'No. None.'

'You have checked with everybody who works in the hotel?'

'Every single person, yes. Monsieur Poirot, we have looked everywhere . . . '

'Signor, a few moments ago you described Jennie Hobbs as a young lady. How old was she, would you say?'

'Oh . . . I must beg your pardon. No, she was not young. But she was not old.'

'Was she, perhaps, thirty?' Poirot asked.

'I believe she might have been forty, but a woman's age is a difficult thing to estimate.'

Poirot nodded. 'A brown hat and a pale brown coat. Fair hair. Panic and distress, and an age that might be forty. The Jennie Hobbs you describe sounds like the Jennie Hobbs I encountered at Pleasant's Coffee House last Thursday evening. But can we say for certain that it was she? Two sightings by two different people . . . ' Suddenly, he fell silent, though his mouth continued to move.

'Poirot?' I said.

He had eyes — intensely green eyes, at that precise moment — only for Lazzari. 'Signor, I must speak to that most observant waiter again, Mr Rafal Bobak. And Thomas Brignell, and John

224

Goode. In fact, I must speak to *every single member of your staff*, as soon as possible and ask how many times they each saw Harriet Sippel, Richard Negus and Ida Gransbury — dead or alive.'

He had evidently realized something important. As I reached this conclusion, I heard myself gasp as I too made a mental leap. 'Poirot,' I murmured.

'What is it, my friend? You have put some pieces of our puzzle together? Poirot, he understands now something that did not strike him before, but there are still questions, still pieces that cannot be made to fit.'

'I have . . . ' I cleared my throat. Speaking, for some reason, was proving rather difficult. 'I have just seen a woman in the hotel gardens.' I could not, at that moment, bring myself to say that she had been in the arms of Thomas Brignell, or to describe the strange way in which she had seemed to crumple, her head falling to one side. It was simply too . . . *peculiar.* The suspicion running through my mind was one I would have felt embarrassed to utter aloud.

Thankfully, however, I did feel able to divulge one important detail. 'She was wearing a pale brown coat,' I told Poirot.

16

A Lie for a Lie

I was engrossed in my crossword puzzle when Poirot returned from the hotel to the lodging house several hours later. 'Catchpool,' he said severely. 'Why do you sit in almost total darkness? I do not believe you can see to write.'

'The fire provides enough light. Besides, I'm not writing at the moment — I'm thinking. Not that it's getting me very far. I don't know how these chaps do it, the ones who invent crosswords for the newspapers. I've been working on this one for *months*, and I still can't get it to fit together. I say, you might be able to help. Can you think of a word that means death and has six letters?'

'Catchpool.' Now Poirot's tone was even sterner.

'Hm?' I said.

'Do you take me to be the fool, or is it that you are a fool yourself? A word for death that has six letters is murder.'

'Yes, that one's rather obvious. That was my first thought.'

'I am relieved to hear it, *mon ami*.'

'That would be perfect, if murder began with a D. Since it doesn't, and since I'm stuck with this D from another word . . . ' I shook my head in consternation.

'Forget crossword puzzles. We have much to discuss.'

'I don't believe, and won't believe, that Thomas Brignell murdered Jennie Hobbs,' I said firmly.

'You feel sympathy for him,' said Poirot.

'I do, and I also would bet my last penny that he is no murderer. Who's to say that he doesn't have a girlfriend with a pale brown coat? Brown is a popular colour for coats!'

'He is the assistant clerk,' said Poirot. 'Why would he stand in the gardens beside a wheelbarrow?'

'Perhaps the wheelbarrow was simply there!'

'And Mr Brignell stands with his lady friend right beside it?'

'Well, why not?' I said, exasperated. 'Isn't that more plausible than the idea that Brignell took Jennie Hobbs' dead body out to the gardens with a plan to wheel it off somewhere in a wheelbarrow, then pretended to embrace her when he saw me looking out of the window? One might just as well say . . . ' I stopped and inhaled sharply. 'Oh, goodness,' I said. 'You *are* going to say it, aren't you?'

'What, *mon ami*? What do you think Poirot will say?'

'Rafal Bobak is a waiter, so why was he pushing a laundry cart?'

'*Exactement*. And why does he push the laundry through the elegant lobby in the direction of the front doors? Is the laundry not washed inside the hotel? Signor Lazzari, he would surely have noticed this if he had not been so concerned about the missing fourth murder victim. Of course, he would not be suspicious of Mr Bobak — all of his staff are beyond reproach in his eyes.'

'Wait a second.' I finally laid down my crossword on the table beside me. 'That was what you meant about the width of the doorway, wasn't it? That laundry cart could easily have been pushed into room 402, so why not wheel it all the way in? Why drag the body instead, which would take more effort?'

Poirot nodded with satisfaction. 'Indeed, mon ami. These are the questions I hoped you might ask yourself.'

'But . . . are you honestly saying that Rafal Bobak might have murdered Jennie Hobbs, thrown her body in with the laundry and pushed it out onto the street, right past us? He stopped to talk to us, for pity's sake!'

'Indeed — even though he has nothing to say. What is it? You think I am uncharitable, thinking the bad thoughts about those who have been so helpful to us?'

'Well . . . '

'Giving everybody the benefit of the doubt is laudable, my friend, but it is no way to apprehend a murderer. While you are displeased with me, let me put one more thought into your head: Mr Henry Negus. He had with him a very large suitcase, did he not? Large enough to contain the body of a slender woman.'

I covered my face with my hands. 'I can't bear much more of this,' I said. 'Henry Negus? No. I'm sorry, but no. He was in Devon on the night of the murders. He struck me as absolutely trustworthy.'

'You mean that both he and his wife *say* that he was in Devon,' Poirot briskly corrected me. 'To return to the matter of the trail of blood, suggesting that the body had been dragged to the door . . . Of course, an empty suitcase can be carried into the middle of a room, to where a dead body waits to be placed inside it. So, again, we must wonder: why pull Jennie Hobbs' body in the direction of the door?'

'Please, Poirot. If we must have this conversation, let us have it some other time. Not now.'

He looked put out by my discomfort. 'Very well,' he said brusquely. 'Since you are in no mood to debate the possibilities, let me tell you what occurred here in London while you were in Great Holling. Perhaps you will feel more comfortable with facts.'

'A great deal more comfortable, yes,' I said.

After making minor adjustments to his moustaches, Poirot lowered himself into an armchair and launched into an account of the conversations he'd had with Rafal Bobak, Samuel Kidd, Nancy Ducane and Louisa Wallace while I was in Great Holling. My mind was reeling by the time he had finished. I risked urging him on to further loquacity by saying, 'Haven't you left out some rather important things?'

'Such as what?'

'Well, this useless, clumsy maid at Louisa Wallace's house — Dorcas. You implied that while you and she were standing together on the upstairs landing, you realized something important, but you didn't say what it was that you realized.'

229

'That is true. I did not.'

'And this mysterious picture you drew and had delivered to Scotland Yard — what's that all about? What was the picture of? And what is Stanley Beer supposed to do with it?'

'That, also, I did not tell you.' Poirot had the nerve to look apologetic, as if he had himself had no choice in the matter.

Foolishly, I persisted. 'And why did you want to know how many times each and every Bloxham Hotel employee saw Harriet Sippel, Ida Gransbury and Richard Negus alive or dead? How is that pertinent to anything? You didn't explain that either.'

'Poirot, he leaves the gaps all over the place!'

'Not to forget your earlier omissions. What, for instance, were the two most unusual features shared by the Bloxham murders and Jennie Hobbs' outburst in Pleasant's Coffee House? You said they had two highly unusual things in common.'

'Indeed I did. *Mon ami*, I do not tell you these things because I want to make of you a detective.'

'This case will make nothing of me but a miserable wretch, of no use to anyone,' I said, allowing my true feelings to have an outing for once in my life. 'It's the most maddening thing.'

I heard a noise that might or might not have been a knock at the drawing-room door. 'Is somebody there?' I called out.

'Yes,' came Blanche Unsworth's apprehensive voice from the hall. 'I'm sorry to disturb you at this time, gentlemen, but there's a lady to see Mr

230

Poirot. She says it can't wait.'

'Show her in, madame.'

A few seconds later, I found myself face to face with the artist Nancy Ducane. Most men, I knew, would have thought her startlingly beautiful.

Poirot made the introductions with perfect courtesy.

'Thank you for seeing me.' Nancy Ducane's swollen eyes suggested that she had done a fair amount of crying. She was wearing a dark green coat that looked expensive. 'I feel dreadful, barging in on you like this. Please pardon the intrusion. I tried to persuade myself not to come, but . . . as you can see, I failed.'

'Please sit down, Mrs Ducane,' said Poirot. 'How did you find us?'

'With help from Scotland Yard, like a proper bona fide detective.' Nancy attempted a smile.

'Ah! Poirot, he chooses a house where he thinks no one will find him, and the police send the crowds to his door! No matter, madame. I am delighted to see you, if a little surprised.'

'I would like to tell you what happened in Great Holling sixteen years ago,' said Nancy. 'I should have done so before, but you gave me such a shock when you mentioned all those names I had hoped never to hear again.'

She unbuttoned her coat and took it off. I gestured towards an armchair.

She sat down. 'It's not a happy tale,' she said.

★ ★ ★

231

Nancy Ducane spoke in a quiet voice and with a haunted look in her eyes. She told us the same story that Margaret Ernst had told me in Great Holling, about the cruel and slanderous treatment of Reverend Patrick Ive. When she spoke of Jennie Hobbs, her voice shook. 'She was the worst of them. She was in love with Patrick, you see. Oh, I can't prove it, but I shall always believe it. She did what she did to him *as someone who loved him*: told an unforgivable lie because she was jealous. He was in love with me, and she wanted to wound him. To punish him. Then when Harriet seized on the lie, and Jennie saw the harm she had done and felt sick about it — and I *do* believe she felt dreadfully ashamed, and must have hated herself — she did nothing to remedy what she had set in motion, nothing! She slunk off into the shadows and hoped not to be noticed. However afraid she was of Harriet, she should have forced herself to stand up and say, 'I told a terrible lie and I'm sorry for it.''

'Pardon, madame. You say you cannot prove that Jennie was in love with Patrick Ive. May I ask: how do you know that she was? As you suggest, it is unthinkable that one who loved him would start so damaging a rumour.'

'There is no doubt in my mind that Jennie loved Patrick,' said Nancy stubbornly. 'She left behind a sweetheart in Cambridge when she moved to Great Holling with Patrick and Frances — did you know that?'

We shook our heads.

'They were supposed to get married. The date was set, I believe. Jennie couldn't bear to let

Patrick go, so she cancelled her wedding and went with him.'

'Could it not have been Frances Ive to whom she was so attached?' Poirot asked. 'Or to both of the Ives? It might have been loyalty and not romantic love that she felt.'

'I don't believe many women would put loyalty to their employers above their own marriage prospects, do you?' said Nancy.

'Assuredly not, madame. But what you tell me does not quite fit. If Jennie were inclined towards jealousy, why was she moved to tell this terrible lie only when Patrick Ive fell in love with you? Why did his marriage to Frances Ive, long before then, not provoke her envy?'

'How do you know that it did not? Patrick lived in Cambridge when he and Frances met and married. Jennie Hobbs was his servant then too. Perhaps she whispered something malicious about him in a friend's ear and that friend, not being Harriet Sippel, chose to spread the malice no further.'

Poirot nodded. 'You are right. It is a possibility.'

'Most people prefer not to spread ill will, and thank goodness for that,' said Nancy. 'Perhaps in Cambridge there is nobody as malevolent as the person Harriet Sippel turned into, and nobody as eager as Ida Gransbury to lead a pious moral crusade.'

'I notice you do not mention Richard Negus.'

Nancy looked troubled. 'Richard was a good man. He came to regret his contribution to the whole awful business. Oh, he regretted it deeply once he understood that Jennie had told a despicable lie, and once he saw Ida for the pitiless creature she was. He wrote to me a few years ago, from Devon, to say that the matter had been preying on his mind. Patrick and I were quite wrong to conduct ourselves as we did, he said, and he would never change his mind about that — marriage vows were marriage vows — but he had come to believe that punishment was not always the right path to follow, even when one knows that an offence has taken place.'

'That is what he wrote to you?' Poirot raised his eyebrows.

'Yes. I expect you disagree.'

'These affairs are complicated, madame.'

'What if, in punishing somebody for the sin of falling in love with the wrong person, one only brings greater sin into the world? And more evil: two deaths — one, of a person who has committed *no* sin.'

'*Oui.* This is precisely the sort of dilemma that creates the complication.'

'In his letter to me, Richard wrote that, Christian as he was, he could not bring himself to believe that God would wish him to persecute a sweet-natured man like Patrick.'

'Punishment and persecution are two separate things,' said Poirot. 'There is also the question: has a rule or law been broken? Falling in love ... *enfin*, we cannot help how we feel, but we can choose whether or not to act upon those feelings. If a crime has been committed, one must ensure that the criminal is dealt with by the law in an appropriate fashion, but always without personal venom and spite — always without the lust for vengeance, which contaminates everything and is indeed evil.'

'Lust for vengeance,' Nancy Ducane repeated with a shudder. 'That was it exactly. Harriet Sippel was filled with it. It was sickening.'

'And yet, in telling the story, you have not once spoken angrily of Harriet Sippel,' I said. 'You describe her behaviour as sickening, as if it saddens you. You do not seem angry with her as you are with Jennie Hobbs.'

'I suppose that's true.' Nancy sighed. 'I used to be devoted to Harriet. When my husband William and I moved to Great Holling, Harriet and George Sippel were our dearest friends. Then George died, and Harriet became a monster. But once you have been very fond of a person, it's difficult to condemn them, don't you find?'

'It is either impossible, or irresistible,' said Poirot.

'Impossible, I should say. You imagine that their worst behaviour is a symptom of an ailment and not their true self. I couldn't forgive Harriet's treatment of Patrick. I couldn't persuade myself to try. At the same time, I felt that it must have been as horrible for her as it was for anybody else — to have turned into *that*.'

'You saw her as a victim?'

'Of the tragedy of losing a beloved husband, yes — and so young! One can be both victim and villain, I think.'

'It was something that you and Harriet had in common,' said Poirot. 'The loss of a husband

235

when you were far too young.'

'This will sound heartless, but there is really no comparison,' said Nancy. 'George Sippel was everything to Harriet, her whole world. I married William because he was wise and safe, and I needed to escape from the home of my father.'

'Ah, yes. Albinus Johnson,' said Poirot. 'It came back to me after I left your house that I do indeed know the name. Your father was one of a circle of English and Russian agitators in London at the end of the last century. He spent a period of time in gaol.'

'He was a dangerous man,' said Nancy. 'I couldn't bear to speak to him about his . . . ideas, but I know that he believed it was acceptable to murder any number of people if those people were delaying the cause of making the world a better place — better only according to *his* definition! How in the name of Heaven can anything ever be made better by bloodshed and mass slaughter? How can any improvement be brought about by men who wish only to smash and destroy, who cannot speak of their hopes and dreams without their faces twisting in hatred and anger?'

'I agree with you absolutely, madame. A movement driven by fury and resentment will not change any of our lives for the better. *Ce n'est pas possible.* It is corrupt at the source.'

I nearly said that I too agreed, but I stopped myself. Nobody was interested in my ideas.

Nancy said, 'When I met William Ducane, I did not fall in love with him, but I liked him. I respected him. He was calm and courteous; he

236

never behaved or spoke intemperately. If he failed to return a book to the library when it was due to be returned, he would suffer agonies of remorse.'

'A man with a conscience.'

'Yes, and a sense of proportion, and humility. If something stood in his way, he would consider moving himself before he would consider moving the obstacle. I knew that he would not fill our home with men intent on making the world uglier with their violent acts. William appreciated art, and beautiful things. He was like me in that respect.'

'I understand, madame. But you did not love William Ducane passionately, in the way that Harriet Sippel loved her husband?'

'No. The man I loved passionately was Patrick Ive. From the first moment I saw him, my heart belonged to him alone. I would have laid down my life for him. When I lost him, I finally understood how Harriet had felt when she had lost George. One thinks one can imagine, but one can't. I remember thinking Harriet morbid when she begged me, after George's funeral, to pray for her death so that she might be quickly reunited with him. I refused to do as she asked. The passing of time would ease her pain, I told her, and one day she would find something else to live for.'

Nancy stopped to compose herself before continuing. 'Regrettably, she did. She found a delight in the suffering of others. Harriet the widow was a joyless harridan. *That* was the woman who was killed at the Bloxham Hotel in London recently. The Harriet I knew and loved died with her husband George.' She looked at me suddenly. 'You observed that I am angry with Jennie. I have no right to be. I am as guilty as she is of letting Patrick down.' Nancy started to cry and covered her face with her hands.

'Come, come, madame. Here.' Poirot passed her a handkerchief. 'How did you let down Patrick Ive? You have told us that you would have sacrificed your life for him.'

'I am as bad as Jennie: a disgusting coward! When I stood up in the King's Head Inn and confessed that Patrick and I were in love and had been meeting in secret, I did not tell the truth. Oh, the secret meetings were real enough, and Patrick and I were desperately in love — that was true too. But . . . ' Nancy appeared too distressed to continue. Her shoulders shook as she wept into the handkerchief.

'I think I comprehend, madame. That day at the King's Head Inn, you told the villagers that your relations with Patrick Ive had been chaste. That was your lie. Poirot, he guesses correctly?'

Nancy let out a wail of despair. 'I couldn't bear the rumours,' she sobbed. 'All those whispered macabre tales of encounters with the souls of the dead in exchange for money; little children hissing in the street about blasphemy . . . I was appalled! You cannot imagine the horror of so many voices of accusation and condemnation, all rounding on one man, a *good* man!'

I could imagine. I could imagine it so vividly that I wished she would stop talking about it.

'I had to *do* something, Monsieur Poirot. So I thought, 'I shall fight these lies with something pure and good: the truth.' The truth was my love for Patrick and his for me, but I was afraid, and I tarnished our truth with lies! That was my mistake. In my frenzy, I could not think clearly. I sullied the beauty of my love for Patrick with faint-hearted dishonesty. Relations between us were not chaste, but I said that they were. I imagined that I had no choice but to lie. That was craven of me. Despicable!'

'You are hard on yourself,' said Poirot. 'Unnecessarily so.'

Nancy dabbed at her eyes. 'How I wish I could believe you,' she said. '*Why* did I not tell the whole truth? My defence of Patrick against those horrible accusations should have been a noble thing, and I ruined it. For that, I curse myself every day of my life. Those braying, spittle-flecked sin-hunters at the King's Head, they all disapproved of me anyway — thought I was a fallen woman, and Patrick the very devil. What would it have mattered if they had disapproved a little more? In point of fact, I'm not sure there was a higher peak of opprobrium for them to ascend to.'

'Why, then, did you not tell the truth?' Poirot asked.

'I hoped to make the ordeal more bearable for Frances, I suppose. To avoid a bigger scandal. But then Frances and Patrick took their own lives, and all hope for ever making anything better was lost. I know they killed themselves, whatever anybody says,' Nancy added as an

239

apparent afterthought.

'Is this a fact that has been disputed?' asked Poirot.

'According to the doctor and all official records, their deaths were accidental, but nobody in Great Holling believed that. Suicide is a sin in the eyes of the Church. The village doctor wanted to protect Patrick and Frances's reputations from greater damage, I think. He liked them very much, and stood up for them when no one else would. He's a good egg, Dr Flowerday — one of very few in Great Holling. He knew a wicked lie when he heard one.' Nancy laughed through her tears. 'A lie for a lie and a tooth for a tooth.'

'Or a truth for a truth?' Poirot suggested.

'Oh. Yes, indeed.' Nancy looked surprised. 'Oh, dear, I've quite ruined your handkerchief.'

'It is not important. I have others. There is one more question I should like to ask you, madame: is the name Samuel Kidd familiar to you?'

'No. Should it be?'

'He did not live in Great Holling when you lived there?'

'No, he did not. Lucky old him, whoever he is,' said Nancy bitterly.

17

The Older Woman and the Younger Man

'So,' said Poirot once our visitor had left us and we were alone. 'Nancy Ducane agrees with Margaret Ernst that the Ives committed suicide, but the official record is of two accidental deaths. Ambrose Flowerday told this lie in order to protect the reputations of Patrick and Frances Ive from further damage.'

'How extraordinary,' I said. 'Margaret Ernst said nothing about that.'

'I wonder, then, if we have found the reason why she made you promise not to speak to the doctor. What if Ambrose Flowerday is proud of the lie he told — proud enough, maybe, to confess if asked. If Margaret Ernst wished to protect him . . . '

'Yes,' I agreed. 'That could have been the reason she wanted to steer me away from him.'

'The desire to protect — this I understand only too well!' Poirot's voice was fierce with emotion.

'You mustn't blame yourself about Jennie, Poirot. You could not have protected her.'

'There you have the wisdom, Catchpool. Protecting Jennie would have been impossible for anyone, even Hercule Poirot. It was too late to save her even before I met her — this I now understand. Much, much too late.' He sighed. 'It is interesting, is it not, that this time there is blood, when before there was poison and no blood?'

'What I keep wondering is: where is Jennie's body? The Bloxham has been searched from top to bottom, and nothing!'

'Do not ask yourself where, Catchpool. Where does not matter. *Ask yourself why.* Whether the body was removed from the hotel by laundry cart, suitcase or wheelbarrow, why was it removed? Why was it not left in the hotel room, as the other three were?'

'Well? What's the answer? You know what it is, so tell me.'

'Indeed,' said Poirot. 'All of this can be explained, but I am afraid it is not a happy explanation.'

'Happy or not, I'd like to hear it.'

'In the fullness of time you will hear everything. For now I will tell you this: no employee of the Bloxham Hotel saw either Harriet Sippel, Ida Gransbury or Richard Negus more than once, apart from one man: Thomas Brignell. He saw Richard Negus twice: once when Negus arrived at the hotel on the Wednesday and Brignell attended to him, and again on Thursday evening when he bumped into Mr Negus in the corridor and Mr Negus asked him for a sherry.' Poirot gave a self-satisfied little chuckle. 'Reflect upon that, Catchpool. Do you start to see what is suggested by that fact?'

'No.'

'Ah!'

'For pity's sake, Poirot!' Never had one syllable — *Ah!* — been enunciated in such an infuriating fashion.

'I have told you, my friend: do not expect always to be given the answer.'

'I'm well and truly stumped! From several angles, it looks as if Nancy Ducane *must* be our killer, but she has an alibi from Lady Louisa Wallace. So. Who else might want to kill Harriet Sippel, Ida Gransbury, Richard Negus and now Jennie Hobbs too?' I stamped up and down the drawing room, angry with myself because I couldn't see a way out of the bind. 'And — though I still think you're crazy to suspect them — if the murderer is Henry Negus, or Rafal Bobak, or Thomas Brignell, what could the motive have been? What connection do any of those people have to the tragic events in Great Holling sixteen years ago?'

'Henry Negus has the oldest and most common motive in the world: money. He told us, did he not, that his brother Richard had been squandering his wealth? He told us, also, that his wife would on no account banish Richard from her home. If Richard Negus dies, Henry Negus does not have to pay for his upkeep. If Richard does not die, he might end up costing his brother a small fortune.'

'And Harriet Sippel and Ida Gransbury? Jennie Hobbs? Why would Henry Negus kill them too?'

'I do not know, though I could speculate,' said Poirot. 'As for Rafal Bobak and Thomas Brignell — I can think of no possible motive for either

243

man, unless one of them is not who he purports to be.'

'I suppose we could do a bit of digging around,' I said.

'While we are compiling a list of possible suspects, what about Margaret Ernst and Dr Ambrose Flowerday?' Poirot suggested. 'They were not in love with Patrick Ive, but they might nevertheless have been motivated by the desire to avenge him. Margaret Ernst was, by her own account, sitting in her house alone on the night of the murders. And we do not know where Dr Flowerday was because you promised you would not seek him out and — alas! — you kept your promise. Poirot will have to go to Great Holling himself.'

'I did say that you ought to come with me,' I reminded him. 'But I suppose if you had, you wouldn't have been able to talk to Nancy Ducane and Rafal Bobak and the others. Incidentally, this younger man and older woman that Bobak overheard Harriet, Ida and Richard Negus talking about, assuming we believe his account — I've been pondering, and I've even made a list of all the romantically linked couples I can think of.' I produced the list from my pocket. (I will admit that I was hoping to impress Poirot, but either he wasn't impressed or else he hid it well.)

'George and Harriet Sippel,' I read aloud. 'Patrick and Frances Ive. Patrick Ive and Nancy Ducane. William Ducane and Nancy Ducane. Charles and Margaret Ernst. Richard Negus and Ida Gransbury. In none of these pairings is the

244

woman older than the man, certainly not by enough to be described as 'old enough to be his mother'.'

'Tsk,' said Poirot impatiently. 'You do not think, my friend. How do you know that this couple exists, with the older woman and the younger man?'

I stared at him, wondering if he had lost his reason. 'Well, Walter Stoakley talked about them at the King's Head, and Rafal Bobak overheard — '

'Non, non,' Poirot interrupted gracelessly. 'You do not pay attention to the details: in the King's Head Inn, Walter Stoakley spoke of *the woman putting an end to her romantic involvement with the man*, did he not? Whereas the conversation that Rafal Bobak overheard between the three murder victims was about *a man no longer romantically interested in a woman who still craved his love.* How can these be the same people, the same couple? The very opposite must be true: they *cannot possibly* be the same people!'

'You're right,' I said, dejected. 'I didn't think of that.'

'You were too delighted with your pattern — that is why. A much older woman and much younger man over *here*, and a much older woman and much younger man over *there*. Voilà, you assume they must be the same!'

'Yes, I did. Perhaps I'm in the wrong job.'

'Non. You are perceptive, Catchpool. Not always, but sometimes. You have helped to steer me through the tunnel of confusion. Do you

245

remember when you said that whatever Thomas Brignell was withholding, he was doing so for reasons of personal embarrassment? That was a remark that proved very helpful to me — very helpful indeed!'

'Well, I'm afraid I'm still in the tunnel and can't see a flicker of light at either end.'

'I will make you a promise,' said Poirot. 'Tomorrow, immediately after breakfast, we will pay a little visit, you and I. After that, you will comprehend more than you do now. I hope that I will also.'

'I don't suppose I am permitted to ask whom we will be visiting?'

'You may ask, *mon ami*.' Poirot smiled. 'I telephoned to Scotland Yard for the address. It is one you would recognize, I think, if I told it to you.'

Which, needless to say, he had no intention of doing.

18

Knock and See Who Comes to the Door

As we made our way across town the following morning to pay our mysterious 'visit', Poirot's mood was as changeable as the London weather, which could not make up its mind between sunny and cloudy. At one moment he would appear to be pleased with himself and at ease, and the next he would furrow his brow as if worrying away at something.

We finally arrived at a modest house on a narrow street. 'Number 3 Yarmouth Cottages,' said Poirot, standing outside it. 'From where do you know this address, Catchpool? It is familiar to you, no?'

'Yes. Hold on a moment. It will come to me. That's right — it's Samuel Kidd's address, isn't it?'

'Indeed. Our helpful witness who saw Nancy Ducane run from the Bloxham Hotel and drop two keys, *even though Nancy Ducane could not have been at the Bloxham Hotel just after eight o'clock on the night of the murders.*'

'Because she was at Louisa Wallace's house,' I agreed. 'So we're here to give Mr Kidd a scare, are we, and find out who put him up to lying?'

'*Non.* Mr Kidd is not at home today. He has gone to work, I expect.'

'Then . . .'

'Let us play a little game, called Knock-and-See-Who-Comes-to-the-Door,' said Poirot with an enigmatic smile. 'Go ahead. I would knock myself if it were not for my gloves. I do not wish to make them dirty.'

I knocked and waited, wondering why Poirot expected anyone to come to the door of a house whose only known occupant was elsewhere. I opened my mouth to ask him, then closed it again. There was, of course, no point. Wistfully, I remembered a time (less than a fortnight ago) when I believed that asking a straight question of someone who knew the answer was a worthwhile thing to do.

The front door of number 3 Yarmouth Cottages opened, and I found myself looking into the large eyes of a person who was not Samuel Kidd. At first I was puzzled, for this was a face I did not know. Then I watched as terror twisted the features, and I knew who it had to be.

'Good morning, Mademoiselle Jennie,' said Poirot. 'Catchpool, this is Jennie Hobbs. And this, mademoiselle, is my friend Mr Edward Catchpool. You might remember that we talked about him at Pleasant's Coffee House. Allow me to express my profound relief at finding you alive.'

That was when I knew for sure that I knew nothing. The few paltry scraps of certainty upon which I had been relying had proved themselves untrustworthy. How the deuce had Poirot known he would find Jennie Hobbs here? It was simply impossible! And yet, here we were.

After Jennie had composed herself and arranged her expression into something less abject and more guarded, she invited us into the house and bade us wait in a small dark room with shabby furniture. She then excused herself, saying that she would be back shortly.

'You said it was too late to save her!' I said angrily to Poirot. 'You lied to me.'

He shook his head. 'How did I know that I would find her here? It is thanks to you, *mon ami*. Again you help Poirot.'

'How?'

'I invite you to think back to your conversation with Walter Stoakley at the King's Head Inn, to what he said about a woman who could have had a husband, children, a home of her own and a happy life. Do you recall?'

'What about it?'

'A woman who devoted her life to a substantial man? Who sacrificed everything for him? Then, later, Mr Stoakley said, 'She couldn't marry some kid, not once she had fallen in love with a man of substance. So she left him behind.' You remember telling me this, *mon ami*?'

'Of course I do! I'm not an imbecile.'

'You thought that you had found our older woman and much younger man, *n'est-ce pas*? Rafal Bobak had referred to them at the Bloxham Hotel — he told us that the three murder victims were talking about them — and you thought Walter Stoakley had in mind the same couple, so you asked Mr Stoakley how much older this woman was than the man whose love she had spurned because you believed that you

249

heard him say, 'She couldn't marry some kid'. *But, my friend, you did not hear him say this!*'

'Yes — I did, as a matter of fact.'

'*Non.* What you heard him say was, 'She couldn't marry *Sam Kidd,*' Mr Samuel Kidd.'

'But . . . but . . . Oh, dash it all!'

'You leapt to an incorrect conclusion because Walter Stoakley had already used the word 'kid' more than once. The young man with whom he had been drinking he had called a kid. *Eh bien,* your error was one that many in your position would have made. Do not chastise yourself too severely.'

'And then, having misunderstood, I asked Stoakley about the difference in age between the woman who could have married but didn't and the ne'er-do-well he had been drinking with before I arrived. He must have wondered why I wanted to know, when Jennie Hobbs had nothing to do with the ne'er-do-well.'

'*Oui.* This he might have asked you, had he not been stupefied by alcohol. Ah, well.' Poirot shrugged.

'So Jennie Hobbs was engaged to Samuel Kidd,' I said, trying to take it all in. 'And . . . she left him behind in Cambridge in order to come to Great Holling with Patrick Ive?'

Poirot nodded his agreement. 'Fee Spring, the waitress from Pleasant's — she told me that Jennie suffered a heartbreak in her past. I wonder what it was.'

'Haven't we just answered that question?' I said. 'It must have been leaving Samuel Kidd behind.'

'I think it is more likely to have been the death

of Patrick Ive, the man Jennie truly loved. Incidentally, I am certain that this is why she altered her way of speaking: to sound more like someone of his class, in the hope that he might see her as an equal and not merely as a servant.'

'Are you not afraid that she might disappear on you again?' I asked, looking towards the closed door of the sitting room. 'What is she doing that is taking so long? You know, we ought to take her straight to a hospital, if she hasn't already been.'

'A hospital?' Poirot looked surprised.

'Yes. She lost a fair amount of blood in that hotel room.'

'You assume too much,' said Poirot. He looked as if he had considerably more to say, but at that moment Jennie opened the door.

★ ★ ★

'Please forgive me, Monsieur Poirot,' she said.

'For what, mademoiselle?'

Silence of an uncomfortable sort filled the room. I wanted to speak and put an end to it, but doubted my ability to contribute anything useful.

'Nancy Ducane,' Poirot said very slowly and deliberately. 'Was she the person from whom you fled, when you sought refuge in Pleasant's Coffee House? Was she the one you feared?'

'I know she killed Harriet, Ida and Richard at the Bloxham Hotel,' Jennie whispered. 'I've read about it in the papers.'

'Since we find you in the home of Samuel Kidd, your former fiancé, can we assume that

251

Mr Kidd has told you what he saw on the night of the murders?'

Jennie nodded. 'Nancy, running from the Bloxham. She dropped two keys on the pavement, he said.'

'It is a coincidence *incroyable*, mademoiselle: Nancy Ducane, who has murdered three people already and wishes to murder you also, is seen running from the scene of her crimes by none other than the man you once intended to marry!'

Jennie uttered an almost inaudible, 'Yes.'

'Poirot, he is suspicious of a coincidence so large. You are lying now, and you were lying when we last met!'

'No! I swear — '

'Why did you take a room at the Bloxham Hotel, knowing it was where Harriet Sippel, Ida Gransbury and Richard Negus had met their deaths? You have no answer for that, I see!'

'Allow me to speak and I shall answer. I was tired of running. It seemed easier to have it over with.'

'Is that so? You calmly accepted the fate that awaited you? You embraced it and moved toward it?'

'Yes.'

'Then why — to Mr Lazzari, the hotel manager — why did you ask him to provide you with a room 'quickly, quickly', as if you were still in flight from your pursuer? And, since you do not appear to be wounded, whose was the blood in Room 402?'

Jennie began to cry, swaying slightly on her feet. Poirot rose and helped her to a chair. He said,

252

'Sit, mademoiselle. It is my turn to stand, and to tell you how I know beyond doubt that *nothing you have ever said to me has been the truth.*'

'Steady on, Poirot,' I cautioned him. Jennie looked as if she might faint.

Poirot seemed unconcerned. 'The murders of Harriet Sippel, Ida Gransbury and Richard Negus were announced in a note,' he said. ''MAY THEY NEVER REST IN PEACE. 121. 238. 317.' Now, I wonder to myself: a killer who walks in a state of brazen calm to a hotel's front desk and places a note there advertising three murders — is this the sort of person who would then panic, run from the hotel panting, and drop two room keys in front of a witness? Are we to believe that the killer Nancy Ducane's panic commenced only *after* she had left the note on the desk? Why would it start only then? And if Nancy Ducane was making her exit from the Bloxham at shortly after eight o'clock, how could she also be dining with her friend Lady Louisa Wallace at that very same moment?'

'Poirot, don't you think you ought to go easy on her?'

'I do not. I ask you, Mademoiselle Jennie: why should Nancy Ducane leave a note at all? Why did the three dead bodies need to be found shortly after eight o'clock that evening? The hotel maids would have found them in due course. What was the hurry? And if Madame Ducane was calm and composed enough to approach the desk and leave the note without arousing suspicion, that must mean she was able to think sensibly about what needed to be done. Why, then, did she not also put the two room keys safely in her deep coat pocket at that point, before she left the hotel? Foolishly, she keeps them in her hand and then drops them in front of Mr Kidd. He is able to see that they have numbers on them: 'one hundred and something' and 'three hundred and something'. He also, by fortunate coincidence, happens to recognize the face of this mysterious woman, and after a short pretence of being unable to recall her name, he is most conveniently able to tell us the name of Nancy Ducane. Does all of this sound plausible to you, Miss Hobbs? It does not sound at all plausible to Hercule Poirot — not when he finds you here, in Mr Kidd's home, and he knows that Nancy Ducane has an alibi!'

Jennie was weeping into her sleeve.

Poirot turned to me. 'Samuel Kidd's testimony was a lie from start to finish, Catchpool. He and Jennie Hobbs conspired to frame Nancy Ducane for the murders of Harriet Sippel, Ida Gransbury and Richard Negus.'

'You don't know how wrong you are!' Jennie cried.

'I know that you are a liar, mademoiselle. I have suspected all along that my encounter with you at Pleasant's was connected to the Bloxham Hotel murders. The two happenings — if we can classify three murders as one happening — had two very important and most unusual features in common.'

That made me sit up straight. I had been waiting to hear these points of likeness for too long.

Poirot went on: 'One, a psychological similarity: in both cases there is the suggestion that *the victims are guiltier than the murderer*. The note left on the desk at the Bloxham — 'MAY THEY NEVER REST IN PEACE' — suggests that Harriet Sippel, Ida Gransbury and Richard Negus deserved to die, and that their killer brought them to justice. And at the coffee house, Mademoiselle Jennie, you said to me that you deserved to die, and that once you had been killed, justice would have been done, finally.'

He was right. How had I missed that?

'Then there is the second similarity, which is not psychological but circumstantial: attached to both the Bloxham Hotel murders and my conversation with the frightened Jennie at the coffee house, there were *too many clues* — too much information available too soon! Too many leads presenting themselves all at once, almost as if someone wanted to offer the hand of help to the police. From a brief meeting in a coffee house, I was able to glean a surprisingly large number of facts. This Jennie, she felt guilty. She had done something terrible. She did not want her killer to be punished. She made sure to say to me, 'Oh, please let no one open their mouths' so that when I hear about three bodies at the Bloxham Hotel with cufflinks in their mouths, I will perhaps remember what she has said and wonder, or perhaps my subconscious will make the connection.'

'You're wrong about me, Monsieur Poirot,' Jennie protested.

Poirot ignored her, and continued with his speech: 'Let us now consider the Bloxham Hotel murders. There again, we found ourselves

255

supplied with much information, suspiciously soon: Richard Negus paid for all three rooms, and for the cars from the railway station to the hotel. All three victims lived or had lived in the village of Great Holling. There was, in addition, the helpful clue of the initials 'PIJ' on the cuff-links, to direct us to the reason these three people needed to be punished — that is, for their callous treatment of Reverend Patrick Ive. Furthermore, the note left on the front desk made it clear that the motive was revenge, or a thirst for justice. It is rare, is it not, for a murderer to write down his or her motive and so helpfully leave it lying in a prominent place?'

'Actually, some murderers *do* wish their motive to be known,' I said.

'*Mon ami*,' said Poirot with exaggerated patience. 'If Nancy Ducane had desired to kill Harriet Sippel, Ida Gransbury and Richard Negus, would she really have done so in a way that led so clearly back to her? Does she wish to go to the gallows? And why did Richard Negus — who, according to his brother, was on the verge of penury — pay for everything? Nancy Ducane is a rich woman. If she is a murderer who enticed her victims to London in order to kill them, why did she not pay for their hotel rooms and transport. None of it fits together!'

'Please let me speak, Monsieur Poirot! I will tell you the truth.'

'I prefer, for the time, being, that *I* tell *you* the truth, mademoiselle. Forgive me, but I find myself to be more reliable. Before you told me your story, you asked me if I was retired, did you not? You made a great show of checking that I had no powers to arrest anybody or enforce the law in this country. Only then, once I had reassured you on this point, did you confide in me. *But I had already told you that I had a friend at Scotland Yard.* You spoke to me not because you believed me to be powerless to arrest a murderer, *but because you knew perfectly well that I had influence with the police* — because you wished to see Nancy Ducane framed and hanged for murder!'

'I wish *no such thing*!' Jennie turned her tear-streaked face to me. 'Please, stop him!'

'I will stop when I am ready,' said Poirot. 'You were a regular visitor to Pleasant's Coffee House, mademoiselle. The waitresses have said so. They talk about their customers a great deal in their absence. I expect you heard them speak about me: the fussy European gentleman with the moustaches who used to be a policeman on the Continent — and my friend Catchpool here, from Scotland Yard. You heard them say that I dine at Pleasant's every Thursday evening at half past seven precisely. Oh, yes, mademoiselle, you knew where to find me, and you knew that Hercule Poirot would be perfect for your devious purposes! You arrived at the coffee house in an apparent state of terror, but it was all a lie, an act! You stared out of the window for a long time, as if fearful of someone in pursuit, but *you cannot have seen anything out of that window except the reflection of the room that you were in.* And one of the waitresses, she saw your eyes reflected and saw that you were watching her, not the street. You were calculating, were you not? 'Will anyone suspect that I am feigning my state of distress? Will that sharp-eyed waitress guess the truth and prevent my plan from being successful?''

I rose to my feet. 'Poirot, I don't doubt that you're right, but you can't simply go on at the poor woman without allowing her to say a word in her defence.'

'Be quiet, Catchpool. Have I not just explained to you that Miss Hobbs is excellent at creating an appearance of great unhappiness while, underneath, her true self is composed and calculating?'

'You are a cold-hearted man!' Jennie wailed.

'*Au contraire, mademoiselle*. In due course you will have your turn to speak, you may rest assured, but first I have another question for you. You said to me, 'Oh, please let no one open their mouths!' How did you know that Nancy Ducane, after killing her three victims, had placed cufflinks in their mouths? It seems to me odd that you should know this. Did Mrs Ducane threaten that it would happen? I can imagine a murderer threatening violence in order to scare — 'If I catch you, I will cut your throat', or something of that nature — but I cannot imagine a killer saying, 'After I have murdered you, I intend to place a monogrammed cufflink in your mouth.' I cannot imagine any person saying that, and I am a man of considerable imagination!

'And — pardon me! — one final observation, mademoiselle. Whatever guilt was yours for the tragic fate of Patrick and Frances Ive, three

258

people were as guilty as you if not more so: Harriet Sippel, Ida Gransbury and Richard Negus. They were the people who believed your lie and turned the whole village against the Reverend Ive and his wife. Now, at Pleasant's you said to me, 'Once I am dead, justice will have been done, finally,' and you placed the stress upon the 'I': 'once *I* am dead'. This indicates to me that you knew that Harriet Sippel, Ida Gransbury and Richard Negus were already dead. But if I look at all the evidence as it has been presented to me, *the three murders at the Bloxham Hotel might not yet have been committed.*'

'Stop, please, *stop!*' Jennie wept.

'In a moment, with pleasure. Let me only say that it was approximately a quarter to eight when you spoke those words to me — 'Once *I* am dead, justice will have been done, finally' — and yet we know that the three Bloxham murders were only discovered by the hotel's staff after ten minutes past eight. Yet somehow you, Jennie Hobbs, had advance knowledge of these murders. How?'

'If you will only stop accusing me, I shall tell you everything! I've been so desperate. Having to keep it all secret and lie constantly — it was a torment. I can't bear it any longer!'

'*Bon,*' said Poirot quietly. He sounded suddenly kinder. 'You have had a severe shock today, have you not? Perhaps you will now see that you cannot deceive Poirot?'

'I do see. Let me tell you the story, from the beginning. It will be such a relief to be able to tell the truth at last.'

Jennie spoke at length then, and neither I nor Poirot interrupted her until she indicated that she had finished. What follows is in her words, and is, I hope, a faithful and complete account of what she said.

19

The Truth at Last

I destroyed the life of the only man I have ever loved, and I destroyed my own life along with it.

I didn't mean for things to take the turn they took. I would never have imagined that a few silly, cruel words spoken by me could lead to such disaster. I ought to have considered, and kept my mouth shut, but I was feeling wounded and, in a moment of weakness, I allowed spite to get the better of me.

I loved Patrick Ive with every bone and muscle in my body. I tried not to. I was engaged to be married to Sam Kidd when I first started working for Patrick — as his bedder, at Saviour College in Cambridge, where he studied. I liked Sam well enough, but my heart belonged to Patrick within a few weeks of first meeting him, and I knew that no amount of trying to feel differently would change that. Patrick was everything good that a person could be. He was fond of me, but to him I was only a servant. Even after I learned to speak like the daughter of a master of a Cambridge college — like Frances Ive — I remained, in Patrick's eyes, a loyal servant and nothing more.

Of course I knew about him and Nancy Ducane. I overheard some of his conversations with her that I wasn't supposed to. I knew how much he loved her, and I couldn't bear it. I had long ago accepted that he belonged to Frances and not to me, but it was intolerable to discover that he had fallen in love with a woman who was not his wife and that that woman was not me.

For a few fleeting seconds — no longer — I wanted to punish him. To cause him grievous hurt of the kind that he had caused me. So I made up a wicked lie about him and, God forgive me, I told that lie to Harriet Sippel. It comforted me for as long as I was telling it: the idea that Patrick's whispered words of love for Nancy — words I had overheard more than once — were not his but the late William Ducane's, conveyed from beyond the grave. Oh, I knew it was nonsense, but when I told Harriet Sippel, for a few seconds it felt true.

Then Harriet set to work, saying dreadful, unforgivable things about Patrick all over the village — and Ida and Richard helped her, which I never understood. They must have known what a venomous creature she had become; everyone in the village knew. How could they turn on Patrick and ally themselves with her? Oh, I know the answer: it was my fault. Richard and Ida knew that the rumour did not come from Harriet in the first place but from a servant girl who had always been loyal to Patrick and who was seen as having no reason to lie.

I saw at once that my jealousy had led me to do a terrible, heinous thing. I witnessed Patrick's suffering and desperately wanted to help him, and Frances — but I didn't see how I could! Harriet had seen Nancy enter and leave the

262

vicarage at night. So had Richard Negus. If I had admitted to lying, I would have had to offer another explanation for Nancy's nocturnal visits to Patrick. And it would not have taken Harriet long to arrive at the correct explanation by her own deductions.

The shameful truth is that I am a dreadful coward. People like Richard Negus and Ida Gransbury — they don't mind what other people think of them if they believe that right is on their side, but I *do* mind. I have always cared about making a good impression. If I had confessed to my lie, I would have been hated by everybody in the village, and rightly so. I'm not a strong person, Monsieur Poirot. I did nothing, said nothing, because I was scared. Then Nancy, horrified by the lie and by people's believing of it, came forward and told the truth: that she and Patrick were in love and had been meeting in secret, though nothing of a carnal nature had taken place between them.

Nancy's efforts on Patrick's behalf only made things worse for him. 'Not only a charlatan who defrauds parishioners and makes a mockery of his Church, but also an adulterer' — that was what they started to say. It became too much for Frances, who took her own life. When Patrick found her, he knew he would not be able to live with the guilt — after all, it was his love for Nancy that had started the trouble. He had failed in his duty to Frances. He, too, took his own life.

The village doctor said that the two deaths were accidents, but that was not true. They were both suicide — another sin in the eyes of those as saintly as Ida Gransbury, and those with an appetite for punishing, like Harriet Sippel. Patrick and Frances both left notes, you see. I found them and passed them on to the doctor, Ambrose Flowerday. I think he must have burned them. He said that he would not give anybody further cause to condemn Patrick and Frances. Dr Flowerday was sickened by the way the whole village had turned on them.

Patrick's death broke my heart, and it has remained broken since that day, Monsieur Poirot. I wanted to die, but with Patrick gone, I felt that I needed to stay alive, loving him and thinking well of him — as if my doing so could ever make up for everybody else in Great Holling believing him to be some sort of devil!

My only consolation was that I was not alone in my misery. Richard Negus felt ashamed of the part he had played. He alone among Patrick's denigrators changed his mind; when Nancy told her story, he saw at once that the outlandish lie I had told was unlikely to be true.

Before he moved to his brother's home in Devon, Richard sought me out and asked me directly. I wanted to tell him that there was not a grain of truth in the rumour I had started, but I didn't dare, so I said nothing. I sat mutely, as if my tongue had been cut out, and Richard took my silence as an admission of guilt.

I left Great Holling shortly after he did. I went to Sammy for help at first, but I couldn't stay in Cambridge — there were too many memories of Patrick there — so I came to London. It was

Sammy's idea. He found work here and, thanks to some people he introduced me to, so did I. Sammy is devoted to me in the way that I was to Patrick. I ought to be grateful to him for that. He asked me again to marry him but I couldn't, though I regard him as a very dear friend.

A new chapter of my life opened with my move to London. I was unable to enjoy it, and thought every single day of Patrick, of the agony of never seeing him again. Then last September I received a letter from Richard Negus. Fifteen years had gone by, but I did not feel as if the past had caught up with me — because I never left it behind!

Richard had been given my London address by the only person in Great Holling who knew it: Dr Ambrose Flowerday. I don't know why, but I wanted someone from there to know where I had gone. I remember thinking at the time that I did not wish to disappear absolutely without trace. I felt that . . .

No, I will not say that. It is not true that I had a vision of the future in which Richard Negus sought me out once again and asked for my help to right an old wrong. I will say instead that I had a powerful premonition, though not one I could have described in words. I knew that the village of Great Holling was not finished with me for ever, nor I with it. That is why I made sure to send my London address to Dr Flowerday.

Richard's letter said that he needed to see me, and it did not occur to me to refuse him. He came to London the following week. Without preamble, he asked if I would help him to make amends for the unforgivable thing we had done all those years ago.

I told him that I did not believe amends could be made. Patrick was dead. There was no undoing that. Richard said, 'Yes. Patrick and Frances are dead, and you and I can never again know happiness. But what if we were to make a corresponding sacrifice?'

I did not understand. I asked him what he meant.

He said: 'If we killed Patrick and Frances Ive, and I believe that we did, is it not fitting that we should pay with our own lives? Do we not find ourselves unable to benefit from the joy that life offers to other people? Why is that? Why does time not heal our wound as it is meant to heal? Could it be because we do not deserve to live while poor Patrick and Frances lie in the ground?' Richard's eyes darkened as he spoke, turning from their usual brown to almost black. 'The law of the land punishes with death those who take the lives of the innocent,' he said. 'We have cheated that law.'

I could have told him that neither he nor I took up a weapon and murdered Patrick and Frances, for that would have been the factual truth of the matter. However, his words resonated so powerfully that I knew he was right, although many would have said he was wrong. As he spoke, my heart filled with something akin to hope for the first time in fifteen years. I could not bring Patrick back, but I could make certain that I did not escape justice for what I had done to him.

266

'Are you proposing that I take my own life?' I asked Richard, because he had not said so explicitly.

'No. Nor that I take mine. What I have in mind is not suicide, but execution — for which we will volunteer. Or at least I shall. I have no wish to force your hand in this.'

'You and I are not the only guilty parties,' I reminded him.

'No, we are not,' he agreed. What he said next nearly caused my heart to stop. 'Would it surprise you greatly, Jennie, to learn that Harriet Sippel and Ida Gransbury have come round to my way of thinking?'

I told him that I could not believe it. Harriet and Ida would never admit to having done something cruel and unforgivable, I thought. Richard said that at one time he too had taken this for granted. He said, 'I persuaded them. People listen to me, Jennie. They always have. I worked on Harriet and Ida, not with harsh condemnation but by expressing, ceaselessly, my own deep regret, and my wish that I could compensate for the harm I had done. It took years — as many as have passed since last you and I spoke — but gradually Harriet and Ida came to see things as I do. They are both profoundly unhappy women, you see: Harriet ever since her husband died, and Ida since I informed her that I no longer wished to marry her.'

I opened my mouth to voice my disbelief, but Richard continued to speak. He assured me that both Harriet and Ida had accepted their responsibility for the deaths of Patrick and Frances Ive, and wanted to correct the wrong they had done. 'The psychology of the matter is fascinating,' he said. 'Harriet is content as long as there is someone she can seek to punish. Presently, that person is herself. Do not forget that she is eager to be reunited with her husband in Heaven. She cannot allow the possibility that she might end up in a different place.'

I was speechless with shock. I said that I would never believe it. Richard told me that I would as soon as I spoke to Harriet and Ida and they confirmed it. I must meet them, he said, so that I could see for myself how changed they were.

I could not imagine Harriet or Ida changed, and feared that I would commit murder if I were to find myself in a room with either one of them.

Richard said, 'You must try to understand, Jennie. I offered them a way out of their suffering — and be assured, they *were* suffering. One cannot do such harm to another and not wound one's own soul in the process. For years Harriet and Ida believed that all they had to cling to was their conviction that they had been right about Patrick, but over time they came to see that I was offering them something better: God's true forgiveness. The sinful soul aches for redemption, Jennie. The more we deny it the chance of finding that redemption, the stronger the ache grows. Thanks to my determined efforts, Harriet and Ida came to see that the revulsion that every day grew harder inside them was disgust at their own behaviour, at the wickedness they tried so hard to drape in a cloak of virtue, and nothing to do with Patrick Ive's imagined sins.'

Listening to Richard, I started to understand that even the most intransigent person — even a Harriet Sippel — might be persuaded by him. He had a way of putting things that made you see the world differently.

He asked for my permission to bring Harriet and Ida to our next meeting and, with doubt and fear in my heart, I granted it.

Although I believed everything Richard had told me by the time he left me, I nevertheless reeled in shock when, two days later, I found myself in a room with Harriet Sippel and Ida Gransbury, and saw with my own eyes that they were as changed as Richard had reported them to be. Or rather, they were the same as always, except that now they strove to apply their compassionless rigidity to themselves. I was filled anew with passionate hatred for them when they spoke of 'poor, kind Patrick' and 'poor, innocent Frances'. They had no right to utter those words.

The four of us agreed that we had to do something to put right the wrong. We were murderers, not according to the law but according to the truth, and murderers must pay with their own lives. Only after our deaths would God forgive us.

'We four are judge, jury and executioner,' said Richard. 'We will execute one another.'

'How will we do it?' Ida asked, gazing adoringly at him.

'I have thought of a way,' he said. 'I shall take care of the details.'

Thus, without noise or complaint, we signed our own death warrants. I felt nothing but immense relief. I remember thinking that I would not be afraid to kill as long as my victim was not afraid to die. Victim is the wrong word. I don't know what the right one is.

Then Harriet said, 'Wait. What about Nancy Ducane?'

★ ★ ★

I knew what she meant before she explained. 'Oh, yes,' I thought to myself, 'this is the same old Harriet Sippel.' Four deaths for a good cause were not enough for her; she craved a fifth.

Richard and Ida asked her what she meant.

'Nancy Ducane must die too,' said Harriet, her eyes as hard as flint. 'She led poor Patrick into temptation, announced their shame to the village and broke poor Frances's heart.'

'Oh, no,' I said, alarmed. 'Nancy would never agree to give up her own life. And . . . Patrick loved her!'

'She's every bit as guilty as we are,' Harriet insisted. 'She must die. We *all* must, all the guilty, or else it will be for nothing. If we are going to do this we must do it properly. It was Nancy's revelation, remember, that prompted Frances Ive to take her own life. And besides, I know something that you don't know.'

Richard demanded that we all be told at once. With a sly glint in her eye, Harriet said, 'Nancy wanted Frances to know that Patrick's heart belonged to her. She said what she said out of jealousy and spite. She admitted it to me. She's just as guilty as we are — more so, if you want to know my true opinion. And if she won't agree to die . . . well, then!'

Richard sat with his head in his hands for a long time. Harriet, Ida and I waited in silence. I realized then that Richard was our leader. Whatever he said when he finally spoke, we would abide by it.

I prayed for Nancy. I did not blame her for Patrick's death, never had and never would.

'All right,' said Richard, though he did not look happy. 'It saddens me to admit it, but yes. Nancy Ducane should not have consorted with another woman's husband. She should not have announced her liaison with Patrick to the village in the way that she did. We do not know that Frances Ive would have taken her own life if that had not happened. Regrettably, Nancy Ducane must also die.'

'No!' I cried out. All I could think of was how Patrick would have felt if he had heard those words.

'I'm sorry, Jennie, but Harriet is right,' said Richard. 'It is a bold and difficult thing that we intend to do. We cannot ask ourselves to make so great a sacrifice and leave alive one person who shares the blame for what occurred. We cannot exonerate Nancy.'

I wanted to scream and run from the room, but I forced myself to stay in my chair. I was certain that Harriet had lied about Nancy's reason for speaking up at the King's Head; I did not believe that Nancy had admitted to being

271

driven by jealousy and a wish to hurt Frances Ive, but, in front of Harriet, I was too afraid to say so, and besides, I had no proof. Richard said that he would need to think for a while about how we would put our plan into action.

Two weeks later, he came to see me again, alone. He had decided what must happen, he said. He and I would be the only ones to know the whole truth — and Sammy, of course. I tell him everything.

We would tell Harriet and Ida, said Richard, that the plan was for us to kill one another, as agreed, and frame Nancy Ducane for our murders. Since Nancy lives in London, this would need to happen in London — in a hotel, Richard suggested. He said that he would pay for everything.

Once at the hotel, it was simple: Ida would kill Harriet, Richard would kill Ida, and I would kill Richard. Each killer, when his or her turn came, would place a cufflink bearing Patrick Ive's initials in the victim's mouth and set up the crime scene to look identical to the other two, so that the police would take for granted that the same killer had committed all three . . . deaths. I was about to say murders, but they weren't. They were executions. You see, it occurred to us that after people are executed there must be a procedure, mustn't there? The prison staff must do the same thing with every body of an executed criminal, we thought. It was Richard's idea that the bodies should be laid out in the way that they were — respectfully and with dignity. *Ceremonially* — that was Richard's word.

Since two of the victims, Ida and Harriet, would have given their home addresses to the hotel as Great Holling, we knew that it would not then take the police long to go to the village, ask around, and begin to suspect Nancy. Who else was so obvious a suspect? Sammy could pretend to have seen her running out of the hotel after the third murder, and dropping the three room keys on the ground. That's right: *three* room keys. Richard's key was part of the plan too, you see. Ida was supposed to take Harriet's key to her own room after killing Harriet and locking Harriet's door. Richard was supposed to do the same: take Harriet's *and* Ida's keys with him when he left and locked Ida's room after killing Ida. Then I would kill Richard, lock his door, take all three keys, meet Sammy outside the Bloxham and give the keys to him. Sammy would then sneak them somehow into Nancy Ducane's home, or, as it turned out, her coat pocket one day on the street, in order to incriminate her.

I don't suppose this matters, but Patrick Ive never wore monogrammed cufflinks. He didn't own a pair as far as I ever knew. Richard Negus ordered all the cufflinks to be specially made, to set the police on the right track. The leaving of the blood and my hat inside the fourth hotel room was also part of our plan, designed to make you believe I had been murdered in that room — that Nancy Ducane had avenged her dead love by killing all four of us. Richard was happy to leave it to Sammy to provide the blood. It came from a stray cat, if you want to know. It was also Sammy's job to leave the note on the hotel's front desk on the night of the killings: 'MAY THEY NEVER REST IN PEACE' and then the three room numbers. He was to place it on the reception desk when no one was looking, shortly after eight o'clock. My task, meanwhile, was to stay alive and make sure that Nancy Ducane hanged for the three murders, and possibly four if the police believed that I too was dead.

How was I to accomplish this? Well, as the fourth person that Nancy would wish to kill — the fourth person responsible for what happened to Patrick — I was to let the police know that I feared for my life. This I did at Pleasant's Coffee House, and you were my audience, Monsieur Poirot. You are quite right: I deceived you. You are right too that I had heard the waitresses at Pleasant's discussing the detective from the Continent who comes in every Thursday evening at precisely half past seven, and who sometimes dines with his much younger friend from Scotland Yard. As soon as I heard the girls talking about you, I knew you would be perfect.

But Monsieur Poirot, one of the conclusions you have drawn is incorrect. You said that my saying, 'Once *I* am dead, justice will have been done, finally' meant that I knew the other three were already dead, but I absolutely did not know whether Richard, Harriet and Ida were dead or alive, because by then I had ruined everything. I was merely thinking, when I spoke those words, that according to the plan Richard and I made, I

274

would outlive them. So you see, they might well still have been alive when I uttered those words.

I should make it clear: there were two plans — one that Harriet and Ida agreed to, and a quite different one known only to Richard and me. As far as Harriet and Ida were concerned it would go like this: Ida would kill Harriet, Richard would kill Ida, I would kill Richard. Then I would fake my own murder, at the Bloxham, using the blood that Sammy would get hold of. I would live only as long as it took to see Nancy Ducane hanged, and then I would take my own life. If by some chance Nancy did not hang, I was to kill her and then take my own life. I had to be the last to die, because of the acting involved. I am a good actress when I want to be. When I contrived to meet you at the coffee house, Monsieur Poirot . . . Harriet Sippel could not have produced such a performance. Neither could Ida, or Richard. So you see, I had to be the one to stay alive.

The plan that Harriet and Ida were party to was not Richard's true plan. When he came to see me alone, two weeks after our first meeting in London with Harriet and Ida, he told me that the question of whether Nancy ought to die had been concerning him greatly. Like me, he did not believe Nancy had admitted to Harriet that she had spoken up at the King's Head for any reason apart from to defend Patrick against lies.

On the other hand, Richard could see Harriet's point. Patrick and Frances Ive's deaths had been caused by the ill-judged behaviour of several people, and it was hard not to count

275

Nancy Ducane among those responsible.

I could not have been more surprised, or frightened, when Richard confessed that he had been unable to reach a decision in the matter of Nancy, and that therefore he had decided to leave it up to me. After he, Harriet and Ida were dead, he said, I was free to choose: either to do my best to ensure that Nancy hanged, or to take my own life and leave a different note for the hotel staff to find — not 'MAY THEY NEVER REST IN PEACE', but a note containing the truth about our deaths.

I begged Richard not to force me to decide alone. Why me? I demanded to know.

'Because, Jennie,' he said — and I shall never forget this — 'because you are the best of us. You were never inflated with a sense of your own virtue. Yes, you told a lie, but you realized your error as soon as the words had left your mouth. I believed your falsehood for an inexcusably long time when I had no proof, and helped to gather support for a campaign against a good, innocent man. A flawed man, yes — not a saint. But who among us is perfect?'

'All right,' I told Richard. 'I will make the choice that you have entrusted to me.' I was flattered to be so praised, I suppose.

And so our plans were made. Now, would you like me to tell you how it all went wrong?

20

How It All Went Wrong

'Indeed,' said Poirot. 'Tell us. Catchpool and I, we are agog.'

'It was my fault,' said Jennie, whose voice was hoarse by now. 'I am a coward. I was afraid to die. Desolate as I was without Patrick, I had grown comfortable in my unhappiness and I didn't want my life to end. Any sort of life, even one filled with torment, is preferable to a state of nothingness! Please don't condemn me as unchristian for saying so, but I'm not sure I believe in an afterlife. I grew more and more afraid as the agreed date for the executions came closer — afraid of having to kill. I thought about what would be involved, imagined standing in a locked room and watching Richard drink poison, and I didn't want to have to do it. But I had agreed! I had promised.'

'The plan that seemed so easy months before started to seem impossible,' said Poirot. 'And of course you could not speak of your fears to Richard Negus, who esteemed you so highly. He might think less of you if you admitted to serious doubts. You perhaps were afraid he would take it upon himself to execute you with or without your consent.'

'Yes! I was terrified that he would. You see, from our discussions of the subject, I knew how

277

important it was to him that all four of us should die. He told me on one occasion that if Harriet and Ida had not allowed themselves to be persuaded, he would have 'done what needed to be done without their consent'. That was how he put it. Knowing that, how could I go to him and tell him I had changed my mind, that I was prepared neither to die nor to kill?'

'I imagine you chided yourself for your reluctance, mademoiselle. You believed, did you not, that this killing and dying was the right and honourable thing to do?'

'With the rational part of my mind, yes, I did,' said Jennie. 'I hoped and prayed that I would discover in myself an extra reserve of courage that would enable me to go through with it.'

'What did you plan to do about Nancy Ducane?' I asked her.

'I did not know. My panic on the night we first met was genuine, Monsieur Poirot. I could not decide what to do about anything! I allowed Sammy to go forward with his story about the keys, and to identify Nancy. I let all that happen, telling myself that at any moment I could go to the authorities with the truth and save her. But . . . I did not do so. Richard thought me a better person than him, but he was wrong — so wrong!

'There is a part of me, still, that envies Nancy because Patrick loved her, the same spiteful part that started all the trouble in Great Holling. And . . . I knew that if I admitted to conspiring in a plot to convict an innocent woman of murder, I would surely go to prison. I was scared.'

'Tell us please, mademoiselle: what did you

278

do? What happened on the day of these . . . executions at the Bloxham Hotel?'

'I was supposed to arrive there at six o'clock. That was when we had agreed to meet.'

'The four conspirators?'

'Yes, and Sammy. I spent the whole day watching the clock tick its way towards the awful moment. When it got close to five o'clock, I simply knew I couldn't do it. I just couldn't! I did not go to the hotel at all. Instead, I ran through the streets of London, crying with fear. I had no notion of where to go or what to do, so I ran and ran. I felt as if Richard Negus was bound to be out looking for me, furious that I had let him and the others down. I went to Pleasant's Coffee House at the agreed time, thinking that I could at least keep that part of my promise, even if I couldn't kill Richard as I was supposed to.

'When I arrived at the coffee house, I *was* afraid for my life. That was no act that you saw. I thought *Richard*, not Nancy, might kill me — and, what is more, I was convinced that if he did, he would be doing the right thing. I *did* deserve to die! I said nothing to you that wasn't true, Monsieur Poirot. Please, recall now what I said:

That I was scared of being murdered? I was — by Richard. That I had done something terrible in the past? I had — and if Richard did catch up with me and kill me, as I believed he one day would, I honestly did not want him to be punished for it. I knew that I had let him down. Can you understand that? Richard might have wanted to die, but I wanted him to live. Despite the harm he did to Patrick, he was a good man.'

'*Oui, mademoiselle.*'

'I longed to tell you the truth that night, Monsieur Poirot, but I lacked the courage.'

'So you believed that Richard Negus would find you and kill you because you did not arrive at the Bloxham Hotel to kill him?'

'Yes. I assumed that he would not be content to die without knowing why I didn't come to the hotel as planned.'

'Yet he was,' I said, thinking furiously.

Jennie nodded.

I could see now that it all made sense: the identical positioning of the three dead bodies for one thing — in a perfectly straight line, feet pointing towards the door, between a small table and a chair. As Poirot had said, Harriet Sippel, Ida Gransbury and Richard Negus were unlikely all to have fallen naturally into that exact position.

There was a suspicious amount of similarity between the three murder scenes, and at last I thought I understood why: the conspirators needed the police to believe there was only one killer. In fact, any detective worth his salt would have assumed this purely from the cufflinks in the mouths and the fact of all three bodies having turned up at the same hotel on the same night, but the killers were in the grip of paranoia. *They* knew they were more than one person, and so they feared, as the guilty tend to, that the truth might be apparent to others. So they went to great lengths to create three murder scenes that were *more similar to one another than they needed to be.*

The laying out of the bodies, perfectly straight and identical, was also consistent with the notion that the killings at the Bloxham Hotel were not murders but executions. There are procedures that one follows after an execution; formalities and rituals. It would have felt important, I thought, to do *something* with the bodies rather than simply leave them lying exactly as they fell, as a common or garden murderer would.

An image of a much younger Jennie Hobbs came to my mind: at Cambridge University's Saviour College, moving from one room to another, making beds. She would have made each one identically, following the prescribed pattern . . . I shuddered, then wondered why a vision of a young woman innocently making beds in a college should give me such a chill.

Beds, and deathbeds . . .

Patterns, and the disruption of patterns . . .

'Richard Negus committed suicide,' I heard myself declare. 'He must have. He tried to make it look like murder — the same pattern as the other two, so that we would suspect the same killer — but he had to lock his door from the *inside.* Then he hid the key behind a fireplace tile to make it look as if the murderer had taken it, and opened a window to its full extent. If the hidden key was ever found, we would have wondered, as we did, why the murderer chose to lock the door from the inside, hide the key in the room and escape via the window, but *we would*

281

still have believed there was a murderer. That was all that mattered to Negus. Whereas if the window was shut and by some chance the key was found, we would draw the only possible conclusion: that Richard Negus had taken his own life. He couldn't risk our arriving at that conclusion — do you see? If we did, then the framing of Nancy Ducane for all three deaths would fail. We would be more likely to assume that Negus killed Harriet Sippel and Ida Gransbury before killing himself.'

'Yes,' said Jennie. 'I think you are right.'

'The different positioning of the cufflink . . . ' Poirot murmured before raising his eyebrows at me, indicating that he wished me to continue.

I said, 'The cufflink was close to Negus's throat because his death convulsions from the poison caused his mouth to open. He had carefully positioned himself in a straight line on the floor and placed the cufflink between his lips, but it fell to the back of his mouth. Unlike Harriet Sippel and Ida Gransbury, Richard Negus did not have a killer present when he died, and so the cufflink could not be carefully positioned in the agreed place.'

'Mademoiselle Jennie, you believe that Mr Negus would swallow the poison, lie down and die without first attempting to discover why you had failed to arrive at the hotel?' Poirot asked her.

'I did not think he would, until I read of his death in the newspaper.'

'Ah.' Poirot's expression was unreadable.

'For so long, Richard had been expecting to

die on that Thursday night, looking forward to the end of his guilt and torment after so many years,' said Jennie. 'I believe that all he wanted, once he arrived at the Bloxham, was for it to be over for him, and so, when I did not arrive to kill him as planned, he did it himself.'

'Thank you, mademoiselle.' Poirot rose to his feet. He wobbled a little to find his balance after so long in a seated position.

'What will happen to me, Monsieur Poirot?'

'Please stay here in this house until I or Mr Catchpool return with more information. If you make the mistake of running away a second time, things will go very badly for you.'

'As they will if I stay put,' said Jennie. There was a blank, faraway look in her eyes. 'It's all right, Mr Catchpool, you needn't be sorry for me. I am prepared.'

Her words, no doubt intended to reassure me, filled me with dread. She had the manner of one who had looked into the future and seen terrible events contained within it. Whatever they were, I knew that I was not prepared and did not wish to be.

21

All the Devils Are Here

Apart from telling me twice that we must go to Great Holling without delay, Poirot remained silent all the way home. He looked preoccupied, and it was clear that he did not want to talk.

We arrived at the lodging house to find young Stanley Beer waiting for us. 'What is the matter?' Poirot asked him. 'Are you here about the work of art I created?'

'Pardon, sir? Oh, your crest? No, that was perfectly all right, sir. As a matter of fact . . . ' Beer reached into his pocket and handed over an envelope. 'You'll find your answer in there.'

'Thank you, Constable. But then it must be that something else is wrong? You are anxious, *non?*'

'Yes, sir. We've had word at Scotland Yard from an Ambrose Flowerday, the Great Holling village doctor. He's asked for Mr Catchpool to go there immediately. He says he's needed.'

Poirot looked at me, then turned back to Stanley Beer. 'It was our intention to go there immediately. Do you know what has provoked Dr Flowerday to request Catchpool's presence?'

'I'm afraid I do. It's not a happy business, sir. A woman by the name of Margaret Ernst has been attacked. She is likely to die — '

'Oh, no,' I murmured.

' — and she says she needs to see Mr Catchpool before she does. After speaking to Dr Flowerday, I would advise you to hurry, sir. There's a car waiting outside to take you to the station.'

Thinking of Poirot's methodical nature and his dislike of any hectic activity, I said, 'Might we take half an hour to ready ourselves?'

Beer looked at his watch. 'Five, ten minutes at a stretch, but no longer, sir — not if you want to catch the next train.'

I must admit with some shame that, in the event, Poirot was downstairs with his suitcase before I was. 'Hurry, *mon ami*,' he urged.

In the car, I decided that I needed to speak, even if Poirot was not feeling talkative. 'If I had only stayed away from that infernal village, Margaret Ernst would not have been attacked,' I said grimly. 'Someone must have seen me go to her cottage and noticed how long I stayed.'

'You stayed long enough for her to tell you everything, or nearly everything. What is achieved by trying to kill her when she has already shared her knowledge with the police?'

'Revenge. Punishment. Though, frankly, it makes no sense. If Nancy Ducane is innocent, and Jennie Hobbs and Samuel Kidd are behind everything — I mean, if they're the only ones still alive who were behind everything — well, why should Jennie and Kidd want to kill Margaret Ernst? She said nothing to me to incriminate either of them, and she never harmed Patrick or Frances Ive.'

'I agree. Jennie Hobbs and Samuel Kidd

would not wish to murder Margaret Ernst as far as I can see.'

Rain lashed at the windows of our car. It made it harder both to hear and to concentrate. 'Then who did?' I asked. 'There we were, thinking we had all the answers — '

'You surely did not think any such thing, Catchpool?'

'Yes, I did. I expect you're about to tell me I'm wrong, but it all seemed to add up, didn't it? All pretty straightforward, until we heard about Margaret Ernst being attacked.'

'He tells me it is straightforward!' Poirot smirked at the rain-spattered car window.

'Well, it looked simple enough to me. All the killers were dead. Ida killed Harriet, with Harriet's consent, and was then killed by Richard Negus — again, with her full consent. Then Negus, when Jennie didn't arrive to kill him as planned, took his own life. Jennie Hobbs and Samuel Kidd have killed nobody. Of course, they conspired to bring about three deaths, but those deaths were not really murders, as I see it. They were — '

'Executions by consent?'

'Exactly.'

'It was a very neat plan they made, was it not? Harriet Sippel, Ida Gransbury, Richard Negus and Jennie Hobbs. Let us call them A, B, C and D for the moment, and we will see the neatness of their plan more clearly.'

'Why should we not call them by their names?' I asked.

Poirot ignored me. 'A, B, C and D — all

286

plagued by guilt and seeking the redemption of the soul. They agree that they must pay for a past sin with their own lives, and so they plan to kill one another: B kills A, then C kills B, then D kills C.'

'Except that D *didn't* kill C, did she? D is Jennie Hobbs, and she didn't kill Richard Negus.'

'Perhaps not, but she was supposed to. That was the plan. Also that D would stay alive to see E — Nancy Ducane — hang for the murders of A, B, and C. Only then could D . . . ' Poirot stopped. 'D,' he repeated. 'Demise. That is the correct word.'

'What?'

'For your crossword puzzle. A word that means death and has six letters. Do you recall? I suggested 'murder' and you said that would only work if murder began . . . ' He fell silent, shaking his head.

'If murder began with a D. Yes, I remember. Poirot, are you all right?' His eyes had that strange green glow about them that they sometimes acquire.

'*Comment? Mais bien évidemment!* If murder began with a D! Of course! That is it! *Mon ami,* you do not know how you have helped me. Now I think . . . yes, that is it. That must be it. The younger man and the older woman — ah, but it is so clear to me now!'

'Please explain.'

'Yes, yes. When I am ready.'

'Why are you not ready *now?* What are you waiting for?'

'You must allow me more than twenty seconds

287

to compose and arrange my ideas, Catchpool. That is necessary if I am to explain to you, who do not understand a thing. Your every word shows me that you comprehend nothing. You talk about having all the answers, but the story we heard from Jennie Hobbs this morning was an elaborate embroidery of lies! Do you not see this?'

'Well . . . I mean . . . um . . . '

'Richard Negus agrees with Harriet Sippel that perhaps Nancy Ducane should hang for three murders she did not commit? He is willing to leave Nancy's fate to be decided by Jennie Hobbs? Richard Negus the leader, the respected authority figure — the same Richard Negus who, for sixteen years, has felt so terribly guilty for unjustly condemning Patrick Ive? The Richard Negus who realized *too late* that it is wrong to condemn and persecute a man for understandable human weaknesses? Who ended his engagement to Ida Gransbury because she dogmatically insisted that every transgression must be punished with the utmost harshness — *this* Richard Negus would entertain the idea of allowing Nancy Ducane, whose only crime was to love a man who could never belong to her, to be condemned by law and face the gallows for three murders of which she is innocent? Pah! It is nonsense! There is no consistency. It is a fantasy dreamed up by Jennie Hobbs to mislead us yet again.'

I listened to most of this with my mouth open. 'Are you sure, Poirot? I believed her, I have to say.'

'Of course I am sure. Did not Henry Negus tell us that his brother Richard spent sixteen years in his home as a recluse, seeing and speaking to nobody? Yet according to Jennie Hobbs, he spent these same years persuading Harriet Sippel and Ida Gransbury that they were responsible for Patrick and Frances Ive's deaths and must pay the price. How was Richard Negus able to do this persuading without his brother Henry noticing his regular communications with two women from Great Holling?'

'You might have a point there. I didn't think of that.'

'It is a minor point. Surely you noticed all that was more substantially wrong with Jennie's story?'

'To frame an innocent person for murder is unquestionably wrong,' I said.

'Catchpool, I am talking not about morally wrong but about *factually impossible*. Is this how you force me to explain before I am ready, by exasperating me? *Bien*, I will draw one detail to your attention in the hope that it will lead you to others. According to Jennie Hobbs, how did the keys to rooms 121 and 317 of the Bloxham Hotel end up in Nancy Ducane's blue coat?'

'Samuel Kidd planted them there. To frame Nancy.'

'He slipped them into her pocket on the street?'

'It's easy enough to do, I imagine.'

'Yes, but how did Mr Kidd get hold of the two keys? Jennie was supposed to find both, along with Richard Negus's key, in Room 238 when

289

she went there to kill Richard Negus. She was supposed to pass all three keys to Samuel Kidd after she had left and locked Room 238. Yet according to her, she did not go to Richard Negus's room or to the Bloxham Hotel at all on the night of the murders. Mr Negus locked his door from the inside and killed himself, having hidden his key behind a loose tile in the fireplace. So how did Samuel Kidd get his hands on the other two keys?'

I waited a few moments in case the answer came to me. It didn't. 'I don't know.'

'Perhaps when Jennie Hobbs did not arrive, Samuel Kidd and Richard Negus improvised: the former killed the latter, then took Harriet Sippel's and Ida Gransbury's keys from Mr Negus's hotel room. In which case, why not also take Mr Negus's key? Why hide it behind the loose tile in the fireplace? The only reasonable explanation is that Richard Negus wanted his suicide to look like murder. *Mon ami*, this could have been achieved just as easily by having Samuel Kidd remove the key from the room. There would have been then no need for the open window to give the impression of the murderer escaping from the room in that way.'

I saw the strength of his argument. 'Since Richard Negus locked his door from the inside, how did Samuel Kidd get into room 238 in order to remove the keys to rooms 121 and 317?'

'*Précisément.*'

'What if he climbed in through the open window, having first climbed a tree?'

'Catchpool — think. Jennie Hobbs says she

did not go to the Bloxham Hotel that night. So, either Samuel Kidd cooperated with Richard Negus to make the plan work without her, or else the two men did not cooperate. If they did not, then why would Mr Kidd enter Mr Negus's hotel room uninvited, by an open window, and remove two keys from it? What reason would he have for doing so? And if the two men did cooperate, surely Samuel Kidd would have ended up with three keys to place in Nancy Ducane's pocket rather than two. Additionally . . . if Richard Negus committed suicide, as you now believe, causing the cufflink to fall far back in his mouth, then who arranged his body in the perfectly straight line? Do you believe that a man could swallow poison and then contrive to die in that exceptionally neat position? *Non! Ce n'est pas possible.*'

'I shall need to think about this another time,' I said. 'You've made my head spin. It's full of a jumble of questions that weren't there before.'

'For example?'

'Why did our three murder victims order sandwiches, cakes and scones and then not eat any of them? And if they didn't eat the food, why wasn't it still on the plates in Ida Gransbury's room? What happened to it?'

'Ah! Now you think like a proper detective. Hercule Poirot is educating you in how to use the little grey cells.'

'Did you think of that — the food discrepancy?'

'*Bien sûr.* Why did I not ask Jennie Hobbs to account for it, when I asked her to explain many

291

other inconsistencies? I did not do so because I wanted her to imagine that we believed her story by the time we left her. Therefore, I could not ask her a question for which she would be unable to provide an answer.'

'Poirot! Samuel Kidd's face!'

'Where, *mon ami?*'

'No, I don't mean that I can see his face, I mean . . . Remember the first time you met him at Pleasant's, he had cut himself shaving? There was a cut on a small shaved area of his cheek, while the rest was covered by a growth of beard?'

Poirot nodded.

'What if that was not a shaving cut that we saw but a cut from a sharp branch of a tree? What if Samuel Kidd cut himself on his way into or out of the open window of Room 238? He knew that he was going to approach us with his lie about having seen Nancy Ducane run from the hotel, and he didn't want us to connect the mysterious scratch on his face with the tree outside Richard Negus's open window, so he shaved a small patch of skin.'

'Knowing that we would assume he had started to shave, cut himself badly and stopped,' said Poirot. 'And then, when he visited me at the lodging house, his beard had disappeared and his face was covered in cuts: *to remind me that he cannot shave without lacerating his face. Eh, bien*, if I believe this then I will assume that every cut I see upon his face is caused by shaving.'

'Why don't you sound more excited?' I asked.

'Because it is so obvious. I arrived at this conclusion more than two hours ago.'

'Oh.' I felt deflated. 'Wait a minute — if Samuel Kidd scratched his face on the tree outside Richard Negus's open window, that means he *might* have climbed into the room and got his hands on the keys to 121 and 317. Doesn't it?'

'There is no time to discuss the meaning now,' said Poirot in a stern voice. 'We arrive at the station. It is clear from your question that you have not listened carefully.'

★   ★   ★

Dr Ambrose Flowerday turned out to be a tall, thick-set man of around fifty with wiry dark hair that was greying at the temples. His shirt was crumpled and missing a button. He had passed on instructions for us to go to the vicarage, and so that was where we were, standing in a chilly hall with a high ceiling and a splintering wooden floor.

The whole place seemed to have been given over to Dr Flowerday, for him to use as a temporary hospital for one patient. The door had been opened by a nurse in uniform. Under different circumstances I might have been curious about this arrangement, but all I could think of was poor Margaret Ernst.

'How is she?' I asked, once the introductions were over.

The doctor's face twisted in anguish. Then he composed himself. 'I am allowed to say only that she is doing well in the circumstances.'

'Allowed by whom?' asked Poirot.

'Margaret. She will not tolerate defeatist talk.'

'And is it true, what she asks you to tell us?'

After a short pause, Dr Flowerday gave a small nod. 'Most people would not survive for this long after such an assault. Margaret has a strong constitution and a strong mind. It was a serious attack, but, damn it, I shall keep her alive if it kills me.'

'What happened to her?'

'Two thoroughly bad pennies from the top end of the village came to the churchyard in the middle of the night and . . . well, they did things to the Ives' grave that do not bear repeating. Margaret heard them. Even in her sleep she is vigilant. She heard metal smashing against stone. When she ran out to try to stop them, they attacked her with a spade they had brought with them. They didn't care if they beat her to death! That much was obvious to the village constable, when he arrested them some hours later.'

Poirot said, 'Pardon me, Doctor. You *know* who did this to Mrs Ernst? The two bad pennies that you refer to . . . they confessed?'

'Proudly,' said Dr Flowerday through gritted teeth.

'So they are arrested?'

'Oh, yes, the police have got them.'

'Who are they?' I asked.

'Frederick and Tobias Clutton, father and son. Drunken good-for-nothings, the pair of them.'

I wondered if the son was the ne'er-do-well I had seen drinking with Walter Stoakley in the King's Head. (I later discovered that I was right: he was.)

'Margaret got in their way, they said. As for

294

the Ives' grave . . . ' Dr Flowerday turned to me. 'Please understand that I am not blaming you for this, but your visit stirred things up. You were seen going to Margaret's cottage. All the villagers know where she stands with regard to the Ives. They knew that the story you were hearing inside that house was one that painted Patrick Ive not as a promiscuous charlatan but as the victim of a sustained campaign of cruelty and slander — theirs. It made them want to punish Patrick all over again. He is dead and beyond their reach, so they desecrated his grave instead. Margaret has always said it would happen one day. She sits by her window day in and day out, hoping to catch them and stop them. Do you know she never met Patrick or Frances Ive? Did she tell you that? They were *my* friends. Their tragedy was my sorrow, the injustice of it my obsession. Yet, from the first, they mattered to Margaret. It horrified her to think that such a thing could happen in her husband's new parish. She made sure that it mattered to him, too. It was the most incredible good fortune, that Margaret and Charles came to Great Holling. One couldn't wish for a better ally. Allies,' Dr Flowerday corrected himself.

'May we speak to Margaret?' I asked. If she was about to die — and I had the sense that she was, in spite of the doctor's determination that she should not — then I wanted to hear what she had to say while there was still time.

'Of course,' said Ambrose Flowerday. 'She would be furious with me for keeping you from her.'

Poirot, the nurse and I followed him up a flight of uncarpeted wooden stairs and into one of the bedrooms. I tried not to show my shock when I saw bandages, blood, and the purple and blue welts and lumps that covered Margaret Ernst's face. Tears came to my eyes.

'Are they here, Ambrose?' she asked.

'Yes.'

'*Bonjour*, Madame Ernst. I am Hercule Poirot. Words cannot express how sorry I am — '

'Please call me Margaret. Is Mr Catchpool with you?'

'Yes, I'm here,' I managed to say. How any man or men could inflict such injury upon a woman was quite beyond me. It was not the act of human beings but of beasts. Monsters.

'Are you both striving for polite expressions that won't alarm me?' Margaret asked. 'My eyes are swollen shut, so I can't see your faces. I expect Ambrose has told you I'm about to die?'

'*Non, madame*. He has said no such thing.'

'Hasn't he? Well, it's what he believes.'

'Margaret, dear — '

'He is wrong. I am far too angry to die.'

'You have something that you wish to tell us?' Poirot asked.

A peculiar noise emerged from Margaret's throat. It had a derisory quality. 'Yes, I do, but I wish you wouldn't ask me so soon and so urgently, as if there's a scrambling hurry about it all — as if my next breath might be my last! Ambrose has given you quite the wrong impression if that is what you believe. Now, I need to rest. I shall no doubt have to defend

296

lied for Patrick and Frances's sake, but she is more cautious than I am. She feared that I would boast to you of my defiant act, as I just have.' He smiled sadly. 'I know that I must now face the consequences. I will lose my medical practice and possibly my liberty, and perhaps I deserve to. The lie I told killed Charles.'

'Margaret's late husband?' I said.

The doctor nodded. 'Margaret and I didn't care if people whispered 'Liar!' after us in the street, but Charles minded dreadfully. His health deteriorated. If I had been less determined to fight the evil in the village, Charles might still be alive today.'

'Where are the Ives' suicide notes now?' Poirot asked.

'I don't know. I gave them to Margaret sixteen years ago. I haven't asked her about them since.'

'I burned them.'

'Margaret.' Ambrose Flowerday hurried to her side. 'You're awake.'

'I remember every word of both of them. It seemed important to remember, so I made sure I did.'

'Margaret, you must rest. Talking is tiring for you.'

'Patrick's note said to tell Nancy that he loved her and always would. I didn't tell her. How could I, without revealing that Ambrose had lied about cause of death at the inquest? But . . . now that the truth is out, you must tell her, Ambrose. Tell her what Patrick wrote.'

'I will. Don't worry, Margaret. I will take care of everything.'

299

'I *do* worry. You have not told Monsieur Poirot and Mr Catchpool about Harriet's threats, after Patrick and Frances were buried. Tell them now.' Her eyes closed. Seconds later, she was fast asleep again.

'What were these threats, Doctor?' Poirot asked.

'Harriet Sippel arrived at the vicarage one day, trailing a mob of ten or twenty behind her, and announced that the people of Great Holling intended to dig up the bodies of Patrick and Frances Ive. As suicides, she said, they had no right to be buried in consecrated ground — it was God's law. Margaret came to the door and told her that she was speaking nonsense: it used to be the law of the Christian Church, but it wasn't any longer. It had not been since the 1880s, and this was 1913. Once dead, a person's soul is entrusted to the mercy of God and that person is beyond earthly judgement. Harriet's pious little helper Ida Gransbury insisted that if it was wrong for a suicide to be buried in a churchyard before 1880, then it must still be wrong. God does not change his mind about what constitutes acceptable behaviour, she said. When he heard about this unconscionable outburst from his fiancée, Richard Negus ended his engagement to the pitiless harridan and left for Devon. It was the best decision he ever made.'

'Where did Frances and Patrick Ive find the Abrin that they used to kill themselves?' Poirot asked.

Ambrose Flowerday looked surprised. 'That's

300

a question I wasn't expecting. Why do you ask?'

'Because I wonder if it originated with you?'

'It did.' The doctor flinched, as if in pain. 'Frances stole it from my house. I spent some years working in the tropics and I brought two vials of the poison back with me. I was a young man then, but I planned to use it later in life if I needed to — in the event of a painful illness from which I would not recover. Having observed the agonies endured by some of my patients, I wanted to be able to spare myself that sort of ordeal. I didn't know that Frances knew I had two vials of lethal poison in my cupboard, but she must have searched it one day, looking for something that would serve her purpose. As I said before, perhaps I do deserve to be punished. Whatever Margaret says, I have always felt that Frances's killer was not Frances but me.'

'*Non*. You must not blame yourself,' said Poirot. 'If she was determined to take her own life, she would have found a way to do so with or without your vial of Abrin.'

I waited for Poirot to move on to a question about cyanide, since a doctor with access to one poison might well have access to two, but instead he said, 'Dr Flowerday, I do not intend to tell anybody that the deaths of Patrick and Frances Ive were not accidental. You will remain at liberty and able to continue in your medical practice.'

'What?' Flowerday looked from Poirot to me in astonishment. I nodded my consent, while resenting Poirot's failure to ask my opinion. I, after all, was the one whose job it was to uphold the law of the land.

Had he consulted me, I would have urged him not to expose the lie that Ambrose Flowerday had told.

'Thank you. You are a fair-minded and generous-spirited man.'

'*Pas du tout.*' Poirot fended off Flowerday's gratitude. 'I have one more question for you, Doctor: are you married?'

'No.'

'If you will permit me to say so, I think you ought to be.'

I breathed in sharply.

'You are a bachelor, are you not? And Margaret Ernst has been a widow for some years. It is evident that you love her very much, and I believe that she returns your affection. Why do you not ask her to be your wife?'

Dr Flowerday seemed to be trying to blink away his surprise, poor chap. Finally he said, 'Margaret and I agreed long ago that we would never marry. It wouldn't have been right. After what we did — necessary as we both felt it was — and after what happened to poor Charles . . . well, it would have been improper for us to allow ourselves to be happy in that way. As happy as we would have been together. There has been too much suffering.'

I was watching Margaret, and saw her eyelids flutter open.

'Enough suffering,' she said in a weak voice.

Flowerday covered his mouth with his clenched fist. 'Oh, Margaret,' he said. 'Without you, what is the point?'

Poirot stood up. 'Doctor,' he said in his most

stringent voice. 'Mrs Ernst is of the opinion that she will survive. It would be a great shame if your foolish resolve to eschew the possibility of true happiness were to survive also. Two good people who love each other should not be apart when there is no need to be.'

With that, he marched from the room.

★ ★ ★

I wanted to make a swift escape back to London, but Poirot said that first he needed to see Patrick and Frances Ive's grave. 'I would like to lay some flowers, *mon ami*.'

'It's February, old chap. Where are you going to find flowers?'

This prompted a lengthy grumble about the English climate.

The gravestone lay on its side, covered in mud smears. There were several overlapping foot-prints in the mud, suggesting that those two feral brutes Frederick and Tobias Clutton had jumped up and down on the stone after digging it out of the ground with their spade.

Poirot took off his gloves. He bent down and, using the forefinger of his right hand, drew the outline of a large flower — like a child's drawing — in the earth. '*Voilà*,' he said. 'A flower in February, in spite of the appalling English weather.'

'Poirot, you've got mud on your finger!'

'*Oui*. Why do you sound surprised? Even the famous Hercule Poirot cannot create a flower in mud while keeping his hand clean. It will come off, the dirt — do not fear. There is always the manicure, later.'

'Of course there is.' I smiled. 'I'm glad to hear you so sanguine on the subject.'

Poirot had produced a handkerchief. I watched in fascination as he used it to wipe the footprints from the gravestone, huffing and puffing as he rocked back and forth, nearly losing his balance once or twice.

'There!' he declared. '*C'est mieux!*'

'Yes. Better.'

Poirot frowned down at his feet. 'There are sights so dispiriting that one wishes one did not have to see them,' he said quietly. 'We must trust that Patrick and Frances Ive rest in peace together.'

It was the word 'together' that did it. It brought to mind another word: apart. My face must have been a picture.

'Catchpool? Something is the matter with you — what is it?'

Together. Apart.

Patrick Ive was in love with Nancy Ducane, but in death, in their shared grave, he was with the woman to whom he had rightfully belonged in life: his wife Frances. Had his soul found peace, or was it pining for Nancy? Did Nancy ask herself this? Did she wish, loving Patrick as she did, that the dead could speak to the living? Anybody who had loved and lost someone precious to them might wish that . . .

'Catchpool! What is in your mind at this moment? I must know.'

'Poirot, I've had the most preposterous idea.

304

Let me tell you, quickly, so that you can tell me I am crazy.' I babbled excitedly until he had heard the whole of it. 'I'm wrong, of course,' I concluded.

'Oh, no, no, no. No, *mon ami*, you are not wrong.' He gasped. 'Of *course!* How, *how* did I fail to see it? *Mon Dieu!* Do you see what this means? What we must now conclude?'

'No, I'm afraid I don't.'

'Ah. *Dommage*.'

'For pity's sake, Poirot! It's hardly fair to make me lay out my idea and then withhold yours.'

'There is not time for discussion now. We must hurry back to London, where you will pack up the clothes and personal effects of Harriet Sippel and Ida Gransbury.'

'What?' I frowned in confusion, wondering if my ears were deceiving me.

'*Oui*. Mr Negus has already had his belongings removed by his brother, if you recall.'

'I do, but . . . '

'Do not argue, Catchpool. It will take you hardly any time to pack two ladies' cases with the clothes in their hotel rooms. Ah, now I see it, I see *all* of it, at last. All the solutions to the many little puzzles, they are in place! You know, it is rather like the crossword puzzle.'

'Please don't make the comparison,' I said. 'You're likely to put me off my favourite pastime if you compare it to this case.'

'Only when one sees all the answers together does one know for certain that one is right,' Poirot went on, ignoring me. 'Until then, for as long as some answers are missing, one may yet discover that a detail that seems to fit in fact does not fit at all.'

'In that case, think of me as an empty crossword grid, with no words filled in,' I said.

'Not for long, my friend — not for long. Poirot, he will require the dining room of the Bloxham Hotel one last time!'

22

The Monogram Murders

The following afternoon at a quarter past four, Poirot and I stood at one end of the Bloxham Hotel's dining room and waited as people took their places at the various tables. The hotel staff had all arrived promptly at four o'clock as Luca Lazzari had promised they would. I smiled at the familiar faces: John Goode, Thomas Brignell, Rafal Bobak. They acknowledged me with nervous nods.

Lazzari was standing by the door, throwing his arms around in wild gesticulation as he spoke to Constable Stanley Beer. Beer kept having to duck and step back in order to avoid being clonked in the face. I was too far away to catch most of what Lazzari was saying, and the room was too noisy, but I did hear 'these Monogram Murders' more than once.

Was that what Lazzari had decided to call them? Everybody else in the country was calling them by the name the newspapers had chosen from the first day: the Bloxham Hotel Murders. Evidently Lazzari had come up with a more imaginative alternative, in the hope that his beloved establishment would not be forever tarnished by association. I found this so transparent as to be irritating, but I knew that my mood was coloured by my failure on the

307

suitcase-packing front. I am easily capable of packing for myself before a trip, but that is because I take as little as possible when I travel. Ida Gransbury's clothes must have expanded during her short stay at the Bloxham; I had spent an infuriating while pressing and leaning down with my full weight, and still I could not fit many of her clothes in her case. No doubt there is a feminine knack to these things that oafish men like me will never master. I was exceedingly relieved to be told by Poirot that I must stop trying and make my way to the hotel's dining room at the appointed hour of four o'clock.

Samuel Kidd, in a smart grey flannel suit, had arrived with a pale-faced Jennie Hobbs on his arm at five minutes past four, followed two minutes later by Henry Negus, Richard's brother, and ten minutes after that by a group of four: a man and three women, one of whom was Nancy Ducane. The skin around her tear-filled eyes was red raw. As she entered the room, she tried unsuccessfully to conceal her face behind a scarf made of diaphanous material.

I muttered to Poirot, 'She doesn't want people to see that she has been crying.'

'No,' he said. 'She wears the scarf because she hopes not to be recognized, not because she is ashamed of her tears. There is nothing reprehensible in allowing a feeling to show outwardly, contrary to what you Englishmen seem to believe.'

I had no wish to be diverted to the topic of myself when I had been talking about Nancy Ducane, in whom I was far more interested. 'I suppose the last thing she wants is to be set upon by eager fans, all falling in an adoring heap at her faraway feet.'

Poirot, as a somewhat famous person himself who should have liked nothing better than a pile of admirers draped all over his spats, looked as if he was about to take issue with this point as well.

I distracted him with a question: 'Who are the three people who came in with Nancy Ducane?'

'Lord St John Wallace, Lady Louisa Wallace and their servant Dorcas.' He looked at his watch and tutted. 'We are fifteen minutes late in starting! Why cannot people arrive on time?'

I noticed that both Thomas Brignell and Rafal Bobak had risen to their feet, both apparently wanting to speak, although the proceedings were not yet officially underway.

'Please, gentlemen, sit down!' Poirot said.

'But Mr Poirot, sir, I must — '

'But I — '

'Do not agitate yourselves, *messieurs*. These things that you are so determined to tell Poirot? You may be assured that he knows them already, and that he is about to tell you, and everybody gathered here, those very same things. Be patient, I beg of you.'

Mollified, Bobak and Brignell sat down. I was surprised to see the black-haired woman sitting next to Brignell reach for his hand. He squeezed hers, and they allowed their hands to remain entwined. I saw the look that passed between them, and it told me all I needed to know: they were sweethearts. This, however, was definitely not the woman I had seen Brignell canoodling with in the hotel gardens.

Poirot whispered in my ear, 'The woman Brignell was kissing in the garden, beside the wheelbarrow — she had fair hair, *non*? The woman with the brown coat?' He gave me an enigmatic smile.

To the crowd, he said, 'Now that everyone has arrived, please may I ask for silence and your full attention? Thank you. I am obliged to you all.'

As Poirot spoke, I cast my eyes over the faces in the room. Was that . . . Oh, my goodness! It was! Fee Spring, the waitress from Pleasant's, was sitting at the back of the room. Like Nancy Ducane, she had made an effort to cover her face — with a fancy sort of hat — and like Nancy she had failed. She winked at me as if to say that it served me and Poirot right for stopping in for a drink and telling her where we were going next. Confound it all, why couldn't the little minx stay in the coffee house where she belonged?

'I must ask for your forbearance today,' said Poirot. 'There is much that you need to know and understand that you do not at present.'

Yes, I thought, that summed up my position perfectly. I knew scarcely more than the Bloxham's chambermaids and cooks did. Perhaps even Fee Spring had a stronger grasp on the facts than I; Poirot had probably invited her to this grand event he had arranged. I must say, I did not and never would understand why he required such a sizeable audience. It was not a theatrical production. When I solved a crime — and I had been lucky enough to do so several times without Poirot's help — I simply presented my conclusions to my boss and then arrested the miscreant in question.

I wondered, too late, if I ought to have demanded that Poirot tell me everything first, before staging this spectacle. Here I was, supposedly in charge of the investigation, and I had no inkling of what solution to the mystery he was about to present.

'Whatever he is about to say, please let it be brilliant,' I prayed. 'If he gets it right and I am standing by his side, no one will suspect that I was once, and so late in the day, as unenlightened as I am now.'

'The story is too long for me to tell it without help,' Poirot addressed the room. 'My voice, I would wear it out. Therefore I must ask you to listen to two other speakers. First, Mrs Nancy Ducane, the famous portrait painter who has done us the honour of joining us here today, will speak.'

This was a surprise — though not to Nancy herself, I noticed. From her face, it was apparent that she had known Poirot would call upon her. The two of them had arranged it in advance.

Awed whispers filled the room as Nancy, with her scarf wrapped round her face, came to stand beside me where everyone could see her. 'You've blown her cover with the adoring fans,' I whispered to Poirot.

'*Oui.*' He smiled. 'Yet still she keeps the scarf around her face as she speaks.'

Everyone listened, rapt, as Nancy Ducane told the story of Patrick Ive: her forbidden love for him, her illicit visits to the vicarage at night, the wicked lies about him taking money from parishioners and, in exchange, passing on communications from their dead loved ones. She did not mention Jennie Hobbs by name when she referred to the rumour that had started all the trouble.

Nancy described how she finally spoke out, at the King's Head Inn, and told the villagers of Great Holling about her love affair with Patrick Ive, which was not chaste, though she had pretended at the time that it was. Her voice shook as she told of the tragic deaths by poisoning of Patrick and Frances Ive. I noted that that was all she said about the cause of death: poisoning. She did not specify accident or suicide. I wondered if Poirot had asked her not to, for the sake of Ambrose Flowerday and Margaret Ernst.

Before sitting down, Nancy said, 'I am as devoted to Patrick now as I ever was. I will never stop loving him. One day, he and I will be reunited.'

'Thank you, Madame Ducane.' Poirot bowed. 'I must now without delay tell you something that I have recently discovered, for I believe it will be a comfort to you. Before his death, Patrick wrote . . . a letter. In it, he asked for you to be told that he loved you and always would.'

'Oh!' Nancy clapped her hands over her mouth and blinked many times. 'Monsieur Poirot, you cannot imagine how happy you have made me.'

'Au contraire, madame. I can imagine only too well. The loving message, conveyed after the death of the loved one . . . It is an echo, is it not, of the untrue rumours about Patrick Ive: that he conveyed messages from beyond the grave? And who, I ask you, would not wish to receive such a message from one they have loved very much and lost?'

Nancy Ducane made her way back to her chair and sat down. Louisa Wallace patted her arm.

'And now,' said Poirot, 'another woman who knew and loved Patrick Ive will speak: his former servant, Jennie Hobbs. Mademoiselle Hobbs?'

Jennie stood up and went to stand where Nancy had stood. She too looked unsurprised to be asked. In a shaking voice, she said. 'I loved Patrick Ive as much as Nancy did. But he did not reciprocate my love. To him, I was no more than a loyal servant. It was I who started the wicked rumours about him. I told an unforgivable lie. I was jealous because he loved Nancy and not me. Although I did not kill him with my own hands, I believe that, in slandering him as I did, I caused his death. I and three others: Harriet Sippel, Richard Negus and Ida Gransbury, the three people who were murdered at this hotel. All four of us later came to regret what we had done. We regretted it profoundly. And so we made a plan to put things right.'

I watched the astonished faces of the Bloxham Hotel staff as Jennie described the same plan that she had described to Poirot and me at Samuel Kidd's house, as well as how and why it went wrong. Louisa Wallace squealed in horror at the part about framing Nancy Ducane for the three murders and making sure she hanged.

'Arranging for an innocent woman to be put to death for three murders she didn't commit is not righting a wrong!' St John Wallace called out. 'That is depravity!'

Nobody disagreed with him, at least not out loud. Fee Spring, I noticed, did not look as shocked as most people did. She seemed to be listening intently.

'I never wanted to frame Nancy,' said Jennie. 'Never! You may believe that or not, as you wish.'

'Mr Negus,' said Poirot. 'Mr *Henry* Negus — do you think it likely that your brother Richard would make such a plan as you have heard?'

Henry Negus stood up. 'I would not like to say, Monsieur Poirot. The Richard I knew would not have dreamt of killing anyone, of course, but the Richard who came to live with me in Devon sixteen years ago *was not the Richard I knew*. Oh, the physicality of him was the same, but he was not the same man on the inside. I'm afraid to say that I never got to know the man that he had become. I cannot, therefore, comment on how likely he was to behave in a particular way.'

'Thank you, Mr Negus. And thank you, Miss Hobbs,' Poirot added with a marked absence of enthusiasm. 'You may now sit down.'

He turned to the crowd. 'So you see, ladies and gentlemen, that Miss Hobbs' story, if true, leaves us with no murderer to arrest and convict. Ida Gransbury killed Harriet Sippel — with her permission. Richard Negus killed Ida Gransbury — again, with her permission — and then killed himself when Jennie Hobbs did not arrive to kill

314

him as she was supposed to. He took his own life and made it look like murder by first locking his door and hiding the key behind a loose tile in the fireplace, and then opening the window. The police were supposed to think that the murderer — Nancy Ducane — took the key with her and escaped through the open window and down a tree. *But there was no murderer*, according to Jennie Hobbs — nobody who killed without permission of the victim!'

Poirot looked around the room. 'No murderer,' he repeated. 'However, even if this were true, there would still be two criminals who are alive and deserving of punishment: Jennie Hobbs and Samuel Kidd, who conspired to frame Nancy Ducane.'

'I hope you're going to lock them both up, Monsieur Poirot!' called out Louisa Wallace.

'I do not lock or unlock the prison gate, madame. That is the job of my friend Catchpool and his associates. I unlock only the secrets and the truth. Mr Samuel Kidd, please stand.'

Kidd, looking uncomfortable, rose to his feet.

'Your part in the plan was to place a note on the front desk of this hotel, was it not? 'MAY THEY NEVER REST IN PEACE. 121. 238. 317.''

'Yes, sir. It was, like Jennie said.'

'You had been given the note by Jennie in good time to do this?'

'Yes. She gave it to me earlier in the day. In the morning.'

'And you were to put it on the desk when?'

'Shortly after eight o'clock in the evening, like

Jennie said. As soon as I could after eight, but first making sure no one was close enough to see me put it there.'

'You had this instruction from whom?' Poirot asked.

'Jennie.'

'And also from Jennie you had the instruction to plant the room keys in the pocket of Nancy Ducane?'

'That's right,' said Kidd in a sullen voice. 'I don't know why you're asking me all this when she's only just now finished telling you.'

'I will explain. *Bon*. According to the original plan, as we have all heard Jennie Hobbs say, the keys to all three rooms — 121, 238 and 317 — would be removed from Richard Negus's room by Jennie after she had killed him, and given to Samuel Kidd, who would place them somewhere that would implicate Nancy Ducane — her coat pocket, as it turned out. *But Jennie Hobbs did not go to the Bloxham Hotel at all on the night of the murders, according to her story.* She was not brave enough. I therefore ask you, Mr Kidd: how did you get hold of the keys to rooms 121 and 317?'

'How did I . . . how did I get hold of the two keys?'

'Yes. That is the question I asked you. Please answer it.'

'I . . . well, if you must know, I got hold of those keys thanks to my own wits. I had a word in the ear of a member of the hotel staff and asked if they'd be good enough to let me have a master key. And they did. I then returned it to

316

them, once I'd used it. All discreet, like.'

I was standing close enough to Poirot to hear the noise of disapproval that he made. 'Which member of staff, monsieur? They are all here in this room. Point to the person who gave you this master key.'

'I can't remember who it was. A man — that's all I can tell you. I've a pitiful memory for faces.' As he said this, Kidd rubbed the red scratches on his own face with his thumb and forefinger.

'So, with this master key you let yourself into all three rooms?'

'No, only Room 238. That's where all the keys ought to have ended up, waiting for Jennie to take them, but I could only find two. As you've said, one was hidden behind a tile in the fireplace. I didn't like to stay and search the room for the third key, what with Mr Negus's body being there and all.'

'You are lying,' Poirot told him. 'It does not matter. You will discover, in due course, that you cannot lie your way out of this predicament. But let us move on. No, do not sit down. I have another question — for you and Jennie Hobbs. It was part of the plan, was it not, that Jennie should bring her tale of mortal fear to me at Pleasant's Coffee House at just after half past seven on the night of the murders?'

'Yes,' said Jennie, looking not at Poirot but at Samuel Kidd.

'Forgive me, then, but I do not understand something important. You were too afraid to go through with the plan, you say, and so you did

317

not arrive at the hotel at six o'clock. Yet the plan went ahead without you, it seems. The only deviation was that Richard Negus killed himself, yes? He put the poison into his own drink, rather than having it put in his drink by you. Is everything that I have said so far correct, mademoiselle?'

'Yes, it is.'

'In that case, if the only altered detail was Richard Negus killing himself instead of being killed, we can assume that the deaths took place as planned: after the ordering of the sandwiches and scones, between a quarter past seven and eight o'clock. Yes, Miss Hobbs?'

'That is right,' said Jennie. She did not sound quite as certain as she had a moment ago.

'Then how, might I ask, can it ever have been part of the plan for you to kill Richard Negus? You have told us that you intended to find me at Pleasant's Coffee House shortly after half past seven on that same night, knowing I would be there for my regular Thursday evening dinner. It is impossible to get from the Bloxham Hotel to Pleasant's Coffee House in less than half an hour. It cannot be done, no matter how one travels. So, even if Ida Gransbury had killed Harriet Sippel and Richard Negus had killed Ida Gransbury as soon as was possible after a quarter past seven, there would not have been time for you to kill Richard Negus in Room 238 after that time, and still arrive at Pleasant's when you did. Are we supposed to believe that, in all the meticulous planning that you undertook, none of you thought of this practical impossibility?'

318

Jennie's face had turned white. I expect mine had too, though I could not see it myself.

It was such an obvious flaw in her account that Poirot had pointed out, and yet I had failed to spot it. It simply had not occurred to me.

23

The Real Ida Gransbury

Samuel Kidd chuckled, turning round so that more people could see him. He said, 'Mr Poirot, for a man who takes pride in his powers of detection, you're not the sharpest of instruments, are you? I've heard Jennie talk about this more often than you have, I think I can safely say. The plan was not for the killings to take place after a quarter past seven. I don't know where you've caught hold of that idea. The plan was for them to happen just after six o'clock. The ordering of food at a quarter past seven wasn't part of it either.'

'That's right,' said Jennie. Offered a way out of the trap by her quick-thinking former fiancé, she appeared to have recovered her composure. 'I can only conclude that my failure to arrive at six as agreed caused a delay. The others would have wanted to discuss my failure to present myself. I should have, in their place. The discussion about what to do might have taken some time.'

'Ah, *bien sûr*. You did not correct me a few moments ago, however, when I asserted that the deaths took place as planned: between a quarter past seven and eight o'clock. Neither did you say that the ordering of the very late afternoon tea was not part of the plan.'

'I'm sorry. I should have corrected you,' said

Jennie. 'I'm . . . I mean, this is all rather overwhelming.'

'You now say that the plan was for the three killings to take place at six o'clock?'

'Yes, and all be done by fifteen minutes before seven so that I could get to Pleasant's by half past.'

'In that case, I have a different question for you, mademoiselle. Why did the plan require Mr Kidd to wait *a full hour* once Harriet, Ida and Richard were all dead, and once you had left the hotel, before placing the note on the front desk? Why was it not agreed that Mr Kidd should do this at, for example, a quarter past seven, or even half past seven? Why eight o'clock?'

Jennie recoiled as if from a blow. 'Why *not* eight o'clock?' she said defiantly. 'What was the harm in waiting a while?

'You ask some daft questions, Mr Poirot,' said Sam Kidd.

'No harm whatever in waiting, mademoiselle — I agree entirely. Therefore we must ask ourselves: why leave a note at all? Why not wait for the hotel maids to find the three bodies the following morning? Jennie? Do not look at Samuel Kidd. Look at Hercule Poirot! Answer the question.'

'I . . . I don't know! I think maybe Richard . . . '

'No! Not maybe Richard!' Poirot spoke over her. 'If you will not answer my question, allow me to do so. You told Mr Kidd to leave the note on the desk just after eight because it was *always part of the plan for the murders to appear to*

321

have been committed between a quarter past seven and eight o'clock!'

Poirot turned once again to the silent wide-eyed crowd. 'Let us think about the afternoon tea for three that was ordered, and delivered to Room 317 — Ida Gransbury's room. Let us imagine that our three voluntary victims, puzzled by the absence of Jennie Hobbs, were unsure what to do, and so went to Ida Gransbury's room to discuss the matter. Catchpool, if you were about to allow yourself to be executed for a past sin, would you order scones and cakes immediately beforehand?'

'No. I would be too nervous to eat or drink anything.'

'Perhaps our trio of executioners thought it important to keep up their strength for the important task ahead,' Poirot speculated. 'Then, when the food arrived, they could not bring themselves to eat it. But to where did all this food disappear?'

'Are you asking me?' said Jennie. 'I'm afraid I don't know, since I wasn't there.'

'To return to the timing of these killings,' said Poirot. 'The police doctor's view was that death occurred in all three cases between four and half past eight. Circumstantial evidence later narrowed this down to between a quarter past seven and ten past eight. *Eh bien*, let us examine that circumstantial evidence. The waiter Rafal Bobak saw all three victims alive at a quarter past seven when he made his delivery to Room 317, and Thomas Brignell saw Richard Negus alive at half past seven in the hotel lobby, when Negus

322

complimented Brignell on his efficiency, asked him to make sure the tea and cakes were put on his bill, and requested a sherry. So it seems that none of the killings can have happened before fifteen minutes past seven, and that the murder of Richard Negus cannot have happened before half past.

'However, there are a handful of details that do not fit to make the neat picture. First, there is the disappearing food that we know was not eaten by Harriet Sippel, Ida Gransbury and Richard Negus. I do not believe that anyone about to kill for the first time would imagine he might first want to eat a scone. So why order food that one has no intention of eating *unless to establish in the eyes of a witness that you are alive at a quarter past seven?* And why should it be necessary for our three victims to be seen alive at that specific time? I can think of just one possible explanation that is consistent with Jennie Hobbs' story: if our conspirators knew, somehow, that Nancy Ducane had no credible alibi for the hour between a quarter past seven and a quarter past eight, they might have wished to make it look as if that was when the killings took place. But Nancy Ducane has a very solid alibi for that hour, does she not, Lady Wallace?'

Louisa Wallace rose to her feet. 'Yes, she does. She was with me and my husband until at around ten o'clock that evening, dining in our home.'

'*Merci beaucoup, madame. Alors,* I can think of only one reason why it should be of such vital importance to create the appearance of the three deaths having taken place between a quarter past seven and ten past eight: between those times, Jennie Hobbs has an unshakeable alibi. I, Hercule Poirot, know perfectly well that she cannot have been at the Bloxham Hotel then. She was with me at Pleasant's Coffee House between thirty-five and fifty minutes past seven, and I have already spoken about the travelling times involved.

'I put all this together with my conviction that the three deaths did not occur between a quarter past seven and ten minutes past eight, and I begin to wonder: why go to such trouble to make it look as if Jennie Hobbs could not have committed these murders, *unless in fact she did commit them?*'

Jennie leapt up out of her chair. 'I didn't kill anybody! I swear I didn't! Of course they died between quarter past seven and eight o'clock — it's clear to everybody but you!'

'Sit down and remain silent, Miss Hobbs, unless I ask you a direct question,' said Poirot coldly.

Samuel Kidd's face was contorted with rage. 'You're making all this up, Mr Poirot! How do you know they didn't order that food because they were ravenous hungry? Just because you wouldn't be or I wouldn't be, doesn't mean they weren't.'

'Then why did they not eat the food, Mr Kidd?' I asked. 'Where did all those sandwiches and cakes vanish to?'

'The finest afternoon tea in all of London!' murmured Luca Lazzari.

324

'I will tell you where it went, Catchpool,' said Poirot. 'Our murderer made a mistake relating to the afternoon tea — one of many. If the food had been left on the plates in Room 317 for the police to find, there would have been no mystery. It would have been assumed that the killer arrived and interrupted the happy occasion before the feast could begin. But the killer thinks it will arouse suspicion, all that uneaten food. He does not want anyone to ask the question, 'Why order food and then not eat it?''

'Then what became of the food?' I asked. 'Where did it disappear to?'

'The conspirators removed it from the scene. Oh, yes, ladies and gentlemen, there was most assuredly a conspiracy to commit these three murders! In case I have not yet made it clear: Harriet Sippel, Ida Gransbury and Richard Negus were all dead long before a quarter past seven o'clock on the Thursday in question.'

Luca Lazzari stepped forward. 'Monsieur Poirot, please forgive my intrusion, but I must tell you that Rafal Bobak, my most loyal of waiters, would not lie. He saw the three murder victims alive and well when he delivered the food at a quarter past seven. Alive and well! You must be mistaken in what you are saying.'

'I am not mistaken. Though in one respect you are correct: your waiter Rafal Bobak is indeed an exemplary witness. He certainly saw three people in Room 317 when he delivered the afternoon tea — *but those people were not Harriet Sippel, Ida Gransbury and Richard Negus.*'

All over the room there were gasps of shock. I

gave one myself, wracking my brains to think who else the three might have been. Not Jennie Hobbs, for she would have been on her way to Pleasant's Coffee House at that time. Who, then?

'Poirot,' I said nervously. 'Is it your contention that three people *impersonated* the murder victims in order to make it look as if they were still alive when the food was delivered?'

'Not precisely, no. In fact, *two* people impersonated *two* of the murder victims. The third person, Ida Gransbury . . . she was not an impersonation, I am sorry to say. No, she was unfortunately the real Ida Gransbury. Mr Bobak, do you remember what you told me about what you overheard and what you witnessed when you took the afternoon tea to Room 317? I recall every word, since you have given me your account twice. Would you mind if I repeat it now for the benefit of us all?'

'No, sir, I would not.'

'*Merci*. You arrived to find the three murder victims apparently alive and talking about people they knew. You heard Harriet Sippel, or the woman later referred to as 'Harriet' by the man in the room, say, 'She had no choice, did she? She's no longer the one he confides in. He'd hardly be interested in her now — she's let herself go, and she's old enough to be his mother. No, if she wanted to find out what was going on in his mind, she had no choice but to receive the woman he *does* confide in, and talk to her.' This was when the man in the room broke off from attending to you and to the food, and said, 'Oh, Harriet, that's hardly fair. Ida's

326

easily shocked. Go easy on her.' Have I been accurate so far, Mr Bobak?'

'You have, sir.'

'You then told me that *either Ida or Harriet* said something else that you could not remember, and then the man you assumed was Richard Negus said, 'His mind? I'd argue he has no mind. And I dispute the old-enough-to-be-his-mother claim. I dispute it utterly.' At which point the woman going by the name of Harriet laughed and said, 'Well, neither of us can prove we're right, so let's agree to disagree!' Correct?'

Rafal Bobak confirmed that, once again, Poirot had got it right.

'*Bon*. May I suggest to you, Mr Bobak, that the remark made by *either Ida or Harriet* that you do not remember was in fact made by Harriet? I am convinced — absolutely convinced! — that you did not hear Ida Gransbury speak *one single word* while you were in that room, and that you did not see her face because she was sitting with her back facing the door.'

Bobak frowned, concentrating. Eventually he said, 'I think you are right, Mr Poirot. No, I did not see the face of Miss Ida Gransbury. And . . . I don't think I heard her speak at all, now that you bring it up.'

'You did not hear her speak, monsieur — for the simple reason that Ida Gransbury, propped up in a chair with her back facing the door, *was already murdered by a quarter past seven. The third person in Room 317 when you took up the afternoon tea was a dead woman!*'

24

The Blue Jug and Bowl

A few people cried out in alarm. There is a strong chance that I was one of them. It is strange: I have seen many dead bodies, thanks to my work for Scotland Yard, and have on occasion found the sight of them disturbing — yet no regular corpse could be as horrifying a prospect as a dead woman propped up as if alive and partaking of a jolly afternoon tea with friends.

Poor Rafal Bobak looked rather shivery and wobbly-lipped, no doubt reflecting that he had been closer to the monstrosity than any sane person would wish to be.

'This is why the food had to be delivered to Ida Gransbury's room,' Poirot went on. 'Richard Negus's room, 238, would have been the most convenient meeting point for the three victims, as it was on the second floor between the other two rooms. The afternoon tea would then have been added to Mr Negus's bill without his having to make a point of requesting this. But of course Room 238 could not be the room in which our three murder victims were seen alive by Rafal Bobak at a quarter past seven! That would have involved carrying Ida Gransbury's dead body from her room, 317, in which she had been killed some hours earlier, through the corridors of the hotel to Richard Negus's room.

It would have been too great a risk. Someone would almost certainly have seen.'

The shocked faces of the bewildered crowd were something to behold. I wondered if Luca Lazzari would soon be seeking new staff. I definitely had no intention of returning to the Bloxham once this unpleasant business was concluded, and I imagined that many in the room felt the same way.

Poirot proceeded with his explanations. 'Reflect, ladies and gentlemen, upon the munificence, the *largesse*, of Mr Richard Negus. Ah, how generous he was, insisting on paying for the food and the tea, also paying for Harriet and Ida each to travel alone to the hotel in a car. Why would they not come by train together and share a car to the hotel? And why should Richard Negus care so passionately about making sure that the bill for the food and beverages was sent to him, when he knew that he, Harriet Sippel and Ida Gransbury were all about to die?'

It was a very good question. All the points that Poirot was making were pertinent, and, moreover, were things I should have thought of myself. Somehow, I had failed to notice that so many aspects of Jennie Hobbs' story did not fit with the facts of the case. How could I have missed such glaring inconsistencies?

Poirot said, 'The man who impersonated Richard Negus at fifteen minutes past seven for the benefit of Rafal Bobak, and again at half past for the benefit of Mr Thomas Brignell, did not care about any bill! He knew that neither he nor his accomplices would have to pay it. He had been outside to dispose of the food. How did he transport it? In a suitcase! Catchpool — do you remember the tramp you saw near the hotel, when we took our trip on a bus? A tramp eating food from a suitcase, *non?* You described him as 'the tramp that got the cream'. Tell me, did you see him eating cream specifically?'

'Oh, my goodness. Yes, I did! He was eating a . . . a cake, with cream in it.'

Poirot nodded. 'From the suitcase he found discarded near the Bloxham Hotel, pleasingly full of afternoon tea for three! Now, here is another test for your memory, *mon ami:* do you remember telling me, on my first visit to the Bloxham, that Ida Gransbury had brought enough clothes with her to fill an entire wardrobe? And yet she had only one suitcase in her room — the same number as Richard Negus and Harriet Sippel, who had brought considerably fewer clothes with them. This afternoon, I asked you to pack Miss Gransbury's garments into her case, and what did you find?'

'They wouldn't fit,' I said, feeling like a prize chump. It seemed that I was doomed to feel idiotic in relation to Ida Gransbury's suitcase, but now for a different reason from before.

'You blamed yourself,' said Poirot. 'It is your preference to do so always, but in fact it was impossible for all the clothes to fit in, because they had been brought to the Bloxham in two suitcases. Even Hercule Poirot, he could not have made them fit!'

To the assembled hotel staff, he said, 'It was on his way back from disposing of the suitcase full of food that this man met the Bloxham's assistant clerk, Thomas Brignell, near the door to this room in which we are gathered. Why did he engage Brignell in discussion about the bill? For one reason only: *to impress upon Brignell that Richard Negus was still alive at half past seven.* Playing the role of Mr Negus, he said something inaccurate: that Negus could afford to pay, whereas Harriet Sippel and Ida Gransbury could not. This was not true! Henry Negus, Richard's brother, can confirm that Richard had no income and very little family money left. But the man impersonating Richard Negus did not know this. He assumed that since Richard Negus was a gentleman, once a lawyer by profession, he was bound to have plenty of money.

'When Henry Negus first spoke to Catchpool and myself, he told us that since moving to Devon, his brother Richard had been morose and doom-laden. He was a recluse with no appetite for life — correct, Mr Negus?'

'Yes, I'm afraid so,' said Henry Negus.

'A recluse! I ask you, does this sound like a man who would indulge himself in sherry and cake, and gossip in a cavalier fashion with two women in a fancy London hotel? No! The man who received the afternoon tea from Rafal Bobak, and for whom Thomas Brignell fetched the sherry, was not Richard Negus. This man, he complimented Mr Brignell on his efficiency and said something approximating the following: 'I know I can rely on you to sort this out, since you are so efficient — bill the food and beverages to me, Richard Negus, Room 238.' His words were

331

calculated to make Thomas Brignell believe that this man, this Richard Negus, was familiar with his level of efficiency, *and that therefore they must have encountered one another before.* Mr Brignell might feel a little guilty, perhaps, because he does not remember his previous dealings with Mr Negus — and he will resolve not to forget him again. He will remember from now on this man whom he has met twice. Naturally, working in a large London hotel, he meets people all the time, hundreds every day! It often happens, I am sure, that guests know his name and face while he has forgotten theirs — after all, they are simply, *en masse,* 'the guests'!'

'Excuse me, Monsieur Poirot, I beg your pardon.' Luca Lazzari hurried forward. 'Broadly speaking, you are quite right, but not, as chance would have it, in the case of Thomas Brignell. He has an exceptional memory for faces and names. Exceptional!'

Poirot smiled appreciatively. 'Is that so? *Bon.* Then I am right.'

'About what?' I asked.

'Be patient and listen, Catchpool. I will explain the sequence of events. The man impersonating Richard Negus was in the lobby of the hotel when Mr Negus checked in on Wednesday, the day before the murders. Probably he wanted to survey the territory in preparation for the role he was to play later. In any case, he saw Richard Negus arrive. How did he know it was Richard Negus? I will come back to that point. Suffice to say, he knew. He saw

332

Thomas Brignell undertake the necessary paperwork and then hand Mr Negus the key to his room. The following evening, after posing as Mr Negus to receive the afternoon tea and then going outside to dispose of it, this man is on his way back to Room 317 and he passes Thomas Brignell. He is a quick-thinking individual, and he sees a superb opportunity to consolidate the misleading of the police. He approaches Brignell and addresses him as if he, this impostor, were Richard Negus. He reminds Brignell of his name and alludes to a previous meeting.

'In fact, Thomas Brignell has never met this man before, but he remembers the name from when he gave the real Richard Negus his room key. Here, suddenly, is a man speaking to him in a confident, friendly and knowledgeable fashion and calling himself by that same name. Thomas Brignell *assumes that he must be Richard Negus*. He does not recall his face, but he blames only himself for this lapse.'

Thomas Brignell's face had turned as red as claret.

Poirot went on, 'The man impersonating Richard Negus asked for a glass of sherry. Why? To extend his encounter with Brignell a little, thereby imprinting it more strongly on the clerk's memory? To soothe agitated nerves with some liquor? Maybe for both of these reasons.

'Now, if you will permit me a small digression: in the remains of this glass of sherry, the poison cyanide was found, as it was in Harriet Sippel's and Ida Gransbury's cups of tea. But it was not the tea or the sherry that killed the three murder

333

victims. It cannot have been. These beverages arrived too late to kill, long after the murders had been committed. The sherry glass and the two teacups on the occasional tables next to the three bodies — they were essential for the staging of the crime scenes, to give the false impression that the killings must have occurred *after* a quarter past seven. In fact, the cyanide that killed Harriet Sippel, Ida Gransbury and Richard Negus was given to them much earlier and by another means. There is a water glass by the basin in each room of the hotel, is there not, Signor Lazzari?'

'*Si*, Monsieur Poirot. Yes, there is.'

'Then I expect that is how the poison was consumed: in water. The glass, in each case, was then carefully washed and replaced by the basin. Mr Brignell,' Poirot addressed him unexpectedly, causing the assistant clerk to duck in his seat as if someone had taken a shot at him. 'You do not like to speak in public, but you plucked up the courage to do so the first time we all gathered in this room. You told us of your encounter with Mr Negus in the corridor, but *you did not mention the sherry, even though I had specifically asked about it.* Later, you sought me out and added the detail about the sherry to your story. When I asked you why you did not originally mention it, you gave me no answer. I did not understand why, but my friend here, Catchpool — he said something most perceptive and illuminating. He said that *you are a conscientious man who would only withhold information in a murder enquiry if it caused you great personal embarrassment, and*

334

if you were sure it had nothing to do with the murder case. He hit upon the head of the nail with this assessment, did he not?'

Brignell gave a small nod.

'Allow me to explain.' Poirot raised his voice, though it was quite loud enough in the first place. 'When we met here in this room before, I asked if anybody had taken sherry to Mr Negus in his room. No one spoke up. Why did Thomas Brignell not say, 'I did not take it up to his room, but I did fetch for him a glass of sherry'? Poirot will tell you! He did not do so because he had doubts in his mind, and he did not want to risk saying something that was not true.

'Mr Brignell was the only member of the hotel staff to see any of the three murder victims more than once — or, to be more precise, *he had been led to believe* that he had seen Richard Negus more than once. He knew that he had given a glass of sherry to a man calling himself Richard Negus who behaved as if he had encountered him before, *but this man did not look like the Richard Negus that Thomas Brignell had met.* Remember, Mr Lazzari has told us that Mr Brignell has an excellent memory for faces as well as names. *That* is why he did not speak up when I asked about the sherry! He was distracted by his thoughts. A voice in his head whispered: 'It must have been him, the same man. But it was not him — I would have recognized him.'

'A few moments later, Mr Brignell said to himself, 'What kind of fool am I? Of course it was Richard Negus if he said that was his name!

For once my memory lets me down. And besides, the man sounded just like Mr Negus, with his educated English accent.' It would seem *incroyable* to the scrupulously honest Thomas Brignell that anyone should wish to impersonate another in order to trick him.

'After reaching the conclusion that the man must have been Richard Negus, Mr Brignell decides to stand up and tell me that he met Mr Negus in the corridor at half past seven on the night of the murders, but he is too embarrassed to mention the sherry, because he fears he will seem an imbecile for sitting in silence in response to my earlier question about the drink. I would surely ask, in front of everybody, 'Why did you not tell me this before?' and Mr Brignell would have been mortified to have to say, 'Because I was too busy wondering how Mr Negus came to have a different face the second time I encountered him.' Mr Brignell, can you confirm that what I am saying is true? There is no need to worry about looking like a fool. You were the opposite. It *was* a different face. It was a different man.'

'Thank goodness,' said Brignell. 'Everything you have said is absolutely correct, Mr Poirot.'

'*Bien sûr*,' said Poirot immodestly. 'Do not forget, ladies and gentlemen, that the same name does not necessarily mean the same person. When Signor Lazzari described to me the woman who took a room in this hotel using the name Jennie Hobbs, I thought that she was probably the same woman I had met at Pleasant's Coffee House. She sounded similar: fair hair, dark brown hat,

336

lighter brown coat. But two men who have each seen a woman fitting this description only once, they cannot be certain they have seen the same woman.

'This led me to ruminate. I already suspected that the dead Richard Negus whose body I saw and the living Richard Negus seen by Rafal Bobak and Thomas Brignell on the night of the murders were two different men. Then I remembered being told that on arrival at the Bloxham on the Wednesday, Richard Negus was dealt with by Thomas Brignell. If I was right in my suppositions, then this would have been a different Richard Negus, the real one. Suddenly I understood Thomas Brignell's predicament. How could he say publicly that this one man appeared to have two faces? Everyone would think him a lunatic!'

'You're the one that sounds half-crazed, Mr Poirot,' said Samuel Kidd with a sneer.

Poirot went on as if he hadn't spoken. 'This impostor might not have resembled Richard Negus in appearance, but I have no doubt that his voice was a perfect imitation. He is an excellent mimic — are you not, Mr Kidd?'

'Don't listen to this man! He's a liar!'

'No, Mr Kidd. It is you who are the liar. You have impersonated me more than once.'

Fee Spring stood up at the back of the room. 'You should all believe Mr Poirot,' she said. 'He's telling the truth, all right. I've heard Mr Samuel Kidd speak in his accent. With my eyes closed, I'd not know the difference.'

'It is not only with his voice that Samuel Kidd

lies,' said Poirot. 'The first time I met him, he presented himself as a man of below average intelligence and slovenly appearance: his shirt with the missing button and the stain. Also the incomplete beard — he had shaved only one small patch of his face. Mr Kidd, please tell everybody here why you went to great lengths to make yourself look so dishevelled the first time we met.'

Samuel Kidd stared resolutely ahead. He said nothing. His eyes were full of loathing.

'Very well, if you will not speak then I shall explain it myself. Mr Kidd cut his cheek while climbing down the tree outside the window of Room 238, Richard Negus's hotel room. A cut on the face of a smartly dressed man might stand out and invite questions, no? One who is careful about his appearance would surely not allow a razor to make an unsightly mark upon his face. Mr Kidd did not want me to think along these lines. He did not want me to wonder if he might recently have climbed out of an open window and down a tree, so he created the general unkempt appearance. He arranged himself to look like the sort of man who would be so careless as to cut himself while shaving and then, to avoid further cuts, walk around with half a beard on and half off! Such a chaotic man would *of course* use his shaving razor recklessly and do damage — this is what Poirot was supposed to believe, and it was what he did believe at first.'

'Hold on a minute, Poirot,' I said. 'If you're saying that Samuel Kidd climbed out of Richard Negus's hotel-room window — '

'Am I saying that he murdered Mr Negus? *Non*. He did not. He assisted the murderer of Richard Negus. As for who that person is . . . I have not yet told you the name.' Poirot smiled.

'No, you haven't,' I said sharply. 'Nor have you told me who were the three people in Room 317 when Rafal Bobak took up the afternoon tea. You've said that the three murder victims were all dead by then — '

'Indeed they were. One of the three in Room 317 at a quarter past seven was Ida Gransbury — dead, but positioned upright in a chair to appear alive, as long as one did not see her face. Another was Samuel Kidd, playing the part of Richard Negus.'

'Yes, I see that, but who was the third?' I asked rather desperately. 'Who was the woman posing as Harriet Sippel, gossiping with spiteful glee? It can't have been Jennie Hobbs. As you say, Jennie would have had to be halfway to Pleasant's Coffee House by then.'

'Ah, yes, the woman gossiping gleefully,' said Poirot. 'I shall tell you who that was, my friend. That woman was Nancy Ducane.'

★ ★ ★

Loud cries of shock filled the room.

'Oh, no, Monsieur Poirot,' said Luca Lazzari. 'Signora Ducane is one of the country's foremost artistic talents. She is also a most loyal friend of this hotel. You must be mistaken!'

'I am not mistaken, *mon ami*.'

I looked at Nancy Ducane, who sat with an air

339

of quiet resignation. She denied nothing that Poirot had said.

Famous artist Nancy Ducane conspiring with Samuel Kidd, Jennie Hobbs' former fiancé? I had never been more flummoxed in my life than I was at that moment. What could it all mean?

'Did I not tell you, Catchpool, that Madame Ducane wears the scarf over her face today *because she does not wish to be recognized?* You assumed that I meant 'recognized as the cele-brated portrait painter'. No! She did not want be recognized by Rafal Bobak as the Harriet he saw in Room 317 on the night of the murders! Please stand and remove your scarf, Mrs Ducane.'

Nancy did so.

'Mr Bobak, was this the woman you saw?'

'Yes, Mr Poirot. It was.'

It was quiet, but audible nonetheless: the sound of breath being drawn into lungs and held there. It filled the large room.

'You did not recognize her as the famous portrait painter, Nancy Ducane?'

'No, sir. I know nothing about art, and I only saw her in profile. She had her head turned away from me.'

'I am sure she did, in case you happened to be an art enthusiast and able to identify her.'

'I spotted her soon as she walked in today, though — her and that Mr Kidd chappy. I tried to tell you, sir, but you wouldn't let me speak.'

'Yes, and so did Thomas Brignell try to tell me that he recognized Samuel Kidd,' said Poirot.

'Two of the three people I'd thought were murdered — alive and well and walking into the

340

room!' From his voice, it was evident that Rafal Bobak had not yet recovered from the shock.

'What about Nancy Ducane's alibi from Lord and Lady Wallace?' I asked Poirot.

'I'm afraid that wasn't true,' said Nancy. 'It is my fault. Please do not blame them. They are dear friends and were trying to help me. Neither St John nor Louisa knew that I was at the Bloxham Hotel on the night of the murders. I swore to them that I had not been, and they trusted me. They are good, brave people who did not want to see me framed for three murders I did not commit. Monsieur Poirot, I believe you understand everything, so you must know that I have murdered nobody.'

'To lie to the police in a murder investigation is not brave, madame. It is inexcusable. By the time I left your house, Lady Wallace, I knew you to be a liar!'

'How dare you speak to my wife like that?' said St John Wallace.

'I am sorry if the truth is not to your taste, Lord Wallace.'

'How did you know, Monsieur Poirot?' his wife asked.

'You had a new servant girl: Dorcas. She is here with you today, only because I asked you to bring her. She is important to this story. You told me that Dorcas had been with you for just a few days, and I saw for myself that she is a little clumsy. She brought me a cup of coffee and spilled most of it. Luckily not all was spilled, and so I was able to drink some. *I immediately recognized it as the coffee made by Pleasant's*

Coffee House. Their coffee is unmistakeable; there is no other like it, anywhere.'

'Blimey!' said Fee Spring.

'Indeed, mademoiselle. The effect upon my mind was profound: at once, I put together several things like pieces of a jigsaw that fit perfectly. The strong coffee, it is very good for the brain.' Poirot looked pointedly at Fee as he said this. She pursed her lips in disapproval.

'This not very capable maid — pardon me, Mademoiselle Dorcas, I am sure you will improve, given time — she was *new*! I put this fact together with the coffee from Pleasant's, and it gave me an idea: what if Jennie Hobbs was Louisa Wallace's maid, before Dorcas? I knew from the waitresses at Pleasant's that Jennie used to go there often to collect things for her employer, who was a posh society lady. Jennie spoke of her as 'Her Ladyship'. It would be interesting, would it not, if Jennie, until a few days ago, worked for the woman providing Nancy Ducane's alibi? An extraordinary coincidence — *or not a coincidence at all!* At first, my thoughts on this matter proceeded along an incorrect track. I thought, 'Nancy Ducane and Louisa Wallace are friends who have conspired to kill *la pauvre* Jennie.''

'What a suggestion!' said Louisa Wallace indignantly.

'A shocking lie!' her husband St John agreed.

'Not a lie, *pas du tout*. A mistake. Jennie, as we see, is not dead. However, I was not mistaken to believe that she was a servant in the home of St John and Louisa Wallace, replaced very

342

recently by Mademoiselle Dorcas. After speaking to me at Pleasant's on the night of the murders, Jennie *had* to leave the Wallaces' house, and quickly. She knew that I would soon arrive there to ask for confirmation of Nancy Ducane's alibi. If I had found her there, working for the woman providing that alibi, I would instantly have been suspicious. Catchpool, tell me — tell us all — what exactly would I have suspected?'

I took a deep breath, praying I hadn't got this all wrong, and said, 'You would have suspected that Jennie Hobbs and Nancy Ducane were colluding to deceive us.'

'Quite correct, *mon ami*.' Poirot beamed at me. To our audience, he said, 'Shortly before I tasted the coffee and made the connection with Pleasant's, I had been looking at a picture by St John Wallace that was his wedding anniversary present to his wife. It was a picture of blue bindweed. It was dated — the fourth of August last year — and Lady Wallace remarked upon this. It was then that Poirot, he realized something: Nancy Ducane's portrait of Louisa Wallace, which he had seen a few minutes earlier, *was not dated*. As an appreciator of art, I have attended countless exhibition premieres in London. I have seen the work of Mrs Ducane before, many times. Her pictures always have the date in the bottom right-hand corner, as well as her initials: NAED.'

'You pay more attention than most who attend the exhibitions,' Nancy said.

'Hercule Poirot always pays attention — to everything. I believe, madame, that your portrait

343

of Louisa Wallace *was* dated, until you painted out the date. Why? Because it was not a recent one. You needed me to believe that you had delivered the portrait to Lady Wallace on the night of the murders, and that, therefore, it was a newly completed portrait. I asked myself why you did not paint on a new, false date, and the answer was obvious: if your work survives for hundreds of years, and if art historians take an interest in it, as they surely will, you do not wish actively to mislead them, these people who care about your work. No, the only people you wish to mislead are Hercule Poirot and the police!'

Nancy Ducane tilted her head to one side. In a thoughtful voice, she said, 'How perceptive you are, Monsieur Poirot. You really do *understand*, don't you?'

'*Oui, madame*. I understand that you found employment for Jennie Hobbs in the home of your friend Louisa Wallace — to help Jennie, when she came to London and needed a job. I understand that Jennie was never part of any plan to frame you for murder, though she allowed Richard Negus to believe otherwise. In fact, ladies and gentleman, *Jennie Hobbs and Nancy Ducane have been friends and allies ever since they both lived in Great Holling.* The two women who loved Patrick Ive unconditionally and beyond reason are the ones who formulated a plan nearly clever enough to fool me, Hercule Poirot — but not quite clever enough!'

'Lies, all lies!' Jennie wept.

Nancy said nothing.

Poirot said, 'Let me return for a moment to

344

the home of the Wallaces. In Nancy Ducane's portrait of Lady Louisa that I inspected so closely and for so long, there is a blue jug and bowl set. When I walked up and down the room and looked at it in different lights, the blue of the jug and bowl remained a solid block of colour, bland and uninteresting. Every other colour on that canvas changed subtly as I moved around, depending on the light. Nancy Ducane is a sophisticated artist. She is a genius when it comes to colour — except when she is in a hurry and thinking not about art but about protecting herself and her friend Jennie Hobbs. To conceal information, Nancy quickly painted blue a jug and bowl set that was not formerly blue. Why did she do this?'

'To paint out the date?' I suggested.

'Non. The jug and bowl were in the top half of the picture, and Nancy Ducane always paints the date in the bottom right-hand corner,' said Poirot. 'Lady Wallace, you did not expect me to ask to be shown round your home from bottom to top. You thought that once we had spoken and I had seen Nancy Ducane's portrait of you, I would be satisfied and leave. But I wanted to see if I could find this blue jug and bowl that were in the portrait, and painted with so much less subtlety than the rest of the picture. And I did find them! Lady Wallace seemed to be puzzled because they were missing, but her puzzlement was a pretence. In an upstairs bedroom, there was a *white* jug and bowl set with a crest on it. This, I thought, might be the jug and bowl set in the portrait — yet it was not blue. Mademoiselle

345

Dorcas, Lady Wallace told me that you must have smashed or stolen the blue jug and bowl.'

'I never did!' said a stricken Dorcas. 'I ain't never seen no blue jug and bowl in the house!'

'Because, young lady, there has never been one there!' said Poirot. 'Why, I asked myself, would Nancy Ducane hurriedly paint over the white jug and bowl with blue paint? What did she hope to hide? It had surely to be the crest, I concluded. Crests are not purely decorative; they belong to families, sometimes, or, at other times, to colleges of famous universities.'

'Saviour College, Cambridge,' I said before I could stop myself. I remembered that just before Poirot and I had left London for Great Holling, Stanley Beer had referred to a crest.

'Oui, Catchpool. When I left the Wallaces' home, I drew a picture of the crest so that I would not forget it. I am no artist, but it was accurate enough. I asked Constable Beer to find out for me where it came from. As you have all heard my friend Catchpool say, the crest on the white jug and bowl set in the Wallaces' house is that of Saviour College, Cambridge, where Jennie Hobbs used to work as a bed-maker for the Reverend Patrick Ive. It was a leaving present to you, was it not, Miss Hobbs, when you left Saviour College and went to Great Holling with Patrick and Frances Ive? And then when you moved into the home of Lord and Lady Wallace, you took it with you. When you left that house in a hurry and went to hide at Mr Kidd's house, you did not take the jug and bowl — you were in no state of mind to think of such things. I believe

346

that Louisa Wallace, at that point, moved the jug and bowl set from the servant's quarters you had previously occupied into a guest bedroom, where it might be admired by those she wished to impress.'

Jennie didn't answer. Her face was blank and expressionless.

'Nancy Ducane did not want to take even the tiniest risk,' said Poirot. 'She knew that, after the murders in this hotel, Catchpool and I would ask questions in the village of Great Holling. What if the old drunkard Walter Stoakley, formerly Master of Saviour College, mentioned to us that he gave Jennie Hobbs a crested jug and bowl as a leaving present? If we then saw a crest in the portrait of Lady Louisa Wallace, we might discover the connection to Jennie Hobbs and, by extension, the link between Nancy Ducane and Jennie Hobbs, which was not one of enmity and envy, as we had been told by both women, but one of friendship and collusion. Madame Ducane could not take the chance that we would arrive at this suspicion because of the crest in the portrait, and so the white jug and bowl set was painted blue — hurriedly, and with little artistry.'

'Not all of one's work can be one's best work, Monsieur Poirot,' said Nancy. It alarmed me to hear how reasonable she sounded — to see somebody who had conspired in three unlawful killings being so polite and rational in conversation.

'Perhaps you would agree with Mrs Ducane, Lord Wallace?' said Poirot. 'You too are a painter, though of a very different kind. Ladies

347

and gentlemen, St John Wallace is a botanical artist. I saw his work in every room of his house when I visited — Lady Louisa was gracious enough to show me around, just as she was generous enough to provide a false alibi for Nancy Ducane. Lady Louisa, you see, is a good woman. She is the most dangerous kind of good: so far removed from evil that she does not notice it when it is right in front of her! Lady Wallace believed in Nancy Ducane's innocence and provided an alibi to protect her. Ah, the lovely, talented Nancy, she is most convincing! She convinced St John Wallace that she was eager to try her hand at his sort of painting. Lord Wallace is well connected and well known, therefore easily able to obtain what plants he needs for his work. Nancy Ducane asked him to obtain for her some cassava plants — from which the cyanide is made!'

'How the devil can you possibly know that?' St John Wallace demanded.

'A lucky guess, monsieur. Nancy Ducane told you that she wanted these plants for the purpose of her art, did she not? And you believed her.' To the sea of open-mouthed faces, Poirot said, 'The truth is that neither Lord nor Lady Wallace would ever believe a good friend of theirs capable of murder. It would reflect so badly upon them. Their social standing — imagine it! Even now, when everything I say fits perfectly with what they know to be true, St John and Louisa Wallace tell themselves that he must be wrong, this opinionated detective from the Continent. Such is the perversity of the human

348

mind, particularly where snobbish *idées fixes* are concerned!'

'Monsieur Poirot, I have not killed anyone,' said Nancy Ducane. 'I know that you know I am telling the truth. Please make it clear to everybody gathered in this room that I am not a murderer.'

'I cannot do that, madame. *Je suis désolé.* You did not administer the poison yourself, but you conspired to end three lives.'

'Yes, but only to save another,' said Nancy earnestly. 'I am guilty of *nothing*! Come, Jennie, let us tell him our story — the *true* story. Once he has heard it, he will have to concede that we did only what we had to do to save our own lives.'

The room was completely still. Everyone sat in silence. I did not think Jennie was going to move, but eventually, slowly, she rose to her feet. Clutching her bag in front of her with both hands, she walked across the room towards Nancy. 'Our lives were not worth saving,' she said.

'Jennie!' Sam Kidd cried out, and suddenly he too was out of his chair and moving towards her. As I watched him, I had the peculiar sense of time having slowed down. Why was Kidd running? What was the danger? He clearly thought there was one, and, though I did not understand why, my heart had started to beat hard and fast. Something terrible was about to happen. I started to run towards Jennie.

She opened her bag. 'So you want to be reunited with Patrick, do you?' she said to

Nancy. I recognized the voice as hers, but at the same time it was not hers. It was the sound of unremitting darkness moulded into words. I hope never again to hear anything like it, as long as I live.

Poirot had also started to move, but both of us were too far away. 'Poirot!' I called, and then, 'Someone stop her!' I saw metal, and light dancing upon it. Two men at the table next to Nancy's rose to their feet, but they were not moving fast enough. 'No!' I called out. There was a rapid movement — Jennie's hand — and then blood, a rush of it, flowing down Nancy's dress and on to the floor. Nancy fell to the ground. Somewhere at the back of the room, a woman started to scream.

Poirot had stopped moving, and now stood perfectly still. '*Mon Dieu*,' he said, and closed his eyes.

Samuel Kidd reached Nancy before I could. 'She's dead,' he said, staring down at her body on the floor.

'Yes, she is,' said Jennie. 'I stabbed her in the heart. Right in the heart.'

25

If Murder Began With a D

I learned that day that I am not afraid of death. It is a state that contains no energy; it exerts no force. I see dead bodies in the course of my work, and it has never bothered me unduly. No, the thing I dread above all else is *proximity to death in the living*: the sound of Jennie Hobbs' voice when the desire to kill has consumed her; the state of mind of a murderer who would, with cold calculation, put three monogrammed cufflinks in his victims' mouths and take the trouble to lay them out: straightening their limbs and their fingers, placing their lifeless hands palms downward on the floor.

'*Hold his hand, Edward.*'

How can the living hold the hands of the dying and not fear being pulled towards death themselves?

If I had my way, no person, while alive and vital, would have any involvement with death at all. I accept that this is an unrealistic hope.

After she had stabbed Nancy, I did not wish to be near Jennie Hobbs. I was not curious to learn why she had done it; I simply wanted to go home, sit by one of Blanche Unsworth's roaring fires, work on my crossword puzzle and forget all about the Bloxham Hotel Murders or Monogram Murders or whatever anybody wanted to call them.

351

Poirot, however, had enough curiosity for both of us, and his will was stronger than mine. He insisted that I stay. This was my case, he said — I had to tie it up neatly. He made a gesture with his hands that suggested meticulous wrapping, as if a murder investigation were a parcel.

So it was that several hours later, he and I were seated in a small, square room at Scotland Yard, with Jennie Hobbs across the table from us. Samuel Kidd had also been arrested, and was being questioned by Stanley Beer. I would have given anything to tackle Kidd instead, who was a crook and a rotten egg for sure, but in whose voice I had never heard the extinction of all hope.

On the subject of voices, I was surprised by the gentleness of Poirot's as he spoke. 'Why did you do it, mademoiselle? Why kill Nancy Ducane, when the two of you have been friends and allies for so long?'

'Nancy and Patrick were lovers in every sense of the word. I did not know that until I heard her say so today. I always thought she and I were the same: we both loved Patrick, but knew we could not be with him in that way — *had not* been with him in that way. All these years, I have believed that their love was chaste, but that was a lie. If Nancy had really loved Patrick, she would not have made an adulterer of him and sullied his moral character.'

Jennie wiped away a tear. 'I believe I did her a favour. You heard her express the desire to be reunited with Patrick. I helped her with that, didn't I?'

352

'Catchpool,' said Poirot. 'Do you recall that I said to you, after we found the blood in the Room 402 of the Bloxham Hotel, that it was too late for me to save Mademoiselle Jennie?'

'Yes.'

'You thought I meant that she was dead, but you misunderstood me. You see, I knew even then that Jennie was beyond help. She had already done things so terrible that her own death was guaranteed, I feared. That was my meaning.'

'In every way that counts, I have been dead since Patrick died,' Jennie said in that same tone of unending hopelessness.

I knew there was only one way that I could get through this ordeal, and that was by concentrating all my attention on questions of logic. Had Poirot solved the puzzle? He seemed to think he had, but I was still in the dark. Who, for instance, had killed Harriet Sippel, Ida Gransbury and Richard Negus, and why had they done so? I asked these questions of Poirot.

'Ah,' he said, smiling fondly, as if I had reminded him of a joke we had once shared. 'I see your dilemma, *mon ami*. You listen to Poirot declaim at great length and then, a few minutes before the conclusion, there is the interruption of another murder, and you do not, after all, hear the answers that you have been waiting for. *Dommage*.'

'Please tell me at once, and let the *dommage* end here,' I said as forcefully as I could.

'It is quite simple. Jennie Hobbs and Nancy Ducane, with the help of Samuel Kidd, conspired to murder Harriet Sippel, Ida Gransbury and Richard Negus. However, while collaborating with Nancy, Jennie *pretended to be part of a quite different conspiracy.* She allowed Richard Negus to believe that *he* was the one with whom she conspired.'

'That does not sound 'quite simple' to me,' I said. 'It sounds inordinately complicated.'

'No, no, my friend. *Vraiment*, it is not at all. You are having trouble reconciling the different versions of the story that you have heard, but you must forget all that Jennie told us when we visited her at Samuel Kidd's house — banish it from your mind completely. It was a lie from start to finish, though I do not doubt that it contained some elements of veracity. The best lies always do. In a moment, Jennie will tell us the whole truth, now that she has nothing to lose, but first, my friend, I must pay you the compliment that you deserve. It was *you*, in the end, who helped me to see clearly with your suggestion in the graveyard of Holy Saints Church.'

Poirot turned to Jennie. He said, 'The lie you told to Harriet Sippel: that Patrick Ive took money from parishioners and, in return, conveyed to them messages from their dead loved ones; that Nancy Ducane had visited him in the vicarage at night for that reason — in the hope of communicating with her deceased husband William. Ah, how often has Poirot heard about this terrible, wicked lie? Many, many times. You yourself admitted to us the other day, Miss Hobbs, that you told the lie in a moment of weakness, inspired by jealousy. But this was not the truth!

'Standing by Patrick and Frances Ive's desecrated grave, Catchpool said to me, 'What if Jennie Hobbs lied about Patrick Ive not to hurt him but to help him?' Catchpool had realized the significance of something that I had taken for granted — a fact that had never been in dispute, and so I had failed to examine it: *Harriet Sippel's passionate love for her late husband George, who died tragically young.* Had Poirot not been told how much Harriet had loved George? Or how the death of George had turned Harriet from a happy, warm-hearted woman into a bitter, spiteful monster? One can hardly imagine a loss so terrible, so devastating, that it extinguishes all joy and destroys all that is good in a person. *Oui, bien sûr*, I knew that Harriet Sippel had suffered such a loss. I knew it so surely that I thought no further about it!

'I knew, also, that Jennie Hobbs loved Patrick Ive enough to abandon Samuel Kidd, her fiancé, in order to remain in the service of Reverend Ive and his wife. This is a very self-sacrificing love: content to serve, and receive little in return. Yet the story told to us by both Jennie and Nancy offered Jennie's jealousy as her reason for telling the terrible lie that she told — jealousy of Patrick's love for Nancy. But this cannot be true! It is not consistent! We must think not only of the physical facts but of the psychological. Jennie did nothing to punish Patrick Ive for his marriage to Frances. She accepted with good grace that he belonged to another woman. She

355

continued as his loyal servant and was a great help to him and his wife at the vicarage, and they, in turn, were devoted to her. Why then all of a sudden, after many years of self-sacrificing love and service, would Patrick Ive's love for Nancy Ducane inspire Jennie to slander him, and to set in motion a chain of events that would destroy him? The answer is that it would not, and *did* not.

'It was not the eruption of envy and longing locked inside for so long that prompted Jennie to tell her lie. It was something altogether different. You were trying — were you not, Miss Hobbs? — to help the man you loved. To save him, even. As soon as I heard the theory of my clever friend Catchpool, I knew it was the truth. It was so obvious, and Poirot, he had been *imbécile* not to see!'

Jennie looked at me. 'What theory?' she asked.

I opened my mouth to answer, but Poirot was too quick for me. 'When Harriet Sippel told you she had seen Nancy Ducane visiting the vicarage late at night, you were straight away alert to the danger. You knew about these trysts — how could you not, when you lived at the vicarage — and you were anxious to protect Patrick Ive's good name. How could this be achieved? Harriet Sippel, once she had sniffed out a scandal, would relish the opportunity to bring public shame to a sinner. How could you explain the presence of Nancy Ducane at the vicarage on nights when Frances Ive was *not* there, except with the truth? What other story would pass the muster? And then, as if by magic, when you had almost given up hope, you thought of something that might work. You decided to use temptation and false hope to eliminate the threat that Harriet represented.'

Jennie stared blankly ahead. She said nothing.

'Harriet Sippel and Nancy Ducane had something in common,' Poirot went on. 'They had both lost their husbands to early tragic death. You told Harriet that, with the help of Patrick Ive, Nancy had been able to communicate with the deceased William Ducane — that money had changed hands. Of course, it would have to be kept secret from the Church and from everybody 'in the village, but you suggested to Harriet that, if she so wished, Patrick would be able to do for her what he was doing for Nancy. She and George could be ... well, if not together again then at least there could be communication of a kind between them. Tell me, how did Harriet respond when you said this to her?'

A long silence followed. Then Jennie said, 'She was foaming at the mouth for it to happen as soon as possible. She would pay any price, she said, to be able to speak to George again. You cannot imagine how much she loved that man, Monsieur Poirot. Watching her face as I spoke ... it was like seeing a dead woman come back to life. I tried to explain it all to Patrick: that there had been a problem, but I had solved it. I made the offer to Harriet without asking him first, you see. Oh, I think I knew in my heart that Patrick would never consent to it, but I was desperate! I didn't want to give him the chance

357

to forbid me. Can you understand that?'

'*Oui, mademoiselle.*'

'I hoped I would be able to persuade him to agree. He was a principled man, but I knew he would want to shield Frances from a scandal, and protect Nancy, and this was a certain way to guarantee Harriet's silence. It was the *only* way! All Patrick would have had to do was say some comforting words to Harriet once in a while and pretend that those words came from George Sippel. There was no need for him to take her money, even. I said all this to him, but he wouldn't hear of it. He was horrified.'

'He was entirely right to be,' said Poirot quietly. 'Continue, please.'

'He said it would be immoral and unfair to do to Harriet what I was proposing; he would sooner face personal ruin. I begged him to reconsider. What harm would it do, if it would make Harriet happy? But Patrick was resolute. He asked me to give her the message that what I had proposed would not, after all, be possible. He was very specific. 'Do not say that you lied, Jennie, or else she will revert to suspecting the truth,' he said. My instructions were to tell Harriet only that she could not have what she wanted.'

'So you had no choice but to tell her,' I said.

'No choice at all.' Jennie started to cry. 'And from the moment I told Harriet that Patrick had refused her request, she made herself his enemy, repeating my lie to the whole village. Patrick could have ruined her reputation in return, by making it known that she had been eager to avail

358

herself of his unwholesome services, and only started to call them blasphemous and unchristian once she had been thwarted, but he wouldn't do it. He said that no matter how maliciously Harriet attacked him, he would not blacken her name. Foolish man! He could have shut her up in an instant, but he was too noble for his own good!'

'Was that when you went to Nancy Ducane for advice?' Poirot asked.

'Yes. I didn't see why Patrick and I should be the only ones to fret. Nancy was part of it too. I asked her if I should publicly admit to my lie, but she advised me not to. She said, 'I fear that trouble is coming to Patrick now one way or another, and to me. You would be wise to recede into the background and say nothing, Jennie. Do not sacrifice yourself. I am not sure you would be strong enough to withstand Harriet's vilification.' She underestimated me. I was upset, you see — I suppose I sort of fell apart a bit, because I was so frightened for Patrick, with Harriet determined to destroy him — but I am not a weak person, Monsieur Poirot.'

'I see that you are not afraid.'

'No. I draw strength from the knowledge that Harriet Sippel — that loathsome hypocrite — is dead. Her killer did the world a great service.'

'Which leads us to the question of that killer's identity, mademoiselle. Who killed Harriet Sippel? You told us that it was Ida Gransbury, but that was a lie.'

'I hardly need tell you the truth, Monsieur Poirot, when you know it as well as I do.'

'Then I must ask you to take pity on poor Mr Catchpool here. He does not yet know the whole story.'

'You'd better tell him, then, hadn't you?' Jennie smiled an absent sort of smile, and I suddenly felt as if there was less of her in the room than there had been only moments ago; she had taken herself away.

'Très bien,' said Poirot. 'I will start with Harriet Sippel and Ida Gransbury: two inflexible women so convinced of their own rectitude that they were willing to hound a good man into an early grave. Did they express sorrow after his death? No, instead they objected to his burial in consecrated ground. Did these two women, after much persuasion by Richard Negus, come to regret their treatment of Patrick Ive? No, of course they did not. It is not plausible that they would. That, Mademoiselle Jennie, was when I knew that you were lying: at that point in your story.'

Jennie shrugged. 'Anything is possible,' she said.

'Non. Only the truth is possible. I knew that Harriet Sippel and Ida Gransbury would never have agreed to the plan of voluntary execution that you described to me. Therefore, they were murdered. How convenient, to pass off their murders as a kind of delegated suicide! You hoped Poirot might disengage his little grey cells once he heard that all the dead had been so willing to die. It was their great opportunity for redemption! What an imaginative and unusual story — the sort that one hears and assumes

360

must be the truth, for who would think to invent such a fabrication?'

'It was my safeguard, to be used if needed,' said Jennie. 'I hoped you would never find me, but I feared you might.'

'And if I did, you expected that your alibi for between quarter past seven and ten past eight would work, and Nancy Ducane's also. You and Samuel Kidd would be charged with attempting to frame an innocent woman, but not with murder or conspiracy to commit murder. It is clever: you confess to wrongdoing in order to avoid punishment for far more serious crimes. Your enemies are murdered, and no one hangs because we believe your story: Ida Gransbury killed Harriet Sippel, and Richard Negus killed Ida Gransbury and then himself. Your plan was ingenious, mademoiselle — but not as ingenious as Hercule Poirot!'

'Richard wanted to die,' said Jennie angrily. 'He was not murdered. He was *determined* to die.'

'Yes,' said Poirot. 'This was the truth in the lie.'

'It's his fault, this whole horrible mess. I would never have killed anybody if it were not for Richard.'

'But you did kill — several times. It was Catchpool who, once again, set me on the right track, by uttering a few innocent words.'

'What words?' Jennie asked.

'He said, 'If murder began with a D . . .''

* * *

It was unsettling to listen to Poirot's appreciation of my helpfulness. I didn't understand how a few careless words of mine could have been so momentous.

Poirot was in full flow. 'After we had heard your story, mademoiselle, we left Samuel Kidd's house and, naturally, we discussed what you had told us: your supposed plan that you made together with Richard Negus . . . If I may say so, it was a compelling idea. There was a neatness about it — like the falling dominoes, except, when I thought carefully, it was not like that at all because the order of knocking over is altered. Not D falls down, then C, then B, then A; instead, B knocks A down, then C knocks B . . . But that is beside the point.'

What on earth was he talking about? Jennie looked as if she was wondering the same thing.

'Ah, I must be more lucid in my explanation,' said Poirot. 'To enable myself to imagine the order of events more easily, mademoiselle, I substituted letters for names. Your plan, as you told it to us at Samuel Kidd's house, was as follows: B kills A, C then kills B, D then kills C. Afterwards, D waits for E to be blamed and hanged for the murders of A, B and C, and then D kills herself. Do you see, Miss Hobbs, that you are D in this arrangement, according to the story you told us?'

Jennie nodded.

'Bon. Now, by chance, Catchpool here is a devotee of the crossword puzzle, and it was in connection with this hobby that he asked me to think of a word that had six letters and meant

362

'death'. I suggested 'murder'. No, said Catchpool, my suggestion would only work 'if murder began with a D.' I recalled his words some time later and made the idle speculation in my mind: what if murder *did* begin with a D? What if the first to kill was not Ida Gransbury but you, Miss Hobbs?

'Over time, this speculation hardened into certainty. I understood why it must have been you who killed Harriet Sippel. She and Ida Gransbury shared neither a train nor a car from Great Holling to the Bloxham Hotel. Therefore each was unaware of the presence of the other, and there was no plan agreed by all for one to kill the other. That had to be a lie.'

'What was the truth?' I asked rather desperately.

'Harriet Sippel believed, and so did Ida Gransbury, that she alone was going to London, for a very private reason. Harriet had been contacted by Jennie, who said she needed to meet with her urgently. The highest level of secrecy was required. Jennie told Harriet that a room at the Bloxham Hotel was booked and paid for, and that she, Jennie, would come to the hotel on Thursday afternoon, perhaps at half past three or four o'clock, so that they could conduct their important business. Harriet accepted Jennie's invitation *because Jennie had written in her letter of invitation something that Harriet could not resist.*

'You offered her what Patrick Ive had refused her all those years ago, *n'est-ce pas, mademoiselle?* Communication with her late beloved

363

husband. You told her that George Sippel had sought to speak to her through you — you, who had tried to help him reach her sixteen years earlier, and failed. And now, again, George was trying to send a message to his dearest wife, using you as his channel. He had spoken to you from the afterlife! Oh, I have no doubt that you made it extremely convincing! Harriet was unable to resist. She believed because she so ardently wished it to be true. The lie you had told her so long ago, about the souls of dead loved ones making contact with the living — she believed it then, and she had never stopped believing it.'

'Clever old you, Monsieur Poirot,' said Jennie. 'Top marks.'

'Catchpool, tell me: do you understand now about the old woman enamoured of a man possibly young enough to be her son? These people with whom you became so obsessed, who featured in the gossip between Nancy Ducane and Samuel Kidd in Room 317?'

'I'd hardly say obsessed. And, no, I don't understand.'

'Let us recall *précisément* what Rafal Bobak told us. He heard Nancy Ducane, posing as Harriet Sippel, say, 'She's no longer the one he confides in. He'd hardly be interested in her now — she's let herself go, and she's old enough to be his mother.' Think about those words: 'he'd hardly be interested in her *now*' — that fact is asserted first, before the two reasons for his lack of interest are given. One of these is that she is old enough to be his mother. *Now*, she is old enough to be his mother. Do you not see, Catchpool? *If she is old enough to be his mother now, then she must always have been old enough to be his mother.* Nothing else is possible!'

'Isn't that stretching it a bit?' I said. 'I mean, without the 'now' it makes perfect sense: he'd hardly be interested in her — she's let herself go and she's old enough to be his mother.'

'But, *mon ami*, what you say, it is ridiculous,' Poirot spluttered. 'It is not logical. The 'now' was there, in the sentence. We cannot pretend to be without it when we are with it. We cannot ignore a 'now' that is right in front of our ears!'

'I'm afraid I disagree with you,' I said with some trepidation. 'If I had to guess, I should say that the intended meaning was something along these lines: before she let herself go, this chap didn't especially mind or notice the age difference between them. Maybe it wasn't quite so visible. However, now that she is no longer in tip-top shape, the chap has moved on to a younger, more attractive companion, the one he now confides in — '

Poirot had begun to speak over me, red faced and impatient. 'There is no point in your *guessing*, Catchpool, when I *know!* Listen to Poirot! Listen one more time to exactly what was said, and in what order: 'He'd hardly be interested in her *now* — she's let herself go, and she's old enough to be his mother'! Reason one that he would no longer be interested in her, followed by reason two! The construction of the sentence makes it clear that *both* of these

365

unfortunate circumstances that are the case *now* were once *not* the case.'

'There is no need to shout at me, Poirot. I have grasped your point, and I still disagree. Not everybody is as precise in their speech as you are. My interpretation has to be the correct one, and yours incorrect, because, as you have pointed out, it makes no sense otherwise. You said it yourself: if she is old enough to be his mother now, then she must always have been old enough to be his mother.'

'Catchpool, Catchpool. How I begin to despair of you! Think of what came later in the same conversation. Rafal Bobak heard Samuel Kidd, posing as Richard Negus, say, 'I dispute the old-enough-to-be-his-mother claim. I dispute it utterly.' To which Nancy, posing as Harriet, replied, 'Well, neither of us can prove we're right, so let's agree to disagree!' But why could neither prove they were right? Surely it is a matter of simple biological fact whether or not a woman is old enough to be a man's mother? If she is four years older than him, then she is not old enough. No one would dispute this! If she is twenty years older, then she is old enough to be his mother — that is equally certain.'

'What if she were thirteen years older?' said Jennie Hobbs, who had closed her eyes. 'Or twelve? One does hear of rare cases . . . That does not apply here, of course.'

So Jennie knew where Poirot was going with all this. I was the only ignorant one in the room.

'Thirteen, twelve — it is irrelevant! One asks a doctor, a medical expert: is it theoretically possible for a female of thirteen, or twelve, to give birth to a child? The answer is either yes or no. Please let us not debate the borderline cases of potential childbearing ages! Have you forgotten the other intriguing statement made by Samuel Kidd in connection with this allegedly younger man: 'His mind? I'd argue he has no mind.' No doubt you will say that Mr Kidd meant nothing more than that the man in question was an imbecile.'

'No doubt I will,' I said peevishly. 'Why don't you tell me what I'm missing, since you're so much cleverer than I am?'

Poirot made a dismissive clicking noise. '*Sacré tonnerre*. The couple under discussion in Room 317 were Harriet Sippel and her husband George. The conversation was not a serious debate — it was mockery. George Sippel died when he and Harriet were both very young. Samuel Kidd argues that he has no mind because, if George Sippel exists at all after his death, it is not in human form. He is a ghost, *n'est-ce pas?* Since the mind is inside the brain, and the soul does not possess human organs, George Sippel the ghost cannot have a mind.'

'I . . . Oh, heavens. Yes, now I see.'

'Samuel Kidd introduces his point of view in the way that he does — 'I would argue . . . ' — because he expects Nancy Ducane to disagree. She might well have said, 'Of course a ghost must have a mind. Ghosts have agency, do they not, and free will? From where do these things come if not the mind?''

Philosophically, it was an interesting point. In

different circumstances, I could imagine taking a view on the matter myself.

Poirot continued: 'Nancy's 'old-enough-to-be-his-mother' remark was based on her belief that, when a man dies, *his age is then fixed forevermore*. In the afterlife, he does not age. George Sippel, if he were to return as a spirit to visit his widow, would be a young man in his twenties, the age he was when he died. And she, as a woman in her forties, is *now* old enough to be his mother.'

'Bravo,' said Jennie in a matter-of-fact tone of voice. 'I was not there, but the conversation was continued later in my presence. Monsieur Poirot really is formidably perceptive, Mr Catchpool. I hope you appreciate him.' To Poirot, she said, 'The argument went on . . . oh, just for ever! Nancy insisted she was right, but Sam would not concede the point. He said ghosts do not exist in the dimension of age — they are timeless, so it is incorrect to say that *anyone* could be old enough to be a ghost's mother.'

Poirot said to me, 'It is distasteful, is it not, Catchpool? When Rafal Bobak delivered the food, Nancy Ducane, with the dead body of Ida Gransbury propped up in a chair beside her, was mocking the woman in whose murder she had conspired earlier that same day. Poor stupid Harriet: her husband is not interested in talking directly to her from beyond the grave. No, he will speak only to Jennie Hobbs, leaving Harriet with no choice if she wants to receive his message: she must meet Jennie at the Bloxham, and, in doing so, meet her own doom.'

'Nobody has ever deserved to be murdered more than Harriet Sippel did,' said Jennie. 'I have many regrets. Killing Harriet is not one of them.'

★ ★ ★

'What about Ida Gransbury?' I asked. 'Why did she go to the Bloxham Hotel?'

'Ah!' said Poirot, who never tired of sharing the endless knowledge that he alone seemed to possess. 'Ida also accepted an irresistible invitation, from Richard Negus. Not to be put in communication with a dead loved one, but to meet, after sixteen years apart, her former fiancé. It is not hard to imagine what the lure would have been. Richard Negus abandoned Ida and, no doubt, broke her heart. She never married. I expect he alluded in a letter to the possibility of a reconciliation, maybe matrimony. A happy ending. Ida agreed — which lonely individual would not choose to give a second chance to true love? — and Richard told her that he would come to her room at the Bloxham Hotel at half past three or perhaps four o'clock on the Thursday. Do you remember your remark, Catchpool, about arriving at the hotel on Wednesday, so that the whole of Thursday could be devoted to getting murdered? That makes more sense now, yes?'

I nodded. 'Negus knew that on the Thursday he would have to commit murder, and also to be killed himself. It is only natural that he would wish to arrive a day early to prepare himself mentally for a double ordeal of that sort.'

'Also to avoid the delayed train or something similar that might have interfered with his plans,' said Poirot.

'So Jennie Hobbs murdered Harriet Sippel, and Richard Negus murdered Ida Gransbury?' I said.

'*Oui, mon ami.*' Poirot looked at Jennie, who nodded. 'At around the same time of day, in rooms 121 and 317 respectively. In both rooms, the same method was used, I imagine, to induce Harriet and Ida to drink the poison. Jennie said to Harriet, and Richard Negus to Ida, 'You will need a glass of water before you hear what I have to say. Here, let me fetch one for you. You sit down.' While fetching the water, using the glass next to the basin, Jennie and Negus slipped in the poison. The glasses were then handed to the two victims to drink. Death would have followed shortly thereafter.'

'What about Richard Negus's death?' I asked.

'Jennie killed him, according to the plan the two of them made.'

'Much of what I told you at Sam's house was true,' said Jennie. 'Richard *did* write to me after years of silence. He *was* torn apart by guilt for what he had done to Patrick and Frances, and he saw no way out — no possibility of justice or peace of mind — unless we all paid with our own lives, all four of us who were responsible.'

'He asked you . . . to help him kill Harriet and Ida?' I said, working it out as I spoke.

'Yes. Them, and him, and myself as well. It had to be all of us, he insisted, or else it was

370

meaningless. He did not want to be a murderer but an executioner — he used that word a lot — and that meant that he and I could not avoid punishment. I agreed with him that Harriet and Ida deserved to die. They were evil. But . . . I didn't want to die, and nor did I want Richard dead. It was enough for me that he was truly sorry for his part in Patrick's death. I . . . I knew it would have been enough for Patrick too, and for any higher authority that might or might not exist. But there was no way to persuade Richard of this. I saw at once that there was no point trying. He was as intelligent as he always had been, but something in his mind had slipped and turned him peculiar, given him weird ideas. All those years of brooding on it, the guilt . . . He had become a strange species of zealot. I knew beyond a shadow of a doubt that he would murder me too if I did not go along with what he was proposing. He didn't say so explicitly. He didn't want to threaten me, you see. He was kind to me. What he wanted and needed was an ally. Someone of like mind. He honestly believed I would agree to his scheme because, unlike Harriet and Ida, I was reasonable. He was so certain he was right — that his solution was the only way for all of us. I thought perhaps he *was* right, but I was afraid. I'm not any more. I don't know what has changed me. Maybe then, even in my unhappiness, I still entertained the notion that my life might improve. Sadness is different from despair.'

'You knew that you would have to pretend in order to save your life,' said Poirot. 'To lie

371

convincingly to Richard Negus — it was your only possible escape from death. You did not know what to do, so you went to Nancy Ducane for help.'

'Yes, I did. And she solved my problem, or so I thought. Her plan was brilliant. Following her advice, I suggested to Richard only one deviation from his proposed plan. His idea was that once Harriet and Ida were dead, he would kill me and then himself. Naturally, as an authoritative man accustomed to being in charge of whatever mattered to him, he wanted to be the one in control until the end.

'Nancy told me I had to persuade Richard that I should kill him rather than have him kill me. 'Impossible!' I said. 'He will never agree.' But Nancy said that he would if I approached him in the right way. I had to pretend to be more committed to our goal than he was. She was right. It worked. I went to Richard and said that it was not enough for the four of us to die: me, him, Harriet and Ida. Nancy had to be punished too. I pretended that I would be happy to die only once she was dead. She was more evil than Harriet, I said. I related an elaborate tale of how Nancy callously plotted to seduce Patrick away from his wife, and would not take no for an answer. I told Richard she had confessed to me that her true motive for speaking up at the King's Head was not to help Patrick but to hurt Frances. She *hoped* that Frances would take her own life, or abandon Patrick at the very least and return to her father in Cambridge, leaving the way clear for Nancy.'

'More lies,' said Poirot.

'Yes, of course more lies — but ones suggested to me by Nancy herself, and ones that did the trick! Richard agreed to die before me.'

'And he did not know that Samuel Kidd was involved, did he?' said Poirot.

'No. Nancy and I brought Sam into it. He was part of our plan. Neither of us wanted to climb out of that window and down the tree — we both feared we would fall and break our necks — and after locking the door from the inside and hiding the key behind the tile, that was the only way to leave Room 238. That's why Sam was needed — that and the impersonation of Richard.'

'And the key *had to be hidden behind the tile*,' I muttered to myself, checking I had it all straight in my mind. 'So that, when you came to tell us your story — the one we heard at Mr Kidd's house — it all appeared to fit: Richard Negus hid the key to make it look as if a murderer had taken it, because he was involved in a plan to frame Nancy Ducane.'

'Which he was,' said Poirot. 'Or rather, he thought he was. When Jennie handed him a glass of poisoned water, as agreed, he believed she would stay alive and do her best to ensure that Nancy was found guilty of the three Bloxham Hotel murders. He believed that she would speak to the police in such a way as to ensure that they suspected Nancy. He did not know that Nancy had arranged a cast-iron alibi with Lord and Lady St John Wallace! Or that, after his death, the cufflink would be pushed to the back

373

of his mouth, the key hidden behind the tile, the window opened . . . He did not know that Jennie Hobbs, Nancy Ducane and Samuel Kidd would arrange it so that it appeared to the police that the killings must have taken place between a quarter past seven and ten minutes past eight!'

'No, Richard was not privy to those details,' Jennie agreed. 'Now you can see why I described Nancy's plan as brilliant, Monsieur Poirot.'

'She was a talented artist, mademoiselle. The best artists, they have the eye for detail and for structure: how all the components fit together.'

Jennie turned to me. 'Neither Nancy nor I wanted any of this. You have to believe me, Mr Catchpool. Richard would have killed me if I had resisted him.' She sighed. 'We had it all worked out. Nancy was supposed to get off scot-free, and Sam and I were to be punished for trying to frame Nancy, but not by death. A short term of imprisonment would suffice, we hoped. After which we intended to marry.' Seeing our surprised faces, Jennie added, 'Oh, I don't love Sam as I loved Patrick, but I am very fond of him. He would have made a good companion, if I had not ruined it all by stabbing Nancy.'

'It was already ruined, mademoiselle. I knew that you had murdered Harriet Sippel and Richard Negus.'

'I did not murder Richard, Monsieur Poirot. That's one thing you're wrong about. Richard wanted to die. I gave him the poison with his full consent.'

'Yes, but under false pretences. Richard Negus agreed to die because you agreed to his plan that

374

all four of you would die. Then it became five when you involved Nancy Ducane. But you did not *really* agree. You betrayed him, and plotted behind his back. Who knows whether Richard Negus would have chosen to die at that moment and in that way if you had told him the truth of your secret pact with Nancy Ducane.'

Jennie's expression hardened. 'I did not murder Richard Negus. I killed him as an act of self-defence. He would have murdered me otherwise.'

'You said that he did not explicitly threaten this.'

'No — but I *knew* it. What do you think, Mr Catchpool? Did I murder Richard Negus or not?'

'I don't know,' I said, confused.

'Catchpool, *mon ami*, do not be absurd.'

'He is not being absurd,' said Jennie. 'He is using his brain where you refuse to, Monsieur Poirot. Please think about it, I beg of you. Before I hang, I hope to hear you say that I did not murder Richard Negus.'

I stood up. 'Let us leave now, Poirot.' I wanted to end the interview while the word 'hope' still hung in the air.

Epilogue

Four days later I was sitting in front of one of Blanche Unsworth's roaring fires, sipping a glass of brandy and working on my crossword puzzle, when Poirot walked into the drawing room. He stood silently by my side for several minutes. I did not look up.

Eventually he cleared his throat. '*Still*, Catchpool,' he said. 'Still you avoid the discussion of whether or not Richard Negus was murdered, was assisted in taking his own life, or was killed in self-defence.'

'I hardly see that it would be a profitable debate,' I said, as my stomach clenched. I did not want to talk about the Bloxham Murders ever again. What I wanted — needed — was to write about them, to set down on paper every detail of what had happened. It mystified me that I was so eager to do the latter and so reluctant to undertake the former. Why should writing about a thing be so different from speaking about it?

'Do not alarm yourself, *mon ami*,' said Poirot. 'I will not raise the matter again. We will talk of other things. For example, I visited Pleasant's Coffee House this morning. Fee Spring asked me to pass the message to you that she would like to speak to you at your earliest convenience. She is displeased.'

'With me?'

'Yes. One moment, she says, she is sitting in the Bloxham Hotel's dining room hearing the explanation of everything, and the next it is all over. A murder takes place in front of all our eyes, and the story, for our audience, is left incomplete. Mademoiselle Fee wishes you to relate the tale to her in its fullest form.'

'It's hardly my fault that there was another murder,' I muttered under my breath. 'Can she not read the story in the newspapers like everybody else?'

'Non. She wishes to discuss it with you in particular. For a waitress, her intelligence is impressive. She is an estimable young woman. Do you not think so, *mon ami?*'

'I know your game, Poirot,' I said wearily. 'Really, you must desist. You are wasting your time, as is Fee Spring, assuming . . . Look, buzz off, can't you?'

'You are angry with me.'

'A little, yes,' I admitted. 'Henry Negus and the suitcase, Rafal Bobak and the laundry cart, Thomas Brignell and his lady friend in the hotel garden, who happened to be wearing a light brown coat like half the women in England. The wheelbarrow . . . '

'Ah!'

'Yes, 'ah'. You knew perfectly well that Jennie Hobbs wasn't dead, so why make such an effort to mislead me into suspecting that her body might have been removed from room 402 by three of the most unlikely means imaginable?'

'Because, my friend, I wanted to encourage

you to imagine. If you do not consider the unlikeliest of possibilities, you will not be the best detective that you can be. It is the education for the little grey cells, to force them to move in unusual directions. From this comes the inspiration.'

'If you insist,' I said doubtfully.

'Poirot, he goes too far, you think — beyond what is necessary. Perhaps.'

'All that fuss you made about the trail of blood in room 402 leading from the pool of blood in the centre of the room towards the door, all your exclaiming about the width of the doorway — what was that about? You knew that Jennie Hobbs had not been murdered and dragged anywhere!'

'I did, but you did not. You believed, as did our friend Signor Lazzari, that Mademoiselle Jennie was dead and that it was her blood on the floor. *Alors*, I wanted you to demand of yourself: a suitcase, a laundry cart on wheels — both of these are objects that could have been brought into room 402, right to the spot where the dead body was. Why, then, would a killer pull the body towards the door? He would not! *She* would not! The trail of blood going in the direction of the door was a hoax; its aim was to suggest to us that the body had been dragged out of the room, since it was not *in* the room. It was the small detail of verisimilitude, so important to lend credence to the murder scene.

'But for Hercule Poirot, it was a detail that allowed him to know what he already strongly suspected: that Jennie Hobbs had not been murdered in that room and neither had anybody else. I could imagine no method of removing a corpse that would necessitate the trail of blood smears going towards the door. No killer would take his victim's body out into the public corridor of a hotel without first hiding it inside some sort of receptacle — a container. Every container I could think of could easily have been taken into the room, travelling towards the body rather than requiring the body to travel towards it. It was such simple logic, Catchpool. I was surprised you did not grasp this point at once.'

'Handy tip for you, Poirot,' I said. 'Next time you'd like me to grasp something at once, open your mouth and tell me facts, whatever they are. Be straightforward about it. You'll find it saves a lot of bother.'

He smiled. '*Bien*. From my good friend Catchpool, I shall endeavour to learn the *comportement* straightforward. I start immediately!' He produced an envelope from his pocket. 'This arrived for me an hour ago. You might not welcome my interference in your personal affairs, Catchpool — you may think, 'Poirot, he sticks in his oar where it is not wanted' — but this letter expresses gratitude for that very vice of mine that you find so intolerable.'

'If you're referring to Fee Spring, she is not my 'personal affairs' and never will be,' I said, eyeing the missive in his hand. 'Which poor stick's private business have you meddled in now? And gratitude for what?'

'For bringing together two people who love

each other very much.'

'Who is the letter from?'

Poirot smiled. 'Dr and Mrs Ambrose Flowerday,' he said. And he handed it to me to read.